Aquarium Suitability

■ These species are almost impossible to keep and should be left on the reef.

◣ Most individuals of these species do not acclimate to the home aquarium, often refusing to feed and wasting away in captivity.

▢ These species are moderately hardy, with many individuals acclimating to the home aquarium if special care is provided.

◥ These species are generally durable and hardy, with most individuals acclimating to the home aquarium.

■ These species are very hardy with almost all individuals readily acclimating to aquarium confines.

V Venomous: These species have spines or barbs that bear toxins with varying degrees of toxicity. The effects range from mild stings to severe pain and even death. They should be handled with caution and not displayed in systems within reach of children or uninformed viewers.

Reef Compatibility

Safe with stony corals.

Occasional threat to some stony corals.

Threat to stony corals.

Safe with soft corals.

Occasional threat to some soft corals.

Threat to soft corals.

Safe with ornamental crustaceans.

Occasional threat to some ornamental crustaceans.

Threat to ornamental crustaceans.

Safe with other invertebrates.

Occasional threat to some other invertebrates.

Threat to other invertebrates.

D1021604

The POCKETEXPERT™ Guide Series ·
for Aquarists and Underwater Naturalists

This book has been published with the intent to provide accurate
and authoritative information in regard to the subject matter
within. While every precaution has been taken in preparation of
this book, the publisher and author assume no responsibility for
errors or omissions. Neither is any liability assumed for damages
resulting from the use of the information herein.

All cover photographs by Scott W. Michael
Front: Yellowfin Flasher Wrasse
(*Paracheilinus flavianalis*), page 270.
Spine: Potter's Angelfish
(*Centropyge potteri*), page 162.

Produced and distributed by:
T.F.H. Publications, Inc.
One TFH Plaza
Third and Union Avenues
Neptune City, NJ 07753
www.tfh.com

REEF AQUARIUM FISHES

500+ ESSENTIAL-TO-KNOW SPECIES

TEXT AND PRINCIPAL PHOTOGRAPHY BY

SCOTT W. MICHAEL

MICROCOSM

t.f.h.

PROFESSIONAL
SERIES™

Produced and distributed by:

T.F.H. Publications
One T.F.H. Plaza
Third and Union Avenues
Neptune City, NJ 07753
www.tfh.com

Printed and bound in China
08 09 10 11 12   3 5 7 9 8 6 4 2

ISBN 978-1-8900-8789-0

Library of Congress Cataloging-in-Publication Data
Michael, Scott W.
A PocketExpert guide reef aquarium fishes : 500+ essential-to-know species / text and principal photography by Scott W. Michael.
p. cm.
Includes bibliographical references and indexes.
ISBN 1-890087-89-0
1. Marine aquarium fishes. 2. Marine aquariums. 3. Coral reef animals. I. Title.
SF457.1.M53 2008
639.34'2--dc22

                    2007044071

Designed by Alice Z. Lawrence and Alesia Depot
Color separations by Digital Engine, Burlington, Vermont

TFH Publications, Inc.
Neptune, NJ 07753
www.tfh.com

Co-published by
Microcosm, Ltd.
Charlotte, VT 05445
www.microcosm-books.com

To my friend and colleague, Dennis Reynolds,
for his unsurpassed enthusiasm for coral reef fishes and
for his vital contribution to this book.

ACKNOWLEDGMENTS

To help make this work more complete and accurate, many scientists, professional aquarists, committed home aquarists, fish wholesalers and dive boat/resort operators have generously shared their observations and facilities with me. (I apologize in advance for those of you that should be in this list that I failed to recognize.) I express immense gratitude to the following: Bob Pascua (Quality Marine), Bill Addison, Mitch Carl, Dr. Bruce Carlson, Millie, Ted, and Edwin Chua (All Seas Marine), J. Charles Delbeek, Mark Ecenbarger (Kungkungan Bay Resort, Sulawesi), Dave Esposito (Hamilton Technology), Tom Frakes, Kevin Gaines (Oceans, Reefs & Aquariums), Kyle and Mark Haeffner (Fish Store Inc.), Richard Harker, Jay Hemdal, Larry Jackson, Kelly Jedlicki, Kevin Kohen (liveaquaria.com), Toshikazu and Junco Kozawa (Anthis Corp.), Morgan Lidster (Inland Aquatics), Chandra Liem (Golden Generation), Martin A. Moe, Jr., Bronson Nagareda, Alf Jacob Nilsen, Michael S. Paletta, Richard Pyle, Dennis Reynolds (Aquamarines), Greg Schiemer, Frank Schneidewind, Mike Schied, Terry Siegel, Julian Sprung, Wayne Sugiyama (Wayne's Ocean World), Leng Sy (Ecosystem Aquariums), Dr. Hiroyuki Tanaka, Takamosa and Miki Tonozuka (Dive and Dives), Jeffrey Turner (Oceans, Reefs & Aquariums), Rob Vanderloss (Chertan, Papua New Guinea), Jeff Voet (Tropical Fish World), Tony Wagner (CaribSea), Randy Walker (Marine Center), Fenton Walsh, Jim Walters (Old Town Aquarium) and Forrest Young and Angus Barnhart (Dynasty Marine Associates).

Dr. Gerald R. Allen, Fred Bavendam, Janine Cairns-Michael, Paul Humann, Rudie H. Kuiter, Dr. John E. Randall, Roger Steene, and Takamosa Tonozuka provided some of the most amazing photographs in this book. Thank you!

I am extremely appreciative of the Microcosm team, especially Alesia Depot, Alice Lawrence, Emily Stetson and Editor James Lawrence, and the folks at T.F.H. Inc., especially Glen Axelrod, for bringing this to fruition.

Thanks also to my U.S. family and New Zealand family for their support over the years. Janine Cairns-Michael, my wonderful spouse, deserves a medal for putting up with years of my chasing, watching, and writing about reef fishes. Without her never-failing support for nearly a quarter of a century, I'm not sure works such as this would ever have seen the light of day.

—*Scott W. Michael, Lincoln, Nebraska*

CONTENTS

Fishes & Invertebrates: A Fine Balance

To me, a reef tank without fishes is like a flower garden without birds, butterflies, squirrels and other life forms. Sessile invertebrates, such as stony corals, have a limited behavior repertoire, to say the least, and many display little if any movement. (I have yet to see a hyperactive sponge, for example.) Fishes add movement and bring their "personalities" and fascinating behaviors to the aquascape, providing flashes of color and greatly enhancing the overall impression of the captive reef being an accurate reflection of a scene in the wild.

However, as marine aquarium keepers master the husbandry skills to maintain, grow, and even propagate corals and other delicate invertebrates, reef fishes sometimes find themselves forgotten— or even banned from some systems.

To succeed with corals and other invertebrates, it is vital to provide optimal water quality and eradicate or control pests or predators that prey on their polyps or delicate, exposed tissues. For this reason, some coral enthusiasts recommend that you introduce few, if any, fishes to the reef aquarium. Fishes and their foods inevitably add to the nutrient load of the tank, thus challenging water quality, and some species may even pick at or eat coral polyps.

While an overload of fishes—or the wrong kind of fishes—can overwhelm a reef aquarium, the right fishes can help in many ways: feeding on pests and parasites, grazing on nuisance algae, sifting the substrate, helping to keep the tank cleaner, and in some cases, even nurturing the corals and anemones with which they may associate.

I believe that the true measure of reefkeeping success today is finding a balance between fishes and invertebrate life, providing as realistic as possible an approximation of a scene in nature.

Reef scene off Bali, Indonesia: akin to birds and butterflies in a garden, fishes bring brilliant colors and movement to the stony coral-dominated aquascape.

Fledgling Science

THE MORE I'VE EXPERIMENTED WITH FISHES in reef aquariums, the more I realize that finding fishes that will coexist with captive corals is still a very inexact science. There are many extremely attractive, durable and reef-safe fish choices, and this guide will attempt to direct the new or intermediate aquarist to the families, genera, and species that have passed the tests of time in captive marine systems.

However, adventuresome reefkeepers are often looking for the unusual or unexpected fish species and may be willing to push the boundaries of what is truly "safe" when assembling their own marine aquarium communities. Coral reef fishes can also be idiosyncratic—well-behaved in some aquariums, exhibiting troublesome habits in others. This guide will attempt to flag the possible troublemakers, as well as the difficult-to-keep species, before you buy them.

Six Things to Consider When Selecting a Fish for Your Reef Aquarium

1. **Will it eat or nip the invertebrates you intend to keep?** The first thing to look at in determining if a particular fish species may be a risk to your invertebrates is its natural diet. If a fish eats coral in the wild, it will most likely do so in the aquarium. If a fish eats shrimp and small fish on the reef, it will probably slurp up all your Blue Green Chromis and cleaner shrimp if it is large enough to do so.

Unfortunately, in the aquarium, some fish develop predilections for foods that they typically will ignore in the wild. Because certain fishes are a threat to some invertebrates and not to others, you will need to decide what types of invertebrates you want to keep in order to determine what species of fish are suitable for your tank. Once you decide on the animals to be included in your invertebrate community, you can then rule out certain fish species.

Exquisite Fairy Wrasse (*Cirrhilabrus exquisitus*) Pacific form, male: perfect for the reef aquarist—modest in size and harmless to corals and most invertebrates.

2. **Will it knock or flip corals over?** When a fish dislodges a piece of coral, the cnidarian's tissue may be torn or it may land on another stinging coral or anemone, resulting in irreparable damage. There are species simply too large and rambunctious for the average home reef tank, and there are also fishes that commonly knock corals over when they forage over the reef. Others will take pieces of coral in their mouths or use chin barbels to flip them over when exposing hidden prey. One way to reduce the damage these species may cause is to use some of the underwater epoxies that are now available to reefkeepers to cement pieces of live rock together or to cement coral pieces to the live rock.

3. **Will it constantly perch on or wallow in your corals?** Special precautions need to be taken with species that perch on corals or that wallow among the tentacles of large-polyped stony corals.

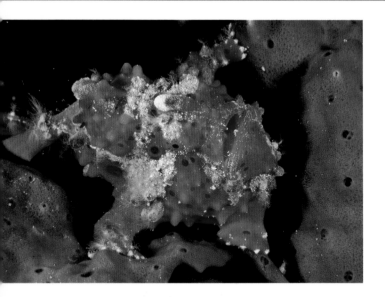

Wartskin Frogfish (*Antennarius maculatus*): an ideal specimen for a nano reef or specimen tank without tempting prey items such as small fishes and shrimps.

Anemonefishes will regularly wallow in the extended polyps of certain species, which sometimes causes the polyps to contract and can lead to the demise of the invertebrate.

4. **Will it cover corals with sand substrate when it feeds or burrows?** Some fishes may bury your invertebrates as a result of their feeding or burrowing activities. The fishes that are most likely to do this are the sleeper gobies (*Valenciennea* species). They take large mouthfuls of sand and eject it out through their gills, and some species rise into the water column before expelling the substrate. If you keep a substrate-sifting goby, you should not keep soft corals (many have a difficult time shedding sand) and species of stony corals that are intolerant of silting well away from the aquarium bottom. Place stony corals on the bottom that can easily shed sediment (e.g., *Alveopora, Catalaphyllia, Cynarina, Goniopora, Fungia, Heliofungia, Herpolitha, Polyphyllia, Scolymia*, and *Trachyphyllia*) and tilt them at

a slight angle that will facilitate shedding. Promptly remove sand from those corals that cannot do it themselves—a turkey baster does this task nicely. Other sessile invertebrates that may be harmed by having substrate deposited on them include mushroom anemones, zoanthids, and clams.

5. **How frequently will this fish have to be fed?** Some reef aquarists feed their aquariums only two or three times a week, depending on the ability of the live rock to provide a sufficient diet of fauna and flora for the fishes. Increased feeding can result in poorer water quality (especially if your tank does not have a proper protein skimmer and/or adequate refugium) and therefore a less healthy environment for your invertebrates. But some of the fishes that feed principally on suspended zooplankton need to be fed at least once, and even twice, a day if they are gong to thrive in captivity. These include anthias (*Pseudanthias* species), fairy wrasses (*Cirrhilabrus* species), flasher wrasses (*Paracheilinus* species), pyramid butterflyfishes (*Hemitaurichthys* species), and swallowtail angelfishes (*Genicanthus* species). If you are resolved to feeding your aquarium less than twice a day, avoid species in these groups. If you would like to keep some of these zooplankton feeders, use a large protein skimmer and live sand to control dissolved organic and nitrate levels that may result from increased feeding. Consider the use of a plant-filled refugium to extract dissolved nutrients and also to serve as a breeding ground for amphipods and other live foods that can help sustain your fishes.

6. **Is this fish disease-resistant?** Although no fish is totally immune to all the parasites common to marine aquariums, some species are less likely to succumb to parasites. For example, the comets (*Calloplesiops* species) are incredibly hardy and rarely, if ever, have problems with parasites. Hawkfishes, damselfishes, certain wrasses, dottybacks, blennies, gobies, dartfishes, and dragonets are also more disease-resistant. On the other hand, there are species, most notably the members of the tang genus *Zebrasoma*, that are virtual parasite magnets. They are commonly hosts to protozoan parasites, such as ich (*Cryptocaryon irritans*) and velvet (*Amyloodinium ocellatum*), and to black flatworms (*Paravortex* sp.).

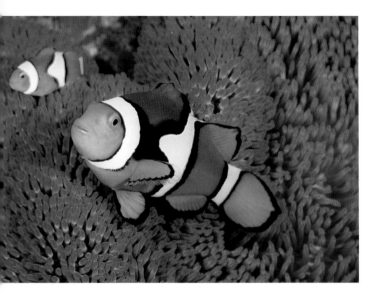

Clown Anemonefish (*Amphiprion percula*) with carpet anemone: a reef aquarium can offer close-up views of fishes with their symbionts and other invertebrates.

One way to avoid parasite problems in the reef tank is to quarantine *every* fish you buy before adding it to the tank and use an ultraviolet sterilizer.

Expect the Unexpected

PART OF THE ALLURE AND CHALLENGE for the marine aquarist is knowing that fishes can be unpredictable. When selecting a fish for your reef tank, be aware there is behavioral variability within families, genera, and even between individuals of the same species. The same specimen may even act differently in different settings, depending on what corals it is kept with or how often it is fed. Therefore, it is not always possible to say that all members of a particular taxonomic group are suitable, or unsuitable for the reef aquarium.

First, there can be variation within a family. For example, most triggerfishes (Family Balistidae) are poor reef aquarium inhabitants because they eat almost anything. But there are several species that feed primarily on zooplankton that will not harm sessile invertebrates.

Second, there can be variations at the genus level. The butterflyfish genus *Heniochus* provides us with a good example. The Schooling Bannerfish (*Heniochus diphreutes*) rarely bothers live corals, but coral polyps are a prime source of nutrition for the Horseface Bannerfish (*Heniochus monoceros*).

Third, there can be variation between individuals within a species. Consider the Flame Angelfish (*Centropyge loriculus*). Some individuals will ignore corals and tridacnid clams, while others will nip them mercilessly. Unfortunately, this individual variability is displayed by all the angelfish species in the *Centropyge* genus, although certain species, like the Lemonpeel Angelfish (*Centropyge flavissimus*), seem more prone to harming corals and clams while others, like the Cherubfish (*Centropyge argi*), are more likely to "behave."

Finally, there can be ontogenetic variability (changes that occur with age). For example, wrasses of the genus *Coris* are well-suited for the reef tank as juveniles, but as adults they eat snails, clams, and shrimp and will flip over coral pieces when searching for food. Other fish that show similar reef-tank suitability changes with age include some of the large angelfishes (e.g., *Pomacanthus* species, *Holacanthus* species), spadefishes (this includes the batfishes), dragon wrasses (*Novaculichthys* species) and the banana wrasses (*Thalassoma* species).

With all species and groups found in this guide, fishes with known behavioral traits that may prove troublesome in a reef aquarium are identified. If you are like most aquarists, you will occasionally want to take a chance on a fish with an imperfect profile, but it always helps to know the rules before breaking them.

Dragon Moray (*Enchelycore pardalis*): an attractive individual from Japan. Although a threat to fish tankmates, this moray can be housed in spacious reef tanks.

Moray Eels (Family Muraenidae)

Contrary to widespread belief, the reef aquarium is an ideal moray venue, as these aquascapes tend to have lots of cracks and crevices in which an eel can refuge. Because morays range in size from 8-inch (20-cm) dwarfs to 13-foot (4-m) giants, proper species selection is critical. A moray downside is that most will eat smaller fishes and ornamental crustaceans, and the larger species may knock corals off the reef structure, which could cause serious damage to these invertebrates. This is particularly true for those morays that get more agitated at feeding time. One advantage in placing an eel in your reef tank is that when it moves behind and between your live rocks, it will stir up some of the detritus that collects in these hidden areas. To keep a moray in your reef aquarium, unless it holds hundreds of gallons, stay away from the larger species. Smaller morays are less likely to dislodge rockwork or coral specimens. Some morays will also dig under rockwork, causing cave-ins (be sure rockwork is placed on the tank bottom before adding a sand bed and use adhesives to bond the rocks together).

Ribbon Eel (*Rhinomuraena quaesita*): although beautiful, the ribbon eels are often difficult to feed and rarely thrive in either a reef or fish-only aquarium.

One of the major causes of moray death is escape. These fishes regularly slither from open tanks or through small holes in the aquarium top. In smaller tanks, larger individuals may even knock off glass tops that are not weighted down. Morays may also go over overflow boxes, so modify the boxes accordingly.

Although live food may be needed to initiate feeding, with time most morays will accept frozen or refrigerated foods on a feeding stick. Field studies indicate that morays typically ingest one large meal every three or four days, so in order to prevent them from over-feeding, be sure your eel eats to satiation roughly twice a week. Numerous smaller prey items are better than fewer, larger items. A moray that eats a food item that is too large may regurgitate its partially digested meal—this can make a mess of your tank. The ribbon eels (*Rhinomuraena* species) tend to be difficult to feed and often live for only short periods in the home aquarium. The handsome Zebra Moray Eel (*Gymnomuraena zebra*) has been housed in reef tanks, but it can be reluctant to feed on anything but live crustaceans (it favors live fiddler crabs).

Gymnothorax melatremus Schultz, 1953
Golden Moray (Dirty Yellow Moray, Pencil Moray)

Maximum Length: 7.1 in. (18 cm).
Range: Indo-Pacific.
Minimum Aquarium Size: 10 gal. (38 L).
Foods & Feeding: Meaty foods, including frozen seafood. May require live ghost shrimp to initiate a feeding response.
Aquarium Suitability/Reef Compatibility:
Aquarium Notes: This is an ideal moray for the reef aquarium. Although it will hide during much of the day, it often does so with its head exposed and can be trained to come out to accept food when the lights are on. It may be difficult to find in a larger reef tank replete with live rock, and is easier to observe in a small or nano-reef. Will eat ornamental crustaceans, but its small maximum size makes it less of a threat to most fishes. The coloration can vary from tan to yellowish orange, with some specimens sporting brown reticulations. There are other small morays (less than 20 in. [51 cm]) that are ideal for reef tanks, but these are not as colorful as *G. melatremus*. They include: Brown Moray (*Gymnothorax brunneus*), Latticetail Moray (*G. buroensis*), Whitelip Moray (*G. chilospilus*), Slendertail Moray (*G. gracilicaudus*), and Herre's Moray (*G. herrei*).

Good Reef Aquarium Morays

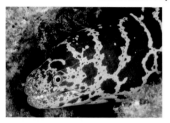

Echidna catenata
Chainlink Moray
Max. Length: 28 in. (71 cm).

Echidna nebulosa
Snowflake Moray
Max. Length: 29.5 in. (75 cm).

Gymnothorax chilospilus
Whitelip Moray
Max. Length: 19.5 in. (20 cm).

Gymnothorax eurostus
Stout Moray
Max. Length: 25.6 in. (65 cm).

Gymnothorax meleagris
Whitemouth Moray
Max. Length: 3.9 ft. (1.2 m).

Siderea thyrsoidea
White-eye Moray
Max. Length: 25.6 in. (65 cm).

Sharptail Snake Eel (*Myrichthys breviceps*): these eels need a deep sand bed, lots of swimming room, and live food.

Snake Eels (Family Ophichthidae)

Most snake eels are not well-suited for reef tanks, doing best in an aquascape devoid of structure. If you devote a significant portion of a large tank (180 gallons [684 L] or more) to an open sand bottom, perhaps with an island of coral, you can keep snake eels healthy in a reef aquarium. They require a thick layer of fine substrate to bury under (minimum depth 4 inches [10 cm]). Live fiddler crabs or ghost shrimp are usually needed to catalyze feeding (some, like the Banded Snake Eel [*Myrichthys colubrinus*] are very difficult to feed). Snake eels often move about the tank when they are not buried, and they may collide with and knock off corals. It is important to provide these fishes with lots of room. Some frantically swim about the tank and attempt to leap out if disturbed by the aquarist. They are very effective at escaping from the aquarium. Try to work in the tank as little as possible, but when you do, move very slowly and stay clear of the eel. They may also collide with and be stung by sea anemones. These eels will eat polychaete worms, crustaceans, sea urchins, and fishes.

Spotted Garden Eel (*Heteroconger hassi*): these eels can make a fascinating addition to a reef tank with a deep sand bed and an expanse of open bottom.

Garden Eels (Family Heterocongridae)

Garden eels are fascinating animals that can be kept in reef aquariums, but they do have special requirements. If you plan to replicate a small colony (as they occur in the wild), you must provide enough space so that individuals can spread out. The substrate on the aquarium bottom must be at least 6 inches (15 cm) deep, preferably deeper, or the eels may damage their tails. In addition, the aquarium should have a gentle current that blows along the bottom of the tank to bring the eels their food.

These fishes can be fed live adult brine shrimp, finely chopped seafood, frozen mysid shrimp, and Cyclop-eeze. They will also eat baby livebearers, free-swimming copepods, and mysids (the latter prey organisms can be provided by connecting an internal or external refugium to your aquarium). Live food may be needed to initiate the first feeding. Feed garden eels at least twice per day. They do best with mild-mannered tankmates and may not compete successful for food with aggressive fishes that intimidate them and gobble up newly introduced prey items before the eels have a chance to eat.

Taylor's Garden Eel (*Heteroconger taylori*): feed these zooplankton-eating eels often and do not house them with aggressive fishes.

These are timid creatures, especially at first, and newly acquired individuals often retract into their burrows as the aquarist approaches the tank. With time, they usually become bolder, spending more time in the open. If you create a high-profile reef, make sure the rocks are securely attached with cable ties or adhesives.

Garden eels can be kept together, but adult males of some species will fight if there is an insufficient distance between them. Avoid keeping them with fish tankmates that may behave aggressively toward them or eat them. They also should not be housed with vigorous substrate displacers (e.g., goatfishes) that may disturb their burrows. These eels will not harm most invertebrates, with the possible exception of delicate shrimps (like smaller *Periclimenes*). Newly acquired garden eels are prone to jumping out of the aquarium until they settle in and dig their burrows.

One interesting trick discovered by some garden eel enthusiasts: place a mirror on the back of the tank and you can create the illusion that the tank is larger than it actually is and that there are twice as many garden eels present—more realistically representing a scene from their natural habitat.

Striped Eel Catfish (*Plotosus lineatus*): while a school of juveniles makes an interesting exhibit, these fish get too large and secretive for most reef tanks.

Eel Catfishes (Family Plotosidae)

J uvenile coral catfish are undeniably cute and make an interesting addition to the reef aquarium. A small to medium-sized group of juveniles is especially fascinating to watch, forming living "balls" when they congregate. They are very effective scavengers, grubbing in the sand and around the aquarium decor to get at any food that hits the bottom.

The biggest drawback to keeping these fish is that they transform from endearing little fish into homely (or at least less attractive) big fish. A group of adults will take up a ponderous amount of room and place a significant burden on the biological filter. Adults are a threat to any fishes or motile invertebrates that they can catch and fit into their mouths. Not only is the coloration of the adult less striking than that of the juvenile, but also larger specimens tend to be secretive, hiding in and around the aquarium decor. These fish are not finicky, eating almost any food particles that land on the aquarium bottom. The eel catfishes have venomous fin spines that can inflict a very painful sting.

Variegated Lizardfish (*Synodus variegatus*): a choice for a reef with large tank-mates only, the lizardfish's toothy grin is a sign of of its predatory prowess.

Lizardfishes (Family Synodontidae)

Lizardfishes make an unusual addition to a reef tank populated with aggressive, predatory fishes. They are a threat to any tank-mate that can fit into their large mouths. They will eat fishes and ornamental shrimps, but are not a threat to most other inverte-brates. They may perch on corals, causing polyps to close, but move often, rarely causing permanent damage. The size of the tank required is species-dependent, as they vary considerably in maxi-mum length. Because they spend most of their time in repose on the bottom, surface area is more important than volume. Some require open sandy areas on which to lie and possibly bury themselves (a sand substrate at least 3 inches [8 cm] deep is important for bury-ing species). They are likely to leap out of an open aquarium. Lizardfishes are often reluctant to ingest anything but live food (e.g., ghost shrimp, feeder fishes). Some can be duped into taking non-living food from the end of a feeding stick. Only one should be kept per tank, unless you can acquire a male-female pair. Larger individ-uals will eat smaller conspecifics or congeners.

Yellow Brotula (*Dinematichthys riukiuensis*): often sold in the trade as gobies, brotulas have a secretive nature that makes them less desirable reef choices.

Livebearing Brotulas (Family Bythitidae)

Although eyecatching, these secretive fishes are not highly desirable reef aquarium inhabitants, often disappearing permanently the moment they are introduced into a new system. It is preferable to house them in a small tank (10 to 30 gallons [38 to 114 L]) with limited decor (provide them with at least one or two desirable hiding places). In a smaller tank, you are much more likely to catch an occasional glimpse of your brotula—and be sure that it is getting fed. In a large reef tank, it is highly unlikely that you will ever see these fishes.

A dim light over the tank will also increase viewing opportunities. At night, you can observe them by using a red bulb (either incandescent or fluorescent). They will eat any animal life that is small enough to be ingested. In a tank with live rock, they will prey on secretive invertebrates, like snapping shrimps, small crabs, isopods, and amphipods. Crustacean-lovers beware: they will also eat ornamental shrimps. It is best to introduce food after dark or by directing meaty food behind the rockwork where the brotula lives.

Gulf Toadfish (*Opsanus beta*): an odd species that may dig under live rock and rearrange a smaller reef tank.

Toadfishes (Family Batrachoididae)

Definitely a choice only for the uncommon reef tank, toadfishes are interesting to observe, but they are a threat to algae-eating snails, small clams, ornamental crustaceans, mantis shrimps, brittle stars, small urchins, and small fishes. Toadfishes can thrive with the many hiding places that are typically found in a reef aquarium, but in a larger reef tank they may be hard to relocate as a result of their reclusive habits. This can present feeding challenges. They should be fed a varied diet, but some individuals may not be eager to ingest nonliving food. Live ghost shrimp may be needed to tempt finicky toadfishes. Most individuals can be trained to take meaty foods off a feeding stick. They will dig under live rock if sand is present in the tank and may cause structural instability. Toadfishes do not require lots of swimming room to survive. Most will do fine in aquariums as small as 15 gallons [57 L]. Toadfishes do not spend a lot of time in the open when first placed in their new home, but with time they should become more brazen and start to make appearances when the aquarium is illuminated.

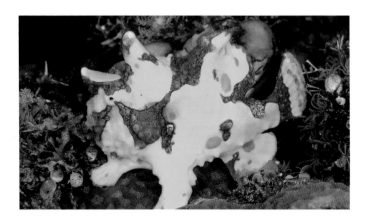

Wartskin Frogfish (*Antennarius maculatus*): this is one of the better species for the reef aquarium because it spends much of its time perching in the open.

Frogfishes (Family Antennariidae)

For the reef aquarium where the fate of small fishes or crustaceans is of no concern, a frogfish can be a truly unusual and interesting inhabitant. Smaller frogfishes are especially well-suited to nano-reefs. It is an ideal captive venue for them, as they do best when housed on their own. They do not contribute greatly to the nitrogenous load of an aquarium—they do not have to be fed frequently, they ingest all the food you give them, and their feces are large and solid and can be easily recognized and removed.

However, in a large reef tank, replete with live rock and coral, the more cryptic species can disappear. For a larger reef tank, select one of the more active, less secretive species. They sometimes perch on hard or soft corals and cause their polyps to stay retracted. This can be problematic if the frogfish remains on the same coral for days at a time. You can encourage a frogfish to move away from a preferred perch by carefully pushing it off with a piece of rigid tubing. Do not keep frogfishes with invertebrates that have a potent sting (e.g., elegance corals, sea anemones) as they may be severely stung if

Scripted Frogfish (*Antennarius scriptissimus*?): a rare, poorly known species that would make a stunning addition to the nano-reef tank.

they inadvertently land on these cnidarians.

Most frogfishes require live food, at least initially. Feed them several prey items, two or three times a week. If you decide to house them with other fishes, select tankmates carefully. Frogfishes will ingest incredibly large prey items. Any slender fishes (e.g., wrasses) kept with a frogfish should be at least twice the length of the frogfish. If the fish is deep-bodied (like a *Dascyllus* damselfish) it should be slightly longer than the frogfish. They are regularly nipped by fishes that scrape or browse on sessile invertebrates (e.g., angelfishes, butterflyfishes, pufferfishes). Do not lift frogfishes from the water, as they regularly ingest air which they can have difficulty purging.

The key to frogfish husbandry is to minimize stress. They apparently suffer from post-stress disorders that can cause an otherwise healthy looking frogfish to die mysteriously. This means not housing them with tankmates that are prone to harassing them, relocating them as infrequently as possible, and maintaining good water quality. They are also susceptible to skin infections that can be difficult to detect because of their normally crusty integument.

Good Aquarium Frogfishes

Antennarius hispidus
Hispid Frogfish
Max. Length: 7.9 in. (20 cm).

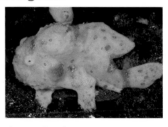

Antennarius pictus
Painted Frogfish
Max. Length: 6.2 in. (16 cm).

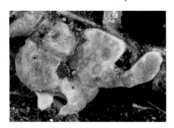

Antennarius pictus (variant)
Painted Frogfish
Max. Length: 6.2 in. (16 cm).

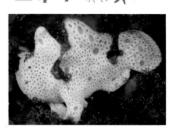

Antennarius pictus (variant)
Painted Frogfish
Max. Length: 6.2 in. (16 cm).

Antennarius striatus
Striated Frogfish
Max. Length: 8.6 in. (22 cm).

Antennarius sp.
Lembeh Frogfish
Max. Length: 3.5 in. (9 cm).

Pink Squirrelfish (*Sargocentron tieroides*): although somewhat secretive, squirrelfishes can be an interesting addition to the large reef tank.

Squirrelfishes & Soldierfishes
(Family Holocentridae)

Squirrelfishes can bring brilliant colors to the large or extra-large reef aquarium, depending on the species in question. Although they are not a threat to sessile invertebrates, they will feed on a variety of motile species, including worms, crustaceans, and serpent stars. They will also eat any fish tankmate that they can swallow. They feed on most meaty food items (e.g., chopped seafood, mysid shrimp, frozen preparations), but it may take a week or more before they come out to feed when the lights are on. Some may require live ghost shrimp. Most of the squirrelfishes are nocturnal. If kept in a brightly lit reef aquarium, these fishes will spend almost all of their time under cover, although some are more secretive than others. Provide them with plenty of good shelter sites (e.g., large caves or overhangs) to refuge in when the lights are on. They are active and will need plenty of swimming space. They are usually not aggressive toward heterospecifics, with the possible exception of congeners and fishes that attempt to enter their preferred refuge.

Blackbar Soldierfish (*Myripristis jacobus*): large eyes and red coloration are two unique soldierfish characteristics. They should be kept in a larger reef tank.

Soldierfishes are relatively easy to keep and do well in a spacious reef aquarium. They form aggregations in the wild, and a captive reef large enough to hold a grouping of soldierfishes can provide an interesting scene not often replicated in home aquariums.

They are nocturnal, and most feed on larger zooplankton after dark. Some species will eat polychaete worms or small crustaceans (e.g., shrimps), but they are not a threat to corals or other sessile invertebrates. They need suitable hiding places (e.g., large caves, overhangs) and will spend more time in the open in a dimly lit tank. You can observe them at night by placing a red bulb over your aquarium. The members of the genus *Myripristis* are not aggressive toward fish tankmates, while members of the genus *Plectrypops* are more likely to pester other crevice-dwellers and will also eat smaller fishes. The *Plectrypops* species are also more secretive.

If a soldierfish needs to be captured, it is best to use a specimen container, not a net, as the latter may damage their large eyes. They can be easily startled as the aquarist works in the tank or if there is sudden activity in the vicinity of the aquarium.

Good Aquarium Squirrelfishes & Soldierfishes

Myripristis hexagona
Doubletooth Soldierfish
Max. Length: 7.9 in. (20 cm).

Myripristis vittata
Whitelip Soldierfish
Max. Length: 7.9 in. (20 cm).

Neoniphon marianus
Longjaw Squirrelfish
Max. Length: 6.7 in. (17 cm).

Neoniphon sammara
Bloodspot Squirrelfish
Max. Length: 12.6 in. (32 cm).

Plectrypops lima
Roughscale Soldierfish
Max. Length: 6.3 in. (16 cm).

Sargocentron diadema
Crown Squirrelfish
Max. Length: 6.7 in. (17 cm).

Common Seahorse (*Hippocampus kuda*): exciting progress has been made in the captive spawning and successful captive husbandry of seahorses.

Seahorses (Family Syngnathidae)

Many aquarists love seahorses but have avoided them because of the husbandry challenges they present. If you've always wanted to keep a seahorse, there is no better time than now. Breeders are now selling captive-raised seahorses that have been weaned on frozen mysid shrimp with no impact on wild populations. But, even the captive-bred individuals can be difficult to keep in a larger community tank where they have to compete for food. Suitable tankmates are nonaggressive, slow-moving fishes like pipefishes, shrimpfishes, dragonets, and some smaller gobies. Seahorses are ideal for the nano-reef. Feeding them in a smaller tank, where they are housed on their own, is easier. Females are somewhat easier to keep than males, and young individuals acclimate more readily than adults. Do not house them with potent stingers (e.g., sea anemones). Provide macroalgae, gorgonians, or dead coral branches for them to grasp with their prehensile tails. Although color is often genetically determined, it may change depending on light levels.

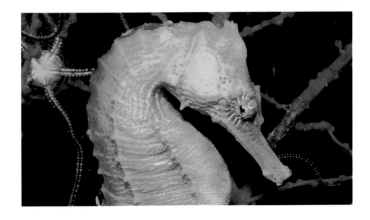

Hippocampus erectus Perry, 1810
Lined Seahorse

Maximum Height: 5.9 in. (15 cm).

Range: Atlantic.

Minimum Aquarium Size: 10 gal. (38 L)

Foods & Feeding: Seahorses may remain healthy for several months on a diet of live brine shrimp, but they will gradually become malnourished and die. Live brine shrimp or frozen mysid shrimp can be fortified with a vitamin supplement (I recommend Vibrance, which is rich in HUFAs and color-enhancing pigments.). Feed 2 to 5 whole, frozen mysid shrimp at least twice per day (larger individuals may take 12 or more mysids per meal). Allow your seahorse to fast one day per week.

Aquarium Suitability*/Reef Compatibility:

Aquarium Notes: This is an ideal candidate for the nano-reef, as well as the larger reef aquarium. It is important to provide stationary objects that it can wrap its prehensile tails around when at rest (e.g., macroalgae, tubular sponges, live gorgonians, dead coral branches, plastic gorgonians). Do not include powerful stingers (sea anemones, stinging corals) and larger, predatory corallimorpharians (elephant ear anemones) with any seahorses.

*FOR CAPTIVE-RAISED SPECIMENS

Good Reef Aquarium Seahorses

Hippocampus barbouri
Zebrasnout Seahorse
Max. Height: 5.9 in. (15 cm).

Hippocampus histrix
Thorny Seahorse
Max. Height: 6.7 in. (17 cm).

Hippocampus kuda
Yellow Seahorse, Spotted Seahorse
Max. Height: 6.7 in. (17 cm).

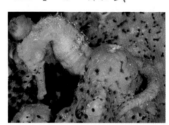

Hippocampus reidi
Longsnout Seahorse
Max. Height: 5.9 in. (15 cm).

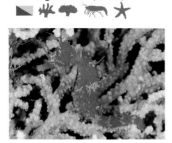

Hippocampus sindonis
Painted Seahorse
Max. Height: 3.1 in. (8 cm).

Hippocampus spinosissimus
Hedgehog Seahorse
Max. Height: 6.3 in. (16 cm).

Orangebanded Pipefish (*Doryrhamphus pessuliferus*): this species and others in this genus are known to clean cryptic fish species that share their hiding places.

Pipefishes (Family Syngnathidae)

Pipefishes can be kept in a peaceful reef aquarium and often do better in this environment because of the availability of natural prey organisms. They are, however, *not* a good choice for beginners. They are often reluctant to accept anything but live foods and require frequent feedings. They will eat live adult brine shrimp. Some pipefishes can be coaxed into eating frozen mysid shrimp and Cyclop-eeze that are being moved by water currents.

A refugium is a great addition to the pipefish aquarium. If you are counting on the live rock or the crustaceans from a refugium to provide your pipefishes with enough to eat, exclude food competitors unless the tank is very large with an ample supply of live rock or the refugium is extremely productive. Avoid tankmates that are likely to pick at them, including larger blennies, wrasses, pufferfishes, triggerfishes, and porcupinefishes. They will not do well if housed in a tank full of fleet-finned food competitors. Keeping a smaller species on its own in a nano-reef can increase the likelihood of success.

YELLOWSTREAKED PIPEFISH (*CORYTHOICHTHYS HAEMATOPTERUS*)

Corythoichthys spp.
Dragon Pipefishes

Maximum Length: 3.7 to 6.7 in. (9 to 17 cm).
Range: Indo-Pacific.
Minimum Aquarium Size: 10 gal. (38 L).
Foods & Feeding: These pipefishes are often reluctant to accept any-thing but live foods, such as live adult brine shrimp, juvenile ghost shrimp, or mysid shrimp. A productive refugium and live rock can aid in getting them enough to eat.
Aquarium Suitability/Reef Compatibility:
Aquarium Notes: Dragon pipefishes spend their time slinking over the substrate, hunting for tiny crustaceans. They are best kept on their own or with other passive fish species. By keeping them in a nano-reef tank, you may be able to ensure that they get enough to eat. They are meticulous micropredators that will have difficulty competing with fishes that eat with gusto. They may eat some of the tiny crustaceans that parasitize stony corals. Before purchasing one of these fishes, be sure the tail is intact and the integument of the bony body is not sloughing off (bacterial infections are often seen in individuals that have been picked on by aquarium tankmates).

Doryrhamphus dactyliophorus (Bleeker, 1853)
Banded Pipefish (Ringed Pipefish)

Maximum Length: 7.9 in. (20 cm).
Range: Indo-Pacific.
Minimum Aquarium Size: 10 gal. (38 L).
Foods & Feeding: Often reluctant to accept anything but live foods.
Aquarium Suitability/Reef Compatibility:
Aquarium Notes: This extremely attractive pipefish is common in the aquarium trade, but should only be purchased by those aquarists willing to spend the time and money to feed and maintain it. Provide it with suitable shelter sites like an overhang or a cave, and choose its tankmates very carefully. It will typically consume only live fare. Living foods to try include adult brine shrimp, mysid shrimp, *Daphnia*, mosquito larvae, baby guppies and mollies, and live ghost shrimp. Some individuals may accept frozen mysid shrimp over time. This species is better suited for the reef aquarium than most of its congeners, because of its less reclusive nature. It may have trouble competing with pugnacious tankmates for food, and will not survive in a competitive community environment. If bullied, it will hide constantly.

Doryrhamphus excisus Kaup, 1856
Bluestripe Pipefish

Maximum Length: 2.8 in. (7 cm).
Range: Indo-Pacific.
Minimum Aquarium Size: 10 gal. (38 L).
Foods & Feeding: Typical of the genus, this species is often reluctant to accept anything but living foods. Offer live adult brine shrimp or some of the other small crustaceans available in the marine fish trade. A productive refugium and live rock can aid in getting it enough to eat. Feed several times a day.
Aquarium Suitability/Reef Compatibility:
Aquarium Notes: The *Doryrhamphus* species are some of the most spectacular members of the pipefish group. They hover over the substrate, rather than slither across it, and often occur in pairs. In nature, they live in caves and under ledges. This species makes a dramatic impact in a nano-reef. It will do better in a tank full of live rock because of the tiny invertebrates that often associate with this substrate. Do not house this fish with food competitors or aggressive species (e.g., dottybacks, angelfishes, wrasses, triggerfishes, puffers). It is a part-time cleaner, picking parasites off of other secretive species (e.g., morays).

Dragon Sea Moth (*Eurypegasus draconis*): a bizarre bottom dweller requiring expert care and an open expanse of sand for hunting live invertebrate prey.

Seamoths (Family Pegasidae)

The seamoths are fascinating fishes, harmless to corals and ornamental invertebrates, but of interest primarily to advanced aquarists willing and able to provide them with live foods and a lagoon-like aquascape. They will reject most preserved foods, preferring live fare, such as black worms, adult brine shrimp, mysid shrimp, and other small benthic crustaceans (e.g., amphipods, isopods). They feed off the substrate, not from the water column, and a productive refugium will help provide enough natural prey. They should be housed in aquariums with little, if any, live rock or other decor. If an aquarium is large enough (100 gallons [380 L] or more), a small patch reef, composed of live rock and soft and stony corals, could be placed in one corner or along the back of the tank. Algae growth can be beneficial because it will encourage the growth of amphipod populations. Sand should be used on the bottom of the tank, although the substrate depth is not a critical factor. Seamoths should be housed with extremely passive tankmates or—even better—in a species tank of their own.

Robust Ghost Pipefish (*Solenostomus cyanopterus*): a short-lived delicate fish that can present feeding challenges.

Ghost Pipefishes (Family Solenostomidae)

These beautiful fishes are delicate and difficult to feed. They will only eat small, live crustaceans. Juveniles need to be fed live, gut-packed brine shrimp and live mysid shrimp, while larger adults will hunt small ghost shrimps. A productive refugium is considered obligatory. A tank that lacks food competitors but has filamentous and macroalgae (to encourage amphipods to thrive) will increase your chances of success. Ghost pipefishes are prone to being picked on by more aggressive tankmates and can become trapped against filter intakes or overflows. The other drawback is their naturally short lifespan—most are thought to live only a year or so. These relatively inactive fishes can be housed in tanks as small as 20 gallons (76 L). Make sure you provide adequate shelter, which can include live gorgonians or other soft corals, sponges (live or artificial), live rock, macroalgae, live sea grass, and artificial plants. Do not house them with invertebrates that pack a potent sting, or with large, potentially dangerous crustaceans (e.g., boxer shrimp, arrow crabs, large hermit crabs, or other large crab species).

Coral Shrimpfish (*Aeoliscus strigatus*): best kept in groups and fed live food, shrimpfishes will do well if their dietary needs are met.

Shrimpfishes (Family Centriscidae)

Shrimpfish have razor-thin bodies, an attribute that has led to their being dubbed razorfishes by some authors. They live upside down, maintaining a posture with the head oriented toward the seafloor. Shrimpfishes can be kept in reef aquariums as small as 30 gallons (114 L) and will thrive in captivity if their dietary needs can be met. This requires providing a source of minute living crustaceans like brine shrimp, amphipods, copepods, and mysid shrimp larvae. These fishes tend do better in tanks with plenty of live rock and/or an attached refugium. A good crop of filamentous algae can help by providing a healthy population of amphipods. You will have better success with these fishes if they are kept on their own. They are not aggressive toward one another, and actually do best if kept in groups. A school of these fishes makes a very interesting display in a reef tank, especially a stony coral display. Do not house them with belligerent fishes or food competitors. Like many other fishes in this order, the shrimpfishes may naturally have a short lifespan.

Cockatoo Waspfish (*Ablabys taenianotus*): doing what it does best, mimicking a leaf. Inset shows a beautiful Longspine Waspfish (*Paracentropogon longispinus*).

Waspfishes (Family Tetrarogidae)

The waspfishes can make interesting additions to the reef aquarium. Because of their less active lifestyles, the smaller species can be kept in a nano-reef. They will eat crustaceans and small, benthic fishes but are no threat to sessile invertebrates. They are relatively easy to keep if fed regularly with live gut-packed ghost shrimp. Some individuals can be trained to take pieces of seafood from a feeding stick, while smaller specimens may need live brine shrimp. Provide them with some open sand bottom—some species bury, others prefer to refuge among macroalgae, while all spend most of their time resting on soft substrates. Waspfishes are often mistaken for food-encrusted substrate by fishes that eat sessile invertebrates, including butterflyfishes, angelfishes, pufferfishes, triggerfishes, and porcupinefishes. Large herbivores may also pick at them, because they look like plant material. When transferring a waspfish, use a specimen container or a fine mesh net to prevent the dorsal and cheek spines from becoming entangled. These fishes are **venomous** and can deliver a painful sting.

Devil Scorpionfish (*Scorpaenopsis diabola*): brightly colored members of this species can enliven the reef aquarium, but they will eat crustaceans and fishes.

Scorpionfishes (Family Scorpaenidae)

Like a peculiar work of art, scorpionfishes are oddities that are appreciated most by the collector of the unusual. They are **venomous** and can inflict a very painful sting, so be sure to take the necessary precautions when moving one of these fishes or working in its aquarium. They spend most of their time perched on the substrate. As a result, they can be kept in smaller aquariums without ill effect. Most species appreciate ledges, caves, and coral rubble where they can seek refuge. If you are not interested in including shrimps and small fishes in your system, they can make colorful additions to a reef community. If you add one of the more secretive forms (e.g., *Parascorpaena* species) to a large tank full of live rock, however, you may never see the fish. Instead, select a species that tends to spend time in the open. Be aware that feeding can present challenges, as most will only accept live food. Gut-packed ghost shrimp are a good staple diet for those scorpionfishes that cannot be weaned onto seafood from a feeding stick. Provide them with a varied diet and feed them to satiation twice a week.

Weedy Scorpionfish (*Rhinopias frondosa*): the allure of keeping one of these is great, but they can be a challenge and collection could be deleterious.

Lacey, Weedy & Eschmeyer's Scorpionfishes
(*Rhinopias* spp.)

In the past few years, these amazing scorpionfishes have become more common in the aquarium trade and will elicit a reaction in even the most jaded marine enthusiasts. But they are not common anywhere they occur in nature, which means fishing pressures could deplete local populations. They also present husbandry challenges. Live food (e.g., gut-packed ghost shrimp, mollies, guppies) is needed for feeding, and many individuals may never accept anything else. Avoid keeping them with species that eat encrusting invertebrates—they mistake these fishes for food. They are highly predatory and will eat any fish they can ingest (do not underestimate the size of their jaws). They are susceptible to bacterial infections if injured and can succumb to skin parasites. They spend most of their time in the open and are relatively inactive—although spectacular, even in repose. Small individuals can be kept in modestly sized aquariums (20 gallons [78 L]). These scorpionfishes are often best kept in a tank with rubble and some open sand bottom.

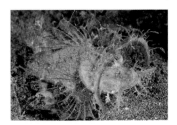

Pteroidichthys amboinensis
Ambon Scorpionfish
Max. Length: 4.7 in. (12 cm).

Rhinopias aphanes
Lacey Scorpionfish
Max. Length: 9.4 in. (24 cm).

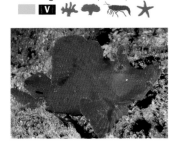

Rhinopias eschmeyeri
Eschmeyer's Scorpionfish
Max. Length: 7.5 in. (19 cm).

Rhinopias eschmeyeri (variant)
Eschmeyer's Scorpionfish
Max. Length: 7.5 in. (19 cm).

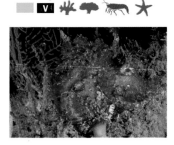

Rhinopias frondosa
Weedy Scorpionfish
Max. Length: 9.1 in. (23 cm).

Rhinopias frondosa (variant)
Weedy Scorpionfish
Max. Length: 9.1 in. (23 cm).

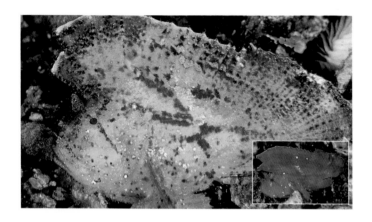

Taenianotus triacanthus Lacépède, 1802
Leaf Scorpionfish

Maximum Length: 3.9 in. (10 cm).
Range: Indo-Pacific.
Minimum Aquarium Size: 15 gal. (57 L).
Foods & Feeding: Meaty foods, including frozen seafood. May require live ghost shrimp or gut-packed livebearers (mollies, guppies) to initiate a feeding response.
Aquarium Suitability/Reef Compatibility:
Aquarium Notes: This lovely scorpionfish comes in many colors, including pink, maroon, yellow, and white. It is a great scorpionfish for the reef aquarium as it tends to spend time in the open. It will do best if not housed with overly aggressive food competitors (a species-dedicated nano-reef would make a wonderful home for this fish). I have never had them become overly aggressive toward each other or toward other fish species, but they may spar with each other. The best way to feed this fish in a reef tank is to train it to "jump" onto the edge of a net that contains its food. With its laterally compressed body and high dorsal fin it resembles a leaf or macroalgae frond. It also mimics bits of plant debris by rocking back and forth or swaying from side to side.

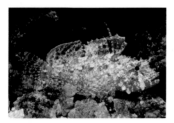

Iracundus signifer
Decoy Scorpionfish
Max. Length: 5.1 in. (13 cm).

Parascorpaena mossambica
Mozambique Scorpionfish
Max. Length: 3.9 in. (10 cm).

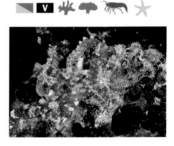

Scorpaenopsis macrochir
Flasher Scorpionfish
Max. Length: 5.1 in. (13 cm).

Scorpaenopsis papuensis
Papuan Scorpionfish
Max. Length: 7.9 in. (20 cm).

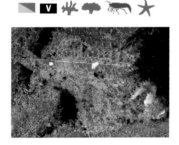

Scorpaenopsis possi
Poss's Scorpionfish
Max. Length: 7.6 in. (19.3 cm).

Sebastapistes cyanostigma
Yellowspotted Scorpionfish
Max. Length: 3.1 in. (8 cm).

Kodipungi Lionfish (*Pterois kodipungi*): larger lionfishes can be successfully housed in a spacious reef aquarium.

Lionfishes (Subfamily Pteroinae)

Although not usually thought of as reef-safe, the majority of lionfishes—among the most spectacular of marine aquarium fishes—are worthy of consideration if their predatory tendencies are recognized. The size of the aquarium used is species-dependent. The *Dendrochirus* species, which tend to be smaller, can be kept in larger nano-reefs. Provide them with suitable hiding places, as they are more secretive. The *Pterois* species will need more room. Lionfishes are ideal candidates for the reef aquarium if small fishes and ornamental shrimps (including cleaner and boxer shrimps) are not important. Some species (e.g., *P. volitans* and *P. russelli*) spend more time in the open but need swimming space. Live food may be needed initially, but most can be switched to nonliving foods presented on a feeding stick. Good live foods include ghost shrimp, fiddler crabs, and small crayfish. Feed them to satiation two or three times a week. It is usually not a problem to house two or more lionfish species together, but conspecifics and closely related forms (e.g., two members of the genus *Dendrochirus*) will occasionally fight.

Shortfin Lionfish (*Dendrochirus brachypterus*): this species comes in a variety of colors, including this rare yellow phase.

Aggressive encounters may include biting and ramming with their venomous spines, which can result in serious injury. If one lionfish is persistently attacked by another, they should be separated.

Special consideration needs to be made when selecting tank-mates for the lionfish. Most will eat any fish tankmate that can fit in their large mouths, but they rarely behave aggressively toward unrelated species. Even though they are **venomous**, lionfishes are not immune from being preyed upon by other marine organisms. Large eels, frogfishes, other scorpionfishes, and octopuses are all known to eat lionfishes. Of these predators, the frogfishes are notorious for ingesting them. Large angelfishes, pufferfishes, and triggerfishes have also been known to harass and damage lionfishes. Lionfishes may occasionally jab their tankmates with their venomous spines. This is more likely to occur in a crowded aquarium. Those fishes that are most prone to being "stung" by a lionfish are slow-moving or sedentary species (e.g., other scorpionfishes, porcupinefishes). Most fishes injected with a large dose of lionfish venom (more than that delivered by a normal "sting") will die within 10 to 30 minutes. Obviously, aquarists should treat them with respect.

Dendrochirus biocellatus
Twinspot Lionfish
Max. Length: 3.9 in. (10 cm).

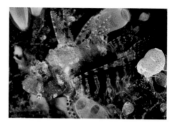

Dendrochirus brachypterus
Shortfin Lionfish
Max. Length: 6.7 in. (17 cm).

Dendrochirus zebra
Zebra Lionfish
Max. Length: 7.1 (18 cm).

Pterois antennata
Spotfin Lionfish
Max. Length: 7.9 in. (20 cm).

Pterois radiata
Clearfin Lionfish
Max. Length: 9.4 in. (24 cm).

Pterois volitans
Volitans Lionfish
Max. Length: 15 in. (38 cm).

Parapterois heterura (Bleeker, 1856)
Bluefin Lionfish (Blackfoot Lionfish)

Maximum Length: 9.1 in. (23 cm).
Range: Indo-Pacific.
Minimum Aquarium Size: 30 gal. (114 L).
Foods & Feeding: Feed marine fish and crustacean flesh. Live, gut-packed ghost shrimp may be needed to initiate feeding. Feed several times a week.
Aquarium Suitability/Reef Compatibility:
Aquarium Notes: The care of this sporadically available species is somewhat of an enigma. Most kept in captivity do not live long. It is known as a very poor shipper (not handling stress well), and so it is often difficult to find a healthy specimen. Aquarists also tend to keep them at higher water temperatures than they are accustomed to. (In the wild, they are usually found at temperatures of less than 74°F [23°C].) This species is unusual among the members of this subfamily in that it often partially buries itself under fine substrate. It also performs an odd behavior when threatened, spinning in circles with its head raised. This species will eat crustaceans and small benthic fishes.

Reef Stonefish (*Synanceia verrucosa*): with highly venomous spines, these fishes demand extreme care, but they can make unusual reef tank inhabitants.

Stonefishes (Family Synanceiidae)

For those reef aquarists interested in the unusual, even potentially deadly, stonefishes may be just what you are looking for, but caution is in order: these fishes are **highly venomous**, having been responsible for a number of human fatalities. Never keep in a home with children, and exercise extreme care when working in a stonefish tank or when moving one of these animals. They will eat crustaceans and fish tankmates (they have large mouths and eat large prey). Members of the genus *Synanceia* perch on hard substrate or bury in the sand. All members of the family require live food (e.g., gut-packed ghost shrimp). Although feeder fish can be used to initiate feeding, these do not constitute a nutritionally adequate diet for predators. Some stonefishes can be enticed to take strips of marine fish flesh off a feeding stick. Larger grazing fishes may nip at a stonefish, which can cause infections. The stonefishes regularly shed their skin to rid themselves of fouling organisms (e.g., algae). They can be kept in smaller tanks (20 gal. [76 L]) because they are not very active.

Inimicus didactylus (Pallas, 1769)
Spiny Devilfish (Sea Goblin)

Maximum Length: 7.1 in. (18 cm).
Range: Indo-west-Pacific.
Minimum Aquarium Size: 30 gal. (114 L).
Foods & Feeding: Feed marine fish and crustacean flesh. Live, gut-packed ghost shrimp may be needed to initiate feeding. Feed several times a week.
Aquarium Suitability/Reef Compatibility:
Aquarium Notes: Flamboyantly finned, this is an interesting species for a reef tank with lots of open, deep sand substrate. When threatened, it throws open its pectoral fins and spreads its caudal fin, exposing bright colors to warn away potential predators. It buries itself so only the top of the head and the dorsal fin is exposed. Be careful when working in the tank, as accidental envenomation is possible (and painful). In a small tank, the devilfish may rub its lower jaw on the sides of the tank and cause itself injury. (Place black plastic along the outside bottom of the tank on all four sides to curb this behavior). Males may behave aggressively toward one another. A startled devilfish may leap out of an open aquarium, so an aquarium cover is required. **Note: Highly venomous.**

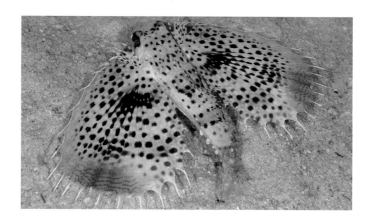

Oriental Helmet Gurnard (*Dactyloptena orientalis*): the magnificent pectoral fins and leglike pectoral rays add to this animal's appeal.

Helmet Gurnards (Family Dactylopteridae)

Young helmet gurnards are occasionally encountered in the aquarium trade. Even youngsters need a large tank (at least 75 gallons [285 L]) with plenty of open, sandy bottom. Adults need a tank of 135 gallons [513 L] or more, and lagoonlike conditions. Select a shallow tank with more surface area than depth, and keep decor to a minimum—it is best to have nothing but a deep sand bed and perhaps a patch reef of corals. Human traffic may cause them to collide with or rub up against the sides of the tank. If this occurs, place a 4-inch (10-cm) wide piece of black plastic along the outside bottom of the aquarium. Keep your hands out of the tank, especially during the acclimation period. Helmet gurnards can be a challenge to feed. Best foods include marine worms (e.g., bristleworms), black worms, brine shrimp, mysid shrimp (they will only pick these off the substrate), amphipods, and ghost shrimp. They are slow feeders and will have difficulty eating enough if kept with fishes that feed with more gusto. Do not house with anemones, as the gurnards may collide with them and be stung.

Harlequin Bass (*Serranus tigrinus*): an ideal reef-aquarium fish, interesting and attractive, although it will prey on small fishes and ornamental crustaceans.

Dwarf Seabasses (*Serranus* spp.)

The dwarf seabasses are well-suited to the home aquarium. They are small, accept most aquarium fare, are color-fast, and disease-resistant. They can be kept in reef tanks, but most species will eat small crustaceans and fishes that are small enough to fit into their mouths. In a reef tank, feed a seabass a minimum of every other day. Keep them in a tank with plenty of hiding places. This will help reduce aggression among the seabasses themselves, as well as between the seabasses and other fish tankmates. The dwarf seabass species vary considerably in their disposition. Some will behave aggressively toward smaller, more docile species. They are also likely to attack and chase other substrate-bound fishes with similar dietary habits, especially if they are introduced to a tank where seabasses are already residing. Although not a common occurrence, these fishes may jump out of an open aquarium. Because of their hardiness and small size, dwarf seabasses are great candidates for captive breeding. Pair formation in the home reef is not uncommon to observe.

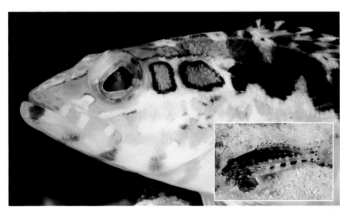

INSET: LANTERN BASS (*SERRANUS BALDWINI*)

Serranus annularis (Evermann & Marsh, 1900)
Orangeback Bass

Maximum Length: 3.5 in. (9 cm).
Range: Tropical Western Atlantic.
Minimum Aquarium Size: 20 gal. (76 L).
Foods & Feeding: Meaty foods, including chopped seafoods, mysid shrimp, and frozen preparation. Feed twice a day.
Aquarium Suitability/Reef Compatibility: ■ ※ ➤ ⁓ ✦
Aquarium Notes: This durable little seabass is a great choice for most reef aquariums, although it will eat smaller ornamental crustaceans. More than once, I have seen one swimming about with the pincers and arms of a tiny *Periclimenes* shrimp sticking out of its mouth. Given its small size and diet, it will not harm other invertebrates. Provide it with rubble and/or reef interstices in which to hide, and keep only one per tank unless your aquarium is at least 135 gallons (513 L). When acquiring a pair, add both fish together. It is a simultaneous hermaphrodite, so acquiring a male and female is not difficult. It may bully some benthic fishes (e.g., small gobies) or be bullied by others (e.g., hawkfishes). *Serranus annularis* inhabits deeper water than the similar Lantern Bass (*S. baldwini*) (inset). The latter is less expensive and slightly smaller.

Serranus tabacarius (Cuvier & Valenciennes, 1829)
Tobacco Bass

Maximum Length: 7.1 in. (18 cm).
Range: Tropical Western Atlantic.
Minimum Aquarium Size: 55 gal. (209 L).
Foods & Feeding: Meaty foods, including chopped seafoods, mysid shrimp, and frozen preparation. Feed twice a day.
Aquarium Suitability/Reef Compatibility:
Aquarium Notes: This larger member of the *Serranus* genus can fit into a predator-dominated reef, and it is a threat to a wider range of motile invertebrates, especially crustaceans, than its smaller genus members. It will eat any fish that can fit into its mouth, but it is not a threat to corals and other sessile invertebrates. Keep one per tank unless your aquarium is quite large (180 gallons [685 L]or more). If you attempt to keep a pair, add two smaller individuals. (They are simultaneous hermaphrodites, so you are guaranteed to end up with a male-female pair.) Larger individuals may pick on smaller specimens. This species may be picked on by more aggressive substrate-bound fishes, such as larger hawkfishes and sand perches. It is a capable jumper, so an aquarium cover is necessary.

Serranus tortugarum Longley, 1933
Chalk Bass

Maximum Length: 3.1 in. (8 cm).
Range: Tropical Western Atlantic.
Minimum Aquarium Size: 20 gal. (76 L).
Foods & Feeding: Meaty foods, including chopped seafoods, mysid shrimp, and frozen preparation. Feed twice a day.
Aquarium Suitability/Reef Compatibility: ▪ ⚑ 🐟 🦐 ★
Aquarium Notes: This is a wonderful little fish, with luminous coloration and a peaceful disposition, to keep in small groups (three to five). It is never aggressive and will not harm most invertebrates, with the possible exception of small ornamental shrimps. It spends most of its time hovering in the water column and is a plankton picker. If you keep a group, make sure your tank is at least 75 gallons (285 L) and add all members of the social unit together. This species is prone to being picked on by other dwarf seabasses and aggressive fish tankmates, especially those that stay on or near the bottom. It has been known to jump out of an open tank or into an overflow box when harassed. This species is a simultaneous hermaphrodite—meaning they possess both functional male and female sex organs.

Shy Hamlet (*Hypoplectrus guttavarius*): this fish and its close kin make colorful and interesting additions to reef tanks without ornamental crustaceans.

Hamlets (*Hypoplectrus* spp.)

Hamlets are rather uncommon in reef aquariums, but are often strikingly beautiful and are quite easy to maintain, although young fishes tend to adjust more readily to captivity than adults. Larger hamlets are more prone to acclimation difficulties, even when transferred from one tank to another. Every time an adult individual is moved, it will have a harder time adjusting. The hamlet's tank should include a number of suitable hiding places. Only one hamlet should be kept per tank, unless the aquarium is large (100 gallons [380 L] or more). Add all hamlets to the tank at once. Even then, some individuals may exhibit aggression toward conspecifics as well as heterospecifics. Hamlets that don't acclimate will hide constantly and refuse to feed. Feed a varied diet of meaty foods—their colors will fade if a pigment-rich diet is not provided. Although these fishes are rarely aggressive toward unrelated species, they are occasionally attacked by more belligerent fishes, such as other groupers, larger dottybacks and triggerfishes. In the reef tank, hamlets will consume shrimps, crabs, and smaller fishes.

Hypoplectrus aberrans
Yellowbelly Hamlet
Max. Length: 4.8 in. (12 cm).

Hypoplectrus chlorurus
Yellowtail Hamlet
Max. Length: 5.1 in. (13 cm).

Hypoplectrus gemma
Blue Hamlet
Max. Length: 5.1 in. (13 cm).

Hypoplectrus gummigutta
Golden Hamlet
Max. Length: 5.1 in. (13 cm).

Hypoplectrus puella
Barred Hamlet
Max. Length: 5.1 in. (13 cm).

Hypoplectrus unicolor
Butter Hamlet
Max. Length: 5.1 in. (13 cm).

Twinspot Anthias (*Pseudanthias bimaculatus*): larger anthias such as this require a large tank with clean, well-oxygenated water and frequent feedings.

Anthias (Subfamily Anthiinae)

Almost nothing underwater is more breathtaking than a large shoal of anthias shrouding the top of a coral reef promontory. Anthias can also make an eyecatching and reef-safe additions to the reef aquarium. They feed exclusively on plankton in the water column and will not harm coral or other ornamental invertebrates. Aquarists often want to keep them in groups, which can be a challenge with certain species. The keys to success are: species selection, shoal composition, size of the tank, and size of the anthias group.

Anthias species vary in their aggressiveness. Shoal maintenance is easier with less pugnacious species. These include the Peach Anthias (*Pseudanthias dispar*), Flame Anthias (*P. ignitus*), and Lori's Anthias (*P. lori*). Unfortunately, these are also some of the least durable anthias species. Some of the more aggressive species (which are also some of the hardiest) include the Redcheek Anthias (*Pseudanthias huchtii*), Redbelted Anthias (*P. rubrizonatus*), and the Lyretail Anthias (*P. squamipinnis*). Most species fall somewhere in between these two groups on the aggression continuum. Chances of

Golden Anthias (*Pseudanthias aurulentus*): some anthias from more remote locations are now making their way into the aquarium hobby.

success will increase if the composition of the group consists principally of juveniles and females. Add only one male to the aquarium, unless the tank is large enough to accommodate more. Even then, the ratio should be highly skewed toward juveniles and/or females (a good rule of thumb would be one male to every six to eight females/juveniles).

In general, the larger the tank, the greater your chances of success in keeping a group of anthias. In a large tank, more submissive members of a shoal may be able to avoid more dominant conspecifics. In a smaller tank, it will be hard for weaker fishes to avoid bullies. Crowd your aquarium with six to eight females or juveniles and you may be able to spread out aggressive interactions so that one or two subordinate fish are not the recipients of all the abuse, which can often end in the weaker fish disappearing. If you decide to try this, it is important to introduce all the shoal members at the same time. On the other hand, many anthias will do fine if kept singly.

The prime challenge in anthias husbandry is ensuring that they get enough to eat. Most of the anthias are zooplankton-feeders that feed throughout the day. Since zooplankton is usually in short sup-

Redstripe Anthias (*Pseudanthias fasciatus*): choose deep-water anthias specimens such as this with care as they may suffer from decompression problems.

ply in the reef aquarium, anthias often suffer from malnutrition, because reef aquarists have traditionally been reluctant to add food as often as these fishes need for fear of polluting the tank. Fortunately, reef aquarists are now employing more effective protein skimmers to help deter the buildup of certain pollutants, and even coral-keepers are beginning to realize that many of their sessile invertebrates will benefit from the addition of these foods. If you are reluctant to feed the fishes in your reef tank frequently, stay away from anthias. Most species need to be fed at least three times a day. If you can, it is best to feed small amounts frequently.

One way to keep anthias nourished is to incorporate a refugium. Live zooplankton cultures (e.g., mysid shrimp, copepods, amphipods) are available to be stocked in the refugium. These will reproduce constantly and provide a natural food source, and because they are highly nutritious, they can facilitate chromatic fidelity in these fishes, which are notorious for losing their color. Anthias also enjoy frozen mysid shrimp and the frozen plankton Cyclop-eeze.

Anthias appreciate strong current and clean, well-oxygenated water. Strong currents may also help discourage aggression in these

Yellowlined Anthias (*Tasanoides flavofasciatus*) male: one of the amazing, rarely available anthias that live in deep water off Japan's rocky reefs.

fishes. Anthias make great "dither" fishes, especially those species that spend considerable time swimming together in the water column. They are often quite frenetic when first added to the tank. Sudden changes in their environment—a light being suddenly turned off or on or an aquarist's hand plunging into the tank—can lead to some spectacular aerial displays. Aggressive tankmates can also be a curse to newly acquired anthias. I have seen dottybacks, angelfishes, hawkfishes, and larger damsels pester anthias to the point of death.

When selecting anthias for your tank, choose fishes that are swimming about, and avoid any specimens that are persistently hiding among the coral (hiding is an atypical behavior unless the fish is threatened by a predator or rival). Also avoid individuals in which the head appears to be enlarged and the back looks sunken. This appearance indicates that the fish has lost weight (including dorsal musculature) and it will be more difficult to recondition and maintain.

MAGENTA SLENDER ANTHIAS (*LUZONICHTHYS WAITEI*)

Luzonichthys spp.
Slender Anthias

Maximum Length: 2.3 to 2.6 in. (5.8 to 6.6 cm).

Range: Indo-Pacific.

Minimum Aquarium Size: 55 gal. (209 L).

Foods & Feeding: Meaty foods, including finely shredded frozen seafood, mysid shrimp, frozen preparations, pigment-enriched flake food and Cyclop-eeze, a great frozen food for these fishes. Feed at least twice a day—preferably more often.

Aquarium Suitability/Reef Compatibility:

Aquarium Notes: The six species in this genus form small to large shoals, which often include other zooplankton-feeding fishes like their cousins, the *Pseudanthias* species. Unlike many of their relatives, *Luzonichthys* males and females do not differ in coloration. Keep them in small groups (five or more individuals) in a reef aquarium with strong water movement. Belligerent fishes may pick on them, including their more aggressive anthias relatives. A small group of chromis damselfishes and dart gobies may encourage slender anthias to come out from hiding and to feed. The anthias in this genus will not behave aggressively toward other fishes.

Plectranthias inermis Randall, 1980
Unarmed Perchlet (Geometric Hawkfish)

Maximum Length: 2 in. (5 cm).
Range: Indo-Pacific.
Minimum Aquarium Size: 10 gal. (38 L).
Foods & Feeding: Meaty foods, including frozen seafood. May require live ghost shrimp to initiate a feeding response.
Aquarium Suitability/Reef Compatibility:
Aquarium Notes: Unlike their close relatives the anthias, which spend their time swimming in the water column, the perchlets rest on the seafloor. They are often secretive, hiding among the coral rubble and coming out to hunt small crustaceans and tiny fishes. As a result of their small size, they are perfect for a nano-reef tank. They are prone to being eaten or picked on by predators or more aggressive tank-mates. They are quite shy, hiding in rocky recesses most of the time when first added to the tank. But as they adjust, they spend more time in the open. If housed with bullies, they spend most, if not all, of their time cowering under shelter and failing to feed. Do not mix them with big dottybacks, hawkfishes, aggressive damsels, pugna-cious wrasses, sand perches, or triggerfishes.

Pseudanthias bartlettorum (Randall & Lubbock, 1981)
Bartlett's Anthias

Maximum Length: 3.5 in. (8.9 cm).
Range: West Pacific.
Minimum Aquarium Size: 55 gal. (209 L).
Foods & Feeding: Meaty foods, including finely shredded frozen seafood, mysid shrimp, pigment-enriched flake food, and various frozen protein-rich plankton-type foods, such Cyclop-eeze. Feed at least twice a day—preferably more often.
Aquarium Suitability/Reef Compatibility:
Aquarium Notes: A true reef beauty, this is also one of the best anthias for the reef aquarium. It can be relatively hardy and long-lived if provided with plenty of swimming room and fed often with protein-rich foods. Males can be quite aggressive. If you want to keep a shoal, add five or more females and one male to a larger tank (100 gallons [380 L] or more)—and be sure to introduce them simultaneously. Males will fight with each other and with other less pugnacious anthias unless in a very large tank. The splendid colors will fade if this species is not given a varied diet that includes food enriched with pigment-enhancing supplements, available at all local shops that cater to marine enthusiasts.

Pseudanthias dispar (Herre, 1955)
Dispar Anthias (Peach Anthias, Redfin Anthias)

Maximum Length: 3.7 in. (9 cm).
Range: Indo-Pacific.
Minimum Aquarium Size: 55 gal. (209 L).
Foods & Feeding: Meaty foods, including finely shredded frozen seafood, mysid shrimp, frozen preparations, pigment-enriched flake food and Cyclop-eeze. Feed at least twice a day, preferably more often.
Aquarium Suitability/Reef Compatibility:
Aquarium Notes: The durability of this anthias species varies—possibly a function of how the fish was captured and treated before arriving in your aquarium. This is not one of the more durable anthias species. It is often difficult to feed and is prone to being picked on by more aggressive tankmates as well as by larger, more aggressive anthias. It is best kept in groups consisting of six or more females and a single male. More than one male can be kept in the same aquarium if the tank is large enough (over 100 gallons [380 L]). Because this species naturally inhabits shallow fore-reef areas, it is a good choice for the well-illuminated shallow-water reef tank.

Pseudanthias pleurotaenia (Bleeker, 1857)
Squarespot Anthias (Squareblock Anthias, Mirror Anthias)

Maximum Length: 7.8 in. (20 cm).
Range: Western Pacific.
Minimum Aquarium Size: 75 gal. (285 L).
Foods & Feeding: Meaty foods, including finely shredded frozen seafood, mysid shrimp, frozen preparations, pigment-enriched flake food and Cyclop-eeze. Feed at least twice per day or preferably more often.
Aquarium Suitability/Reef Compatibility:
Aquarium Notes: This is a truly spectacular fish, best kept by aquarists with some experience and larger reef systems. Acclimation of this species is often slow. Individuals may hide for a week or more before they emerge from hiding. Juveniles and smaller females (under 3.9 in. [10 cm]) adjust more readily to aquarium confines. Only one specimen should be kept per aquarium, unless the tank is large enough (135 gallons [513 L] or more); you can keep one male per tank with six or more females. This fish may also behave aggressively toward other zooplankton feeders, but it will not harm invertebrates. This anthias does best at lower light levels and needs plenty of swimming room. In a brightly lit tank, its color often fades.

Serranocirrhitus latus Watanabe, 1949
Fathead Anthias (Sunburst Anthias, Hawkfish Anthias)

Maximum Length: 5.1 in. (13 cm).
Range: Indo-Pacific.
Minimum Aquarium Size: 30 gal. (114 L).
Foods & Feeding: Meaty foods, including finely shredded frozen seafood, mysid shrimp, frozen preparations, pigment-enriched flake food, and Cyclop-eeze. Feed at least twice per day, preferably more often.
Aquarium Suitability/Reef Compatibility:
Aquarium Notes: This is a gloriously colorful species, but one that needs plenty of hiding places, such as caves or overhangs. If it feels secure, it will be more likely to spend time in the open. A dimly lit tank may help it to more quickly overcome its initial timidity, but it is possible to keep it in more brightly lit aquariums. It should be kept with more aggressive tankmates, especially when the Fathead is added to the tank first, and more than one can be kept in the same tank. Males are more likely to quarrel among themselves, while females tend to be less aggressive. To increase the chances of acquiring a pair, purchase individuals that differ significantly in size—males are typically larger.

Best Aquarium Anthias

Pseudanthias huchtii (female)
Red Cheek Anthias
Max. Length: 4.7 in. (12 cm).

Pseudanthias huchtii (male)
Red Cheek Anthias
Max. Length: 4.7 in. (12 cm).

Pseudanthias rubrizonatus (male)
Redbelted, Redgirdled, Tricolor Anthias
Max. Length: 3.9 in. (10 cm).

Pseudanthias squamipinnis (female)
Lyretail Anthias, Scalefin Anthias
Max. Length: 4.7 in. (12 cm).

Pseudanthias squamipinnis (male)
Lyretail Anthias, Scalefin Anthias
Max. Length: 4.7 in. (12 cm).

Pseudanthias squamipinnis (male)
Lyretail Anthias, Scalefin Anthias
Max. Length: 4.7 in. (12 cm).

Moderately Hardy Anthias Species

Pseudanthias cooperi (male)
Cooper's Anthias, Redbar Anthias
Max. Length: 5.5 in. (14 cm).

Pseudanthias hutomoi (male)
Hutomo's Anthias
Max. Length: 4.5 in. (11 cm).

Pseudanthias hypselosoma (male)
Stocky Anthias
Max. Length: 7.5 in. (19 cm).

Pseudanthias luzonensis (male)
Luzon Anthias
Max. Length: 3.9 in. (10 cm).

Pseudanthias parvirostris (male)
Diadem Anthias
Max. Length: 3.1 in. (8 cm).

Pseudanthias sp. (male)
Bloodspot Anthias
Max. Length: 4 in. (10 cm).

Delicate Anthias Species

Pseudanthias hawaiiensis (male)
Hawaiian Anthias
Max. Length: 3 in. (7.6 cm).

Pseudanthias lori (male)
Lori Anthias, Tiger Queen Anthias
Max. Length: 4.7 in (12 cm).

Pseudanthias pascalus (male)
Purple Queen Anthias
Max. Length: 6.7 in. (17 cm).

Pseudanthias smithvanizi (male)
Princess Anthias
Max. Length: 3.7 in. (9.4 cm).

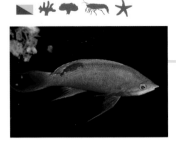

Pseudanthias tuka (male)
Yellowstripe Anthias, Purple Anthias
Max. Length: 4.7 in. (12 cm).

Pseudanthias ventralis (male)
Longfin Anthias
Max. Length: 2.1 in. (5.3 cm).

Coral Hind (*Cephalopholis miniata*) juv.: not suited for most reef aquariums, groupers tend to grow too large and, as here, feed on ornamental crustaceans.

Groupers (Tribe Epinephelini)

The groupers are hardy, disease-resistant fishes that will live for many years in a home setting. Groupers can be kept in a predatory reef aquarium, but they will eat crustaceans. If you want to try housing cleaner shrimps (*Lysmata* spp.) or boxer shrimps (*Stenopus* spp.) with these fishes, adding the crustaceans to the tank before the grouper will increase your chances of success. Groupers will also eat any fish they can swallow whole. In some cases, depending on the prey item's shape, the groupers can ingest fishes almost as long as themselves. Long, slender fishes, such as eels, certain wrasses, blennies, gobies, and dartfishes are easy prey for a grouper to swallow and will curl up in its stomach. Deep-bodied spiny fishes, such as butterflyfishes, angelfishes, and *Dascyllus* damselfishes, are more difficult to engulf and may even become lodged in the mouth or pharynx of an overzealous grouper. When selecting a grouper species, consider how large it may grow. Many will quickly outgrow a home aquarium if well fed. Some of the groupers are very secretive, spending much of the day peering out from under ledges and

Harlequin Hind (*Cephalopholis polleni*): provide this cave-dweller with a suitable refuge and tankmates that they are unable to swallow whole.

caves. Once these species become acclimated, they will usually begin to spend more of the daylight hours hovering near or sitting on the bottom close to their favorite shelter site.

Groupers should be fed a varied diet, consisting, in part, of fresh marine fish and crustacean flesh. They will also eat freeze-dried and frozen krill, mysid shrimp, brine shrimp, pellet foods; smaller specimens will even take flake food. An occasional grouper may require live food (e.g., feeder fish, ghost shrimp) to catalyze feeding, but they should switch to nonliving foods over time. Feed to satiation two or three times a week. Efficient skimming will be needed to handle their wastes. They usually ignore unrelated species in a large tank unless their favorite hiding places are invaded. They may bully newly introduced tankmates, especially if space is tight. The grouper should be the last fish introduced to a community tank. Groupers will behave aggressively toward conspecifics and will often fight with their relatives. It is best to keep only one per aquarium, although if you have a large tank (100 gallons [380 L] or larger) with ample shelter sites, individuals with disparate color patterns can be housed together successfully.

Anyperodon sp.
Metallic Blue Grouper

Maximum Length: 5.9 in. (15 cm)?.
Range: Red Sea.
Minimum Aquarium Size: 75 gal. (285 L).
Foods & Feeding: Meaty foods, including frozen seafood. May require live ghost shrimp to initiate a feeding response.
Aquarium Suitability/Reef Compatibility:
Aquarium Notes: This spectacular grouper has been coming into the aquarium trade with greater frequency. It is a durable fish that can be housed in the predatory reef aquarium. Provide it with a ledge or cave in which to hide, and it will spend much of its time peering from a preferred refuge, dashing out dramatically to snap up food items. Offering live, gut-packed ghost shrimp is a good way to initiate feeding. With time, it should take nonliving foods placed in the current. It will eat small fishes (its mouth is bigger than it may appear, so use care when selecting fish tankmates) and crustaceans, including cleaner shrimps. Keep only one per tank. The Metallic Blue Grouper is a close relative of the Whitelined Grouper (*Anyperodon leucogrammicus*).

CORAL HIND (*CEPHALOPHOLIS MINIATA*)

Cephalopholis spp.
Hinds

Maximum Length: 10.2 to 17 in. (26 to 43 cm).
Range: Circumtropical.
Minimum Aquarium Size: 75 gal. (285 L) and larger.
Foods & Feeding: Meaty foods, including frozen seafood. May require live ghost shrimp or feeder fish to initiate a feeding response. Feed several larger meals per week.
Aquarium Suitability/Reef Compatibility:
Aquarium Notes: The hinds are some of the best groupers for the large, predatory reef aquarium. Many are colorful and most do not exceed a maximum length of 14 in. (36 cm). Hinds tend to be shy, spending most of their time under overhangs or in caves, but over time they will become bolder. They are fish-eaters that will eat any piscine tankmate that can be swallowed whole. They have even been know to eat cleaner wrasses (*Labroides* spp.). Cleaner shrimps and wrasses may survive if added to the tank before the hind is introduced and if the hind is fed frequently. Although you can keep two hinds of different species in a large aquarium, do not attempt to house conspecifics together. They do not tend to be aggressive toward unrelated fishes unless their favorite refuge is invaded.

Best Reef Aquarium Groupers

Cephalopholis boenak
Chocolate Hind
Max. Length: 10.2 in. (26 cm).

Cephalopholis fulva
Coney
Max. Length: 12.9 in. (33 cm).

Cephalopholis leopardus
Leopard Hind
Max. Length: 9.4 in. (24 cm).

Cephalopholis sexmaculata
Sixspot Grouper
Max. Length: 18.5 in. (47 cm).

Cephalopholis urodeta
Darkfin Hind, V-tail Grouper
Max. Length: 10.6 in. (27 cm).

Gracila albomarginata (juv.)
Whitemargin Grouper
Max. Length: 15 in. (38 cm).

ADULT WITH ISOPOD PARASITE

Paranthias colonus (Valenciennes, 1828)
Creolefish

Maximum Length: 13.7 in. (35 cm), most less than 7.8 in. (20 cm).
Range: Tropical Western Atlantic.
Minimum Aquarium Size: 75 gal. (285 L).
Foods & Feeding: Meaty foods, including finely shredded frozen seafood, mysid shrimp, frozen preparations, pigment-enriched flake food, and Cyclop-eeze (adults will ignore the latter). Feed two or three times per day.
Aquarium Suitability/Reef Compatibility:
Aquarium Notes: This atypical Caribbean grouper is a zooplankton feeder that forms groups in the water column. It is more fusiform in shape than most groupers and avoids predators by racing back to the protection of the reef. It is a very durable aquarium species and is less of a threat to crustaceans and fishes in the reef tank. Adults will eat delicate shrimp species. Although they form shoals in the wild, they are best kept singly in the aquarium. In captive confines, they are often aggressive toward each other, and they will pester smaller, passive fishes. Adults should not be housed with passive anthias species, flasher wrasses, dartfishes, or other more passive zooplanktivores. A tank cover is needed, as they are capable jumpers.

Reynold's Reef Basslet (*Liopropoma* sp.): although highly secretive, this beautiful basslet makes an interesting addition to the reef aquarium.

Reef Basslets (Genus *Liopropoma*)

These small, shy-but-beautiful seabasses are ideal for the reef aquarium. They are very fond of the numerous hiding places in a typical reef aquascape. A smaller *Liopropoma* species can make the perfect centerpiece for a specimen nano-reef aquarium. Be forewarned: they eat crustaceans and small fishes and have relatively large jaws that enable them to consume larger prey items. These fishes will also make short work of some of the tiny gobies that are popular for nano-reefs.

They take a variety of captive fare as well as the small crustaceans (e.g., amphipods, copepods) that live among the live rocks of a reef aquarium. They only need to be fed two or three times a week if live rock is present. These lovely basslets are relatively colorfast, but color loss may occur unless you offer them a varied diet with a pigment-enhanced food. A new reef basslet may hide for several days or even a couple of weeks before coming out to inspect its new surroundings. If kept with aggressive fishes in a large system, they often remain hidden and will not eat.

Yellowtail Reef Basslet (*Liopropoma* sp.): this deep-water species often dies from decompression-related maladies.

One appealing attribute of the smaller *Liopropoma* species is that they are rarely aggressive toward unrelated fishes. Two reef basslets of different species can also be kept in the same aquarium if they are introduced simultaneously and if plenty of hiding places are provided. However, members of the same species should not be kept together unless you have a large aquarium with lots of hiding places or you can acquire a mated pair. Even then, a larger, more dominant individual may harass a subordinate when they cross paths. Fighting between conspecifics can be violent, often involving vicious jaw-locking behavior, and can lead to the death of the subordinate individual. Some of the deep-water forms (e.g., the Yellowtail Reef Basslet) regularly perish due to maladies related to improper decompression. Avoid selecting fishes that display labored swimming with the tail held above the head (these individuals often wedge themselves in the live rock). Reef basslets will occasionally skirmish over a hiding place with other basslets or other cryptic fish species (e.g., cardinalfishes), but this can be prevented by providing numerous refuges. These fishes acclimate best with a steep wall of rock in their aquarium home, replete with caves and crevices.

INSET: THE MORE EXPENSIVE AND LESS COMMON CANDY BASSLET (*LIOPROPOMA CARMABI*)

Liopropoma swalesi (Fowler & Bean, 1930)
Swale's Reef Basslet (Swalesi Reef Basslet)

Maximum Length: 2.5 in. (6.4 cm).
Range: Indonesia.
Minimum Aquarium Size: 20 gal. (76 L).
Foods & Feeding: Meaty foods, including frozen seafood. May require live ghost shrimp to initiate a feeding response.
Aquarium Suitability/Reef Compatibility:
Aquarium Notes: Once a prized rarity, this species is now common-place in the aquarium trade. Although eye-catchingly comely in appearance, it is very secretive. Provide it with plenty of small caves and crevices in which to hide. You will need to be sure it gets enough to eat if housed with aggressive tankmates. This can be difficult, as it tends to spend most of its time hiding. It may remain hidden for weeks or even months, especially in a large reef tank. Keep one per tank, unless your aquarium is larger (135 gallons [513 L] or more) with lots of rockwork, or if you can acquire a heterosexual pair. A tank cover is necessary, as it may jump out of an open aquarium. A similar species, Reynold's Reef Basslet (*Liopropoma* sp.), is shown on page 81. Reynold's is similar in husbandry to *L. swalesi*.

Liopropoma eukrines
Wrasse Bass
Max. Length: 5.1 in. (13 cm).

Liopropoma mitratum
Headband Reef Basslet
Max. Length: 3.1 in. (8 cm).

Liopropoma mowbrayi
Ridgeback Basslet
Max. Length: 3.5 in. (8.9 cm).

Liopropoma multilineatum
Many-lined Reef Basslet
Max. Length: 3.1 in. (8 cm).

Liopropoma rubre
Swissguard Basslet
Max. Length: 3.1 in. (8 cm).

Liopropoma susumi
Pinstripe Reef Basslet
Max. Length: 3.6 in. (9.2 cm).

Sixline Soapfish (*Grammistes sexlineatus*): for the large, unconventional reef tank only, soapfishes such as this are proverbial eating machines.

Soapfishes (Tribe Diploprionini)

The soapfishes are durable aquarium inhabitants that can be kept in big, boisterous reef aquariums. However, they will eat any crustacean or fish that will fit in their maws (it can be quite surprising what they are capable of ingesting). Most spend the majority of their daylight hours hiding among the aquarium decor, occasionally slinking from one crevice to another. After a while, they recognize their keepers as a source of food and become quite tame. It may be necessary to induce feeding by offering live food (e.g., ghost shrimp), but most are easily trained to accept bite-sized pieces of seafood, frozen preparations, or frozen mysids. Although most soapfishes behave aggressively toward conspecifics or congeners, they are rarely aggressive toward unrelated fish species. A downside to soapfish ownership is the potential risk to their tankmates due to their toxic body slime. If harassed by a tankmate, aquarist, or if they are ill, they may secrete copious amounts of grammistin, which could result in the death of the soapfish and any other fishes in the tank. Fortunately, this happens very rarely in the home aquarium.

Diplioprion bifasciatum (Cuvier, 1828)
Twobanded Soapfish (Barred Soapfish)

Maximum Length: 10 in. (25 cm).
Range: Indo-Pacific.
Minimum Aquarium Size: 75 gal. (285 L).
Foods & Feeding: Meaty foods, including frozen seafood. May require live ghost shrimp or guppies to initiate a feeding response.
Aquarium Suitability/Reef Compatibility:
Aquarium Notes: The Twobanded Soapfish is attractive and well-suited to captivity in a larger reef setting. It may hide when initially introduced to its new home, but usually within hours it will start swimming about the tank. Be sure to provide plenty of suitable hiding places. This species will eat finely chopped fresh seafood, frozen brine shrimp, frozen mysid shrimp, frozen preparations, and even flake food. The Twobanded Soapfish is not aggressive toward other fishes and will ignore all corals, but it will eat any small tankmate—fish or crustacean—it can swallow whole. Two or more of these fish can be kept together, rarely behaving aggressively toward each other. They may be picked on by overly aggressive tankmates.

Belonoperca chabanaudi Fowler & Bean, 1930
Arrowhead Soapfish (Chabanaud's Soapfish)

Maximum Length: 5.9 in. (15 cm).
Range: Indo-Pacific.
Minimum Aquarium Size: 40 gal. (152 L).
Foods & Feeding: Meaty foods, including frozen seafood. May require live, gut-packed ghost shrimp to initiate a feeding response.
Aquarium Suitability/Reef Compatibility:
Aquarium Notes: This beguiling fish but predatory species is not for every reef, and it will spend more time in the open in a dimly lit tank. The tank should have a cover because this species is likely to launch itself out of an open aquarium if it is startled or harassed. Authentic aquascaping will help; provide it with an arch, overhang, or cave in which it can hover as it does in the wild. Otherwise it will spend much of its time resting on its pelvic fins behind aquarium decor. It rarely displays interspecific aggression. This species is a voracious predator that will eat any fish or shrimp that will fit into its mouth. It slowly approaches its prey by undulating its median fins and then, with incredible speed, swoops down to capture its quarry. Only one should be kept per tank, but it can be kept with related forms (i.e., other soapfishes, groupers).

Raja Dottyback (*Pseudochromis* sp.): many members of this often colorful, often bold, genus are among the very best candidates for the reef aquarium.

Dottybacks (Family Pseudochromidae)

All the dottybacks are very durable aquarium fishes that are ideal for the reef aquarium. Most feed on polychaete worms, small crustaceans (including delicate shrimps), and zooplankton. There are a few larger species that also consume larger shrimps, crabs, and small fishes (e.g., *Labracinus*). Some are prone to severe color loss. To prevent this, provide dottybacks with a varied diet that includes pigment-rich foods (e.g., color-enhanced flake foods, frozen preparations, and the frozen food Cyclop-eeze). In a tank with live rock, they will feed on associated populations of worms and crustaceans. In the reef tank, you should have to feed them only once a day or even less often. Keep an eye on their girth to be sure they are getting enough to eat. They vary in their aggressiveness, but many become bullies, especially in a smaller tank. (Dottybacks can be some of the most aggressive fishes on the reef.) Some of the smaller species are more timid and less likely to cause problems. The nano-reef aquarium makes a wonderful species tank for a more aggressive, flamboyant dottyback—and some are truly worthy of the special attention.

Tono's Dottyback (*Pseudochromis tonozukai*) female: a sexually dichromatic dottyback species from Indonesia.

When keeping a large, feisty dottyback species in a community tank, be sure to mix it only with species of similar disposition or add fishes that are large enough that their size alone will intimidate the dottyback. It is possible to keep more than one dottyback in the same aquarium. The secret is to have a big tank with lots of hiding places. Do not keep conspecifics together, unless you can acquire a male and female.

Dottybacks are protogynous hermaphrodites and some can reverse sex (male back to female). To acquire a male-female pair, purchase two smaller individuals. The more dominant fish will eventually change into a male, while the subordinate will be the female. In some species, males may harass their mates to the point of killing them. Dottybacks regularly spawn in captivity. In fact, many of the dottybacks available in the aquarium trade today are captive-raised. Some of these captive-raised species (e.g., *Pseudochromis aldabraensis*) have become more domesticated and placid than their notoriously fierce wild-caught cousins. Captive-raised individuals are often more tolerant of conspecifics and easier to pair up for spawning.

Congrogadus subducens (Richardson, 1843)
Carpet Eel Blenny (Green Wolf Eel)

Maximum Length: 17.6 in. (45 cm).
Range: Indo-Pacific.
Minimum Aquarium Size: 55 gal. (209 L).
Foods & Feeding: Meaty foods, including fresh or frozen seafood. May require live ghost shrimp to initiate a feeding response. Feed several large food items at least every other day. If fed daily, it will grow very quickly.
Aquarium Suitability/Reef Compatibility: ▬ ⚜ 🐟 🦐 ⭐
Aquarium Notes: This odd pseudochromoid makes an interesting addition to the spacious, predatory reef aquarium. It is a voracious predator that will eat small fishes and ornamental crustaceans, but it will do fine with squirrelfishes, soldierfishes, surgeonfishes, rabbitfishes, and other larger tankmates. It is very hardy and a good choice for the beginner. The aquarium should be covered, as this fish is prone to jumping. Keep only one per tank, unless you can acquire a known heterosexual pair. When threatened, it will open its jaws and flare its gill covers. Once adjusted to its captive home, it will learn to recognize its keeper as a source of food and will swim about the tank begging for food when the aquarist comes near.

MALE

Cypho purpurascens (De Vis, 1884)
Oblique-lined Dottyback (McCulloch's Dottyback)

Maximum Length: 2.9 in. (7.4 cm).
Range: Western Pacific.
Minimum Aquarium Size: 20 gal. (76 L.)
Foods & Feeding: Meaty foods, including finely shredded frozen seafood, mysid shrimp, frozen preparations, pigment-enriched flake food, and Cyclop-eeze. Feed every other day in a reef tank.
Aquarium Suitability/Reef Compatibility:
Aquarium Notes: This stunning dottyback is a great reef aquarium species, provided that certain vulnerable tankmates are excluded. It may attack ornamental shrimps (I have seen one attack and bite the legs off a mantis shrimp) and, like many in this family, it may bully smaller, more docile fishes. It is less likely to be a problem in a large tank with plenty of hiding places. It is also more likely to attack other dottybacks, grammas, and red-colored fishes (e.g., cardinal-fishes). It can be kept in male-female pairs, but only in a tank of 100 gallons [380 L] or more. If you succeed in acquiring a pair, there is a good chance they will spawn (if you can keep the male from killing the female). See page 106 for a photo of a female.

RED DOTTYBACK (*LABRACINUS CYCLOPHTHALMUS*)

Labracinus spp.
Lined Dottybacks

Maximum Length: 7.8 to 9.8 in. (20 to 25 cm).

Range: Western Pacific.

Minimum Aquarium Size: 30 to 55 gal. (114 to 209 L).

Foods & Feeding: Meaty foods, including chopped marine fish and crustacean flesh. Feed two to four times per week.

Aquarium Suitability/Reef Compatibility:

Aquarium Notes: *Labracinus* dottybacks can be glamorous, interesting additions to the predatory reef aquarium. Before acquiring one, however, know that they are some of the most aggressive members of the dottyback family and are only suitable for tanks that contain larger, more belligerent fish species. They are a threat to ornamental crustaceans and regularly eat small fishes. Although it is a risky proposition, they can be kept in male-female pairs if the aquarium is large enough (over 135 gallons [513 L]) and if the two in the pair are introduced simultaneously. One effective way to introduce potential pair members (and keep them from fighting) is to divide the aquarium with a pane of glass or acrylic and let them habituate to each other for several days before pulling out the divider.

SPLENDID DOTTYBACK (*MANONICHTHYS SPLENDENS*)

Manonichthys spp.
Bigfinned Dottybacks

Maximum Length: 2.7 to 5.1 in. (6.9 to 13 cm).
Range: Indo-Pacific.
Minimum Aquarium Size: 30 gal. (114 L).
Foods & Feeding: Meaty foods, including finely shredded frozen seafood, mysid shrimp, frozen preparations, pigment-enriched flake food, and Cyclop-eeze. Feed every other day in a reef tank.
Aquarium Suitability/Reef Compatibility:
Aquarium Notes: These are wonderful reef aquarium fishes and are some of the most elegant of all the dottybacks. The five species in the genus are deeper bodied with long pelvic fins. While perfectly safe with all corals and giant clams, they will feed on ornamental shrimps and will prey on bristleworms. These medium-sized dottybacks can be quite scrappy in the home aquarium, especially in a smaller tank. They may pester smaller and more passive fish tankmates, but this is less of a concern in a larger reef aquarium. (For photos of others in this genus, see page 106.)

QUEENSLAND DOTTYBACK (*OGILBYINA QUEENSLANDIAE*)

Ogilbyina spp.
Australian Dottybacks

Maximum Length: 3.9 to 5.9 in. (10 to 15 cm).

Range: Great Barrier Reef.

Minimum Aquarium Size: 30 gal. (114 L).

Foods & Feeding: Meaty foods, including chopped marine fish and crustacean flesh. Feed two to four times per week.

Aquarium Suitability/Reef Compatibility:

Aquarium Notes: A terror with fins, this fish is one of two very similar species, the Australian (*Ogilbyina novaehollandiae*) and the Queensland Dottyback (*O. queenslandiae*, that come in a variety of different color forms. These fishes are fairly large, most common in shallow water on the reef flat or reef face, and are some of the most aggressive members of their subfamily. Because they attain larger sizes than many other dottybacks, they are also better equipped to inflict damage to their tankmates. They will make short work of any ornamental shrimps in your reef tank, but will also consume small mantis shrimps and bristleworms. Another positive trait they possess is that they are extremely durable and often survive when other fishes in the tank succumb to poor water quality or disease. These dottybacks are sexually dichromatic.

Oxycercichthys velifera (Lubbock, 1980)
Sailfin Dottyback

Maximum Length: 4.7 in. (12 cm).
Range: Great Barrier Reef.
Minimum Aquarium Size: 30 gal. (114 L).
Foods & Feeding: Meaty foods, including chopped marine fish and crustacean flesh. Feed two to four times per week.
Aquarium Suitability/Reef Compatibility:
Aquarium Notes: Although delicately hued, this is a large and pugnacious dottyback that (like many members of the group) is most suitable for the more aggressive reef aquarium community. Much care should be taken when selecting suitable tankmates for this fish. It will pick on smaller fishes, ornamental shrimps, and porcelain crabs. I have seen the Sailfin Dottyback living with relatively peaceful fishes in large reef tanks, but even in a spacious aquarium, any fish that enters its preferred shelter site will be vigorously attacked. As with many of the dottybacks, this fish can become a character study when kept in a smaller species tank, where it is no threat to tankmates and where it can be closely observed as the indomitable ruler of its own domain.

Pholidochromis cerasina Gill & Tanaka, 2004
Cherry Dottyback

Maximum Length: 3.1 in. (7.9 cm).
Range: Western Pacific.
Minimum Aquarium Size: 20 gal. (76 L).
Foods & Feeding: Meaty foods, including finely shredded frozen seafood, mysid shrimp, frozen preparations, pigment-enriched flake food, and Cyclop-eeze. Feed every other day in a reef tank.
Aquarium Suitability/Reef Compatibility:
Aquarium Notes: This is an unusual dottyback that is a relative rarity in aquarium stores. It is a moderately aggressive member of the genus that is well-suited to the reef aquarium, although it is a threat to ornamental shrimps. I have found small adults to be fairly placid for a dottyback, but Japanese aquarists report that adults can be quite belligerent. This makes it a better candidate for large systems where aggression is spread over a greater area, or for smaller species tanks. Unlike many in its family, it tends to spend a considerable amount of time in the open.

Pictichromis diadema Lubbock & Randall, 1978
Diadem Dottyback

Maximum Length: 2.3 in. (6 cm).
Range: Western Pacific.
Minimum Aquarium Size: 20 gal. (76 L).
Foods & Feeding: Meaty foods, including finely shredded frozen seafood, mysid shrimp, frozen preparations, pigment-enriched flake food, and Cyclop-eeze. Feed every other day in a reef tank.
Aquarium Suitability/Reef Compatibility:
Reef Aquarium Notes: This is one of the more popular reef aquarium dottybacks, and not nearly as problematic as its bullying cousin, the Royal Dottyback (following page). It is quite common in aquarium stores and reasonably priced. Most are collected from the wild, not tank-raised. It is less likely to kill ornamental shrimps, although it may harass smaller, more delicate specimens. It may pester smaller, more docile fishes (this is especially true once it has established residence in its new home), but it is less feisty than many of its more muscular congeners. When kept with larger fishes (e.g., tangs, angelfishes, butterflyfishes) in a larger reef system, it is much less belligerent. Although it is moderately hardy, it is prone to radical color loss if not adequately fed.

Pictichromis paccagnellae Axelrod, 1973
Royal Dottyback

Maximum Length: 2 in. (5.1 cm).
Range: Western Pacific.
Minimum Aquarium Size: 20 gal. (76 L).
Foods & Feeding: Meaty foods, including finely shredded frozen seafood, mysid shrimp, frozen preparations, pigment-enriched flake food, and Cyclop-eeze. Feed every other day in a reef tank.
Aquarium Suitability/Reef Compatibility:
Aquarium Notes: Although it makes a stunning addition to the reef aquarium, ounce for ounce this is regarded by many (this writer included) as one of the most aggressive marine fishes. I have seen it tangle with, and beat up, other hellions that had already been well-established in a reef community tank. It may bother shrimps, but is less likely to do so than larger relatives. Like others in this genus, its brilliant colors often fade in captivity. Feed it a color-enhancing food to prevent this from happening. Keep only one per tank. It is also prudent not to house it with other dottybacks. This is a fish that can wreck the balance of small or average-sized marine community, and one that very often will need to be hunted down and removed to restore peace to the system.

Pictichromis porphyrea Lubbock & Goldman, 1974
Magenta Dottyback (Purple Dottyback, Strawberry Dottyback)

Maximum Length: 2.3 in. (5.8 cm).
Range: Western Pacific.
Minimum Aquarium Size: 20 gal. (76 L).
Foods & Feeding: Meaty foods, including finely shredded frozen seafood, mysid shrimp, frozen preparations, pigment-enriched flake food, and Cyclop-eeze. Feed every other day in a reef tank.
Aquarium Suitability/Reef Compatibility:
Aquarium Notes: This, simply enough, is a wonderful reef aquarium fish. It is less of a threat to ornamental crustaceans than many others in the family. It is best not to keep this fish with members of its own kind or others in the genus, unless you have a bigger tank (100 gallons [380 L] or larger) with lots of hiding places. Although it can create behavioral issues in the passive community tank, it is less aggressive than many members of the genus. It has been known to harass grammas, small wrasses, dart gobies, and other small, mild-mannered reef fishes, especially in smaller aquariums. It tends to lose its brilliance as its color gradually fades. Feed it a varied diet with enriched foods to help prevent this from occurring.

Pseudochromis aldabraensis Bauchot-Boutin, 1958
Arabian Bluelined Dottyback (Neon Dottyback)

Maximum Length: 3.3 in. (8.4 cm).
Range: Indian Ocean.
Minimum Aquarium Size: 20 gal. (76 L).
Foods & Feeding: Meaty foods, including finely shredded frozen seafood, mysid shrimp, frozen preparations, pigment-enriched flake food, and Cyclop-eeze. Feed every other day in a reef tank.
Aquarium Suitability/Reef Compatibility:
Aquarium Notes: This attractive fish is a stunning addition to the reef aquarium. It is a shrimp-eater that will also ferret out and feed on bristleworms. It does have a dark side—it can be dangerous when housed with small, competitive tankmates. It is thus best kept with larger, more aggressive species (surgeonfishes, large damselfishes, hawkfishes). It has been observed to pick at the body surfaces of larger fishes (apparent cleaning behavior) in captivity. Courtship in wild-caught pairs is often brutal, with the male biting the abdomen of the female to elicit egg deposit. Injuries resulting from mating are often lethal to the female. In captive-bred individuals, courtship is not nearly as aggressive.

Pseudochromis bitaeniatus (Fowler, 1931)
Twolined Dottyback

Maximum Length: 2.7 in. (6.9 cm).
Range: Western Pacific.
Minimum Aquarium Size: 20 gal. (76 L).
Foods & Feeding: Meaty foods, including finely shredded frozen seafood, mysid shrimp, frozen preparations, pigment-enriched flake food, and Cyclop-eeze. Feed every other day in a reef tank.
Aquarium Suitability/Reef Compatibility:
Aquarium Notes: This handsome little dottyback is a worthy addition to the reef tank. It is especially suited to smaller systems or to larger aquariums that have communities of smaller or similarly sized fishes. The downside is that it has been known to attack and kill smaller fishes and eat ornamental shrimps. If placed in a larger tank with plenty of hiding places, it will often ignore its tankmates, unless they venture too close to its preferred hiding places. Juveniles lack yellow coloration on the head.

Pseudochromis coccinicauda (Tickell, 1888)
Orangetail Dottyback

Maximum Length: 2.3 in. (5.8 cm).
Range: Indian Ocean.
Minimum Aquarium Size: 20 gal. (76 L).
Foods & Feeding: Meaty foods, including finely shredded frozen seafood, mysid shrimp, frozen preparations, pigment-enriched flake food, and Cyclop-eeze. Feed every other day in a reef tank.
Aquarium Suitability/Reef Compatibility:
Aquarium Notes: This small dottyback is a great addition to the reef aquarium. It is less of a threat to shrimps and other crustaceans than others in the family. It is also one of the more docile dottybacks. However, larger males may terrorize small, passive species (e.g., gobies, dartfishes) in smaller tanks. I have had larger individuals beat up other dottybacks that were of similar size but added after the Orangetail was well-established in the tank. It will spend much of its time slinking around among the live rock. If kept with more aggressive tankmates, it is likely to spend most of its time hiding. A male-female pair can be housed in a larger reef aquarium. The females are brown with an orange tail. The Bluelined Dottyback (*Pseudochromis cyanotaenia*) is a similar species (see page 106).

Pseudochromis fridmani Klausewitz, 1968
Orchid Dottyback (Orchid Dottyback)

Maximum Length: 2.7 in. (6.9 cm).
Range: Red Sea.
Minimum Aquarium Size: 20 gal. (76 L).
Foods & Feeding: Meaty foods, including finely shredded frozen seafood, mysid shrimp, frozen preparations, pigment-enriched flake food, and Cyclop-eeze. Feed every other day in a reef tank.
Aquarium Suitability/Reef Compatibility:
Aquarium Notes: Once nearly priceless and reserved for tycoon aquarists only, this is a five-star, drop-dead-beautiful dottyback. Now captive-bred and easily available, it is a near-perfect reef species. It is not much of a threat to ornamental shrimps and is typically less aggressive than most of its congeners. That said, an occasional individual will pester smaller, more passive species (e.g., smaller wrasses, fire gobies). It will also defend its shelter sites from intrusion. It tends not to fade in color like the other magenta dottybacks. This species can be home-bred, following the advice of pioneering breeder Martin Moe and others. Sankey's Dottyback (*Pseudochromis sankeyi*)(page 106) is similar in form, behavior, and husbandry.

Pseudochromis springeri Lubbock, 1975
Springer's Dottyback

Maximum Length: 1.6 in. (4.1 cm).
Range: Red Sea.
Minimum Aquarium Size: 20 gal. (76 L).
Foods & Feeding: Meaty foods, including finely shredded frozen seafood, mysid shrimp, frozen preparations, pigment-enriched flake food, and Cyclop-eeze. Feed every other day in a reef tank.
Aquarium Suitability/Reef Compatibility:
Aquarium Notes: This is a great reef aquarium dottyback. An elegantly pigmented species, it often spends its time among branching small-polyped stony corals, which can aid the water circulation within these colonies. It is less of a threat to ornamental shrimps and is not as aggressive as many of the other dottybacks. It can be kept in male-female pairs or housed with other *Pseudochromis* species in a larger reef tank. It has been observed to clean other fishes in captivity. Its color may serve to mimic sympatric cleaner fishes, which may provide some protection against predators. Captive-raised individuals are available and highly desirable. This species spawns in holes in live rock, producing a white egg ball.

ORANGE DOTTYBACK (*PSEUDOPLESIOPS* SP.)

Pseudoplesiops spp.
Secretive Dottybacks

Maximum Length: 2.3 in. (6 cm).
Range: Indo-Pacific.
Minimum Aquarium Size: 2 gal. (8 L).
Foods & Feeding: Meaty foods, including finely shredded frozen seafood, mysid shrimp, frozen preparations, pigment-enriched flake food. Feed every other day in a reef tank.
Aquarium Suitability/Reef Compatibility:
Aquarium Notes: These are lovely, albeit secretive, additions to the reef aquarium. They hide most of the time, but will dash out from cover to snag pieces of food. Once fully acclimated to the aquarium, they will spend more time in open. Unfortunately, but true to the instincts of the family, they can be quite aggressive, especially in a nano-reef setting. They can be especially aggressive toward smaller fishes like tiny wrasses, gobies, and blennies. Keep only one per tank, unless the aquarium is large. Secretive Dottybacks will fight with more aggressive dottybacks or other crevice dwellers. Feed color-enhancing foods to prevent fading of wild pigmentation.

Cypho purpurascens (female)
Oblique-lined Dottyback
Max. Length: 2.9 in. (7.4 cm).

Manonichthys alleni
Allen's Dottyback
Max. Length: 4.7 in. (12 cm).

Manonichthys cf. *alleni*
Red-dot Dottyback
Max. Length: 4.7 in. (12 cm).

Manonichthys polynemus
Longfin Dottyback
Max. Length: 4.7 in. (12 cm).

Pseudochromis cyanotaenia
Bluelined Dottyback (male & female)
Max. Length: 2.4 in. (6.1 cm).

Pseudochromis dilectus
Esteemed Dottyback
Max. Length: 3.5 in. (8.9 cm).

Pseudochromis elongatus
Elongate Dottyback
Max. Length: 2.5 in. (6.4 cm).

Pseudochromis flammicauda
Firetail Dottyback
Max. Length: 2.2 in. (5.6 cm).

Pseudochromis flavivertex
Sunrise Dottyback
Max. Length: 3.1 in. (7.9 cm).

Pseudochromis fuscus
Dusky Dottyback
Max. Length: 3.9 in. (10 cm).

Pseudochromis sankeyi
Sankey's Dottyback
Max. Length: 3.1 in. (8 cm).

Pseudochromis steenei
Steene's Dottyback (male)
Max. Length: 4.7 in. (11.9 cm).

Blackcap Basslet (*Gramma melacara*): like others in the genus, this species is susceptible to prodigious color loss, but is still a lovely reef tank inhabitant.

Grammas (Family Grammatidae)

Perhaps the quintessential reef fishes, grammas are not only beautiful but durable and relatively congenial to their tankmates. Hailing from the Caribbean and tropical Western Atlantic, the grammas are not a threat to most ornamental invertebrates, with the possible exception of small shrimps. On the other hand, grammas have been known to fall prey to invertebrates, including elephant ear anemones, carpet sea anemones, and large crabs. (The latter will eat small fishes like grammas when they are torpid at night.) They should be housed with relatively peaceful tankmates. Once established, however, grammas should be able to hold their own with a variety of tankmates as long as they are kept in a larger tank, replete with shelter sites. Avoid housing them with dottybacks, large damselfishes, some hawkfishes, and other highly malevolent fishes. If kept with potentially aggressive tankmates, the gramma should be added to the aquarium before the others are introduced. If incessantly picked on, grammas will hide constantly or cower in an upper corner of the aquarium until they perish.

Gramma loreto Poey, 1868
Royal Gramma (Fairy Basslet)

Maximum Length: 3.1 in. (8 cm).
Range: Tropical Western Atlantic.
Minimum Aquarium Size: 20 gal. (76 L).
Foods & Feeding: Meaty foods, including finely shredded frozen seafood, mysid shrimp, frozen preparations, pigment-enriched flake food, and Cyclop-eeze. Feed once a day in a reef tank. May require live ghost shrimp to initiate a feeding response.
Aquarium Suitability/Reef Compatibility:
Aquarium Notes: This is a stellar reef species that can be kept in small groups in the large reef aquarium. Provide enough space to meet their territorial requirements and try to add the group simultaneously or add the largest member of the group last. Other gramma species are a greater challenge to keep in groups because they tend to be more aggressive and will also fight with congeners. All grammas tend to fade in color in captivity—this is probably due to a dietary deficiency, but bright lighting and low dissolved oxygen levels are also possible causes. The Blackcap Basslet (*Gramma melacara*) (page 108) is a larger, more aggressive species but with similar care requirements.

THREELINE BASSLET (*LIPOGRAMMA TRILINEATUM*)

Lipogramma spp.
Deepwater Grammas

Maximum Length: ~ 1.6 in. (4.1 cm).
Range: Tropical Western Atlantic.
Minimum Aquarium Size: 10 gal. (38 L).
Foods & Feeding: Meaty foods, including frozen seafood. May require live ghost shrimp to initiate a feeding response.
Aquarium Suitability/Reef Compatibility:
Aquarium Notes: Although they can make interesting additions to the reef aquarium, deep-water grammas such as this often succumb to shipping stress. If they make it through those rigors, they will do well in a tank that contains plenty of hiding places and peaceful tankmates—or no other fishes at all (a single-species nano-reef). They are more likely to spend time in the open if the tank is dimly lit. In a larger reef tank, you may not see these fishes often, as they tend to be quite secretive. I recommend keeping them in a smaller tank with several suitable hiding places so that they can be observed more frequently. One potential malady is swim bladder problems resulting from improper decompression. Avoid buying any individuals that have a difficult time maintaining their position in the water column and exhibit labored swimming.

Yellow Assessor (*Assessor flavissimus*): One of a group of exemplary fishes for the reef aquarium. Inset: Blue Assessor (*Assessor macneilli*).

Assessors (*Assessor* spp.)

This outstanding group of stunningly colored fishes is a welcome addition to virtually all reasonably peaceful reef aquariums. Two species are most commonly available: the Yellow Assessor (*Assessor flavissimus*) and the Blue Assessor (*Assessor mcneilli*). Both live in caves, under overhangs, or in large crevices, where they typically swim upside down. The Yellow Assessor usually occurs singly, in pairs, or in small groups. The Blue Assessor is more often found in large groups. Both feed on zooplankton and are very hardy. To keep more than one in your reef tank, be sure the tank is large enough (100 gallons [380 L] or more) with ample hiding spaces. Add the pair or small group members all at once. It is also better if the fish differ in size to increase the chances of getting both sexes. Males are larger and more likely to fight. It is best not to include them in a tank with overly boisterous species as they are likely to be the targets of aggression. Neither species will bother ornamental invertebrates. Both reach a length of just over 2 in. (5.1 cm). They are ideally suited for the nano-reef aquarium.

Comet (*Calloplesiops altivelis*): a great fish for the reef aquarium, here guarding an egg mass. Inset: Finespotted Comet (*Calloplesiops argus*).

Comets (*Calloplesiops* spp.)

The comets are some of the most bulletproof fishes in the aquarium trade and a favorite with reefkeepers. They do not harm corals or other sessile invertebrates, but are a threat to ornamental shrimps. Small fishes are also at risk when introduced to a tank with a resident comet. The comets are secretive and do not spend much time moving about in the open, especially in a brightly illuminated aquarium. Feeding them can be tricky; live gut-packed ghost shrimp are a good starter. They will also feed on worms and crustaceans associated with live rock. Adults can be housed in tanks as small as 30 gallons (114 L), but 55 gallons (209 L) or more is preferable. Comets rarely exhibit interspecific aggression, but they may quarrel with each other. To keep two together, add them to a larger aquarium (100 gallons [380 L] or more) with plenty of hiding places. Comets may be harassed and physically damaged by larger, more aggressive fishes (e.g., large dottybacks or hawkfishes). They may also have some difficulty competing for food in a crowded tank lacking sufficient live rock.

Goldspecs Jawfish (*Opistognathus* sp.): provide this digger with a deep sand bed with substrate of varying grades.

Jawfishes (Family Opistognathidae)

Jawfishes make comical and fascinating reef aquarium inhabitants. They can be kept in reef aquariums if provided with enough open sand/rubble substrate for burrowing. When they dig, they may inadvertently cover corals that are situated near the bottom of the aquarium. Be sure that any stony corals kept near jawfish burrows are those that can readily shed sediment. Do not place soft corals in an area where they can be buried. It is also possible that the digging activities of a larger jawfish could cause the reef structure to collapse. Rockwork should be put in place before sand is added to the aquarium. This will ensure that jawfishes cannot dig beneath the reef structure. Some species will eat ornamental crustaceans and other motile invertebrates (e.g., worms, serpent stars), but most are relatively easy to keep. Smaller species can be kept in tanks as small as 10 to 20 gallons (38 to 76 L). Larger species will require more substantial accommodations (75 gallons [285 L or more]).

Because they are industrious diggers, it is important to provide a mixed blend of coral sand, bits of rubble, shells, and/or bits of

Yellowhead Jawfish (*Opistognathus aurifrons*): males orally incubate the eggs until they hatch.

shells, etc. With this array of materials, they will pick and choose what they need and can create more stable burrows. Substrate depth depends on the maximum length of the species or individual in question. For the smaller species, 3 to 4 in. (7.6 to 10 cm) of substrate depth should suffice. They will often dig under flat rocks resting on the sand, using them as a roof for their burrow chamber.

Fortunately, jawfishes are fairly disease-resistant. The leading cause of captive jawfish death is leaping out of aquariums. This is especially true when the fishes are new to the tank. It is best to let them find shelter before you turn the lights off. A small nightlight over the tank will also help prevent them from jumping.

It is important to keep jawfishes (at least the smaller varieties) with more passive fishes. This is especially the case if you are keeping them in a smaller tank. Some jawfishes do very well in colonies, although if they are crowded, quarreling may occur. Some jawfish species are very aggressive toward each other and only one should be kept per tank.

Opistognathus aurifrons (Jordan & Thompson, 1905)
Yellowhead Jawfish (Pearly Jawfish)

Maximum Length: 3.9 in. (10 cm).
Range: Tropical Western Atlantic.
Minimum Aquarium Size: 20 gal. (76 L).
Foods & Feeding: Meaty foods, including chopped seafood, mysid shrimp, and frozen preparations for carnivores. Feed three times/day.
Aquarium Suitability/Reef Compatibility:
Aquarium Notes: Colonies of these opalescent beauties can make an incredible display. It is best to add all the individuals at once or add the smaller individuals to the tank first. When first introduced, this species may engage in "gulping" behavior (the fish swims along the surface and appears to gulp air) and is prone to leaping from the tank at this time. A good rule of thumb is approximately one jawfish per 2 to 2.5 ft.^{2} (13 to 16 cm^2) of tank surface area. (In the wild, individual burrows are from 6 to 45 in. [15 to 114 cm] apart.) If there are too many individuals in a tank, the subordinate fish will be forced to hide in the upper corners of the aquarium. A jawfish will chase smaller fishes away from its burrow, like dwarf seabass, goatfishes, small wrasses, and sharpnose puffers. This species regularly spawns in captivity.

Opistognathus rosenblatti Allen & Robertson, 1991
Bluespotted Jawfish

Maximum Length: 3.9 in. (10 cm).
Range: Tropical Eastern Pacific.
Minimum Aquarium Size: 20 gal. (76 L).
Foods & Feeding: Meaty foods, including chopped seafood, mysid shrimp, and frozen preparations for carnivores. Feed three times/day.
Aquarium Suitability/Reef Compatibility:
Aquarium Notes: This is a magnificent aquarium fish with a near-fluorescent color pattern whose appearance and behavior never fails to incite wonder. Its husbandry is similar to that of the other small members of the family. This is a more aggressive species toward conspecifics: unless you can acquire a heterosexual pair or you have a tank with an expansive surface area (e.g., a standard 180 gallon [684 L]), I would only keep one per tank. On the other hand, it is rarely aggressive toward unrelated species unless they try to enter its burrow. If they do intrude, it will display at them and push them away with its open mouth, or it may spit sand at them. Like others in the family, it is a very effective jumper that will find the smallest of holes in the aquarium top to leap through.

Opistognathus castelnaui
Blackcapped Jawfish
Max. Length: 4.7 in. (12 cm).

Opistognathus whitehurstii
Dusky Jawfish
Max. Length: 3.9 in. (10 cm).

Opistognathus sp.
Chestnut Jawfish
Max. Length: 3.9 in. (10 cm).

Opistognathus sp. (variant)
Chestnut Jawfish
Max. Length: 3.9 in. (10 cm).

Opistognathus sp.
Variable Jawfish
Max. Length: 3.9 in. (10 cm).

Opistognathus sp.
Brownheaded Jawfish
Max. Length: 3.5 in. (8.9 cm).

Bloch's Bigeye (*Priacanthus blochii*): the bigeyes make unusual additions to the larger reef aquarium, but good hiding places are a must to keep them happy.

Bigeyes (Family Priacanthidae)

With flaming scarlet color and a curious appearance, the bigeyes are interesting candidates for the larger reef system. Members of the genus *Priacanthus* should be housed in tanks of 100 gallons (380 L) or more, while the less active *Pristigenys* species will thrive in aquariums as small as 75 gallons (285 L). Be aware that bigeyes have large mouths and will eat smaller fishes and ornamental crustaceans. The tank should have one or two suitable hiding places, such as caves or overhangs offering dark shelter. Bigeyes will make better display animals and more readily acclimate in a deep-water reef aquarium. If exposed to bright lights for extended periods without shelter, their vision may be impaired. They will usually accept chopped seafood, frozen mysid shrimp, and frozen preparations. Live guppies or ghost shrimp may be needed to elicit feeding. In a large tank (180+ gallons [684+ L]), more than one *Priacanthus* can be kept, but add the individuals simultaneously and make sure each has its own hiding place. Only one *Pristigenys* should be kept per tank. Bigeyes are best housed with nonaggressive tankmates.

Spotted Hawkfish (*Cirrhitichthys aprinus*): some of the hawkfishes can be found living near the bases or even among the tentacles of sea anemones.

Hawkfishes (Family Cirrhitidae)

Hawkfishes are wonderful aquarium inhabitants, bringing beauty and personality into any system. They are durable, disease-resistant and will feed on a wide array of aquarium foods. Many are well-suited to the reef tank. That said, the hawkfishes' dark side includes a predilection for dining on ornamental crustaceans. The larger species also consume small fishes. If you want to try to keep shrimp with a cirrhitid, choose larger varieties like boxer shrimp (*Stenopus* species), and add the shrimp first. Hermit crabs and arrow crabs are also at risk from hawkfish predation. Except for crustaceans (and to a lesser degree tubeworms and snails), hawkfishes are not a threat to ornamental invertebrates. It is possible that hawkfishes can cause irritation by perching on live corals. When a hawkfish lights on a piece of soft coral it will cause the coral's polyps to contract. If an individual consistently rests on the same coral, this could interfere with the coral's normal behavior, but this usually does not cause problems. The key to maintaining their brilliance is to offer a varied diet, including some color-enhancing foods.

Amblycirrhites pinos (Mowbray, 1927)
Redspotted Hawkfish

Maximum Length: 3.7 in. (9.5 cm).
Range: Western Atlantic.
Minimum Aquarium Size: 20 gal. (76 L).
Foods & Feeding: Meaty foods, including finely shredded frozen seafood, mysid shrimp, frozen preparations, pigment-enriched flake food, and Cyclop-eeze. Feed at least once a day, preferably twice.
Aquarium Suitability/Reef Compatibility:
Aquarium Notes: This is a smaller hawkfish that is usually well-behaved in the reef aquarium. It is shy when first added to the tank, but once it has settled in it becomes bolder. It may bully newly introduced tankmates in smaller tanks. This species can be kept in pairs in aquariums of 75 gallons (285 L) or more. Your chances of success will be greater if the two fish differ in size and they are added simultaneously. This species will spend most of its time sitting in the open. It feeds mainly on zooplankton (including copepods and shrimp larvae) but does feed to a lesser degree on small shrimps, isopods, crabs, and polychaete worms.

FALCO HAWKFISH (*CIRRHITICHTHYS FALCO*)

Cirrhitichthys spp.
Spotted Hawkfishes

Maximum Length: 2.7 to 5.5 in. (7 to 14 cm).
Range: Indo-Pacific.
Minimum Aquarium Size: 20 gal. (76 L).
Foods & Feeding: Meaty foods, including finely shredded frozen seafood, mysid shrimp, frozen preparations, pigment-enriched flake food, and Cyclop-eeze. Feed once a day or preferably twice a day.
Aquarium Suitability/Reef Compatibility:
Aquarium Notes: The members of this genus are well-suited to the reef tank, although they do prey on crustaceans. In the wild, these hawkfishes feed on small crustaceans, small fishes, fish eggs, and polychaete worms. They may feed on ornamental shrimps. They are prone to aggression if crowded or once they are established in the tank. Newly introduced fishes (especially those that sit on the bottom) may be bullied by these hawkfishes. Do not house them with smaller gobies, dartfishes, or other passive fishes (unless the passive fishes are added to the tank first). The *Cirrhitichthys* species may lose color over time in captivity. Be sure to feed a varied diet, including some color-enhancing flake foods.

Cirrhitichthys aprinus
Spotted Hawkfish, Threadfin Hawkfish
Max. Length: 4.9 in. (12.5 cm).

Cirrhitichthys aprinus (variant)
Spotted Hawkfish, Threadfin Hawkfish
Max. Length: 4.9 in. (12.5 cm).

Cirrhitichthys aureus
Yellow Hawkfish, Golden Hawkfish
Max. Length: 2.7 in. (7 cm).

Cirrhitichthys falco
Falco's Hawkfish, Dwarf Hawkfish
Max. Length: 2.7 in. (7 cm).

Cirrhitichthys oxycephalus
Coral Hawkfish, Pixy Hawkfish
Max. Length: 3.3 in. (8.5 cm).

Cirrhitichthys oxycephalus (variant)
Coral Hawkfish, Pixy Hawkfish
Max. Length: 3.3 in. (8.5 cm)

Cirrhitops fasciatus (Bennett, 1828)
Blood Red Hawkfish (Redbar Hawkfish, Banded Hawkfish)

Maximum Length: 5 in. (12.7 cm).
Range: Japan, Hawaii, Madagascar, and Mauritius.
Minimum Aquarium Size: 20 gal. (76 L).
Foods & Feeding: Meaty foods, including finely shredded frozen seafood, mysid shrimp, frozen preparations, pigment-enriched flake food, and Cyclop-eeze. Feed at least once a day, preferably twice.
Aquarium Suitability/Reef Compatibility:
Aquarium Notes: This is an attractive and durable aquarium fish. It is a threat to small fishes and crustaceans and is best housed with larger or more aggressive species. It will ignore corals and giant clams, but will take almost all food offered, including flake and frozen rations, but should be fed a varied diet, including some color-enhancing foods (e.g., some of the flake foods that contain added pigments, krill, and shrimp). In the wild, it feeds mainly on small fishes, xanthid crabs, and shrimps, but also consumes zooplankters (including larval shrimps, copepods, amphipods, and larval gastropods), octopuses, sipunculid worms, and serpent stars on occasion. Unlike most hawkfishes, *C. fasciatus* feeds during both the day and night.

AMONG TENTACLES OF *MACRODACTYLA DOREENSIS*

Cyprinocirrhites polyactis (Bleeker, 1874)
Lyretail Hawkfish (Swallowtail Hawkfish)

Maximum Length: 5.5 in. (14 cm).

Range: Indo-Pacific.

Minimum Aquarium Size: 20 gal. (76 L).

Foods & Feeding: Meaty foods, including finely shredded frozen seafood, mysid shrimp, frozen preparations, pigment-enriched flake food, and Cyclop-eeze. Feed at least once a day or preferably twice.

Aquarium Suitability/Reef Compatibility:

Aquarium Notes: This is an exception to the usual rules of the hawkfish family, spending more time swimming in the water column, where it feeds on zooplankton. It is also one of the better reef aquarium hawkfishes. It is less of a threat to ornamental invertebrates (larger individuals will eat shrimps) and is also not as aggressive as most of the cirrhitids, although it has been known to pick on more passive fish tankmates. In a quiet aquarium, it will spend most of its time in repose on the reef structure, but when the tank has a considerable amount of water movement it will often swim against the current up in the water column. On occasion, it will hide near the base and under the tentacles of large anemones (especially *Heteractis* species) or large-polyped corals (like *Goniopora* species).

Neocirrhites armatus Castlenau, 1873
Flame Hawkfish

Maximum Length: 3.5 in. (9 cm).
Range: Indo-Pacific.
Minimum Aquarium Size: 20 gal. (76 L).
Foods & Feeding: Meaty foods, including finely shredded frozen seafood, mysid shrimp, frozen preparations, pigment-enriched flake food, and Cyclop-eeze. Feed at least once a day—preferably twice.
Aquarium Suitability/Reef Compatibility:
Aquarium Notes: In the wild, this distinctive fish spends most of its time within the branches of *Pocillopora* corals. In the reef tank, it will hide in larger small-polyped stony coral colonies or within live rock interstices. Its movements may facilitate water circulation in the colony and its feces may provide a source of nitrogen for coral tissue growth. It will sometimes refuge next to the base and under the tentacles of the Magnificent Sea Anemone (*Heteractis magnifica*). It is a threat to shrimps, hermit crabs, snails, and Christmas tree worms. If you keep more than one, provide plenty of suitable hiding places (preferably live *Pocillopora* corals) and add one larger fish and one or more smaller individuals, increasing your chances of eventually getting a mated pair.

Oxycirrhites typus Bleeker, 1857
Longnose Hawkfish

Maximum Length: 5.1 in. (13 cm).
Range: Indo-Pacific.
Minimum Aquarium Size: 20 gal. (76 L).
Foods & Feeding: Meaty foods, including finely shredded frozen seafood, mysid shrimp, frozen preparations, pigment-enriched flake food, and Cyclop-eeze. Feed at least once a day or preferably twice.
Aquarium Suitability/Reef Compatibility:
Aquarium Notes: This is a perennial favorite with reef aquarists. It is, however, a real threat to ornamental crustaceans (it will take shrimp in its jaws and bash them against the coral until they are broken into bite-sized pieces) and smaller or more elongated fishes (adults have a predilection to attack and attempt to eat dartfishes and firefishes). Longnose Hawkfishes like to perch in soft corals and gorgonians. They can be kept in heterosexual pairs, although sexing them can be tricky. If they begin to fight, you will need to separate them. To have a better chance of avoiding aggression, choose two fish that differ in size. This species is often picked on by other hawkfishes and is notorious for jumping out of open aquariums.

FRECKLED HAWKFISH (*PARACIRRHITES FORSTERI*) WITH CHROMIS IN ITS MOUTH

Paracirrhites spp.

Arc-Eye Hawkfishes (Freckled Hawkfishes)

Maximum Length: 5.5 to 11.3 in. (14 to 29 cm).

Range: Indo-Pacific.

Minimum Aquarium Size: 20 gal. (76 L).

Foods & Feeding: Meaty foods, including frozen seafood, mysid shrimp, frozen preparations, and pigment-enriched flake food. Feed daily.

Aquarium Suitability/Reef Compatibility:

Aquarium Notes: These brawny hawkfishes spends most of their time perching in coral colonies, ready to ambush passersby. Although they will not harm corals, small crabs, cleaner, boxer, anemone, and *Saron* shrimp are all fair game. *Paracirrhites* species are some of the most aggressive members of the hawkfish family. They will attack, maim, and occasionally ingest fish tankmates. Any small damselfish, dottyback, wrasse, goby, or blenny is potential prey. They will even attack fishes larger than themselves. Because of their predatory tendencies, it is imperative that they be the last fish placed into a community tank, unless of course they are being kept with more aggressive fishes. They are best housed with larger, more aggressive species (e.g., large angels, surgeonfishes, triggerfishes).

Paracirrhites arcatus
Arc-eye Hawkfish
Max. Length: 5.5 in. (14 cm).

Paracirrhites forsteri
Freckled Hawkfish
Max. Length: 8.8 in. (22.5 cm).

Paracirrhites forsteri (juv.)
Freckled Hawkfish
Max. Length: 8.8 in. (22.5 cm).

Paracirrhites forsteri (variant)
Freckled Hawkfish
Max. Length: 8.8 in. (22.5 cm).

Paracirrhites hemistictus
Whitespot Hawkfish
Max. Length: 11.3 in. (29 cm).

Paracirrhites xanthus
Golden Hawkfish
Max. Length: 4.7 in. (12 cm).

Orangestriped Cardinalfish (*Apogon cyanosoma*) juveniles: mild-mannered, often nicely pigmented fishes that will form authentic social groupings in the aquarium.

Cardinalfishes (Family Apogonidae)

Cardinalfishes are ideal for the reef aquarium and are underutilized by many aquarists. There are many attractive species that are very durable, and a group of gregarious apogonids makes an attractive addition to a larger reef tank (although not all species get along with each other). Cardinalfishes' activity above and among branching stony corals can increase coral growth rates, and their movement among coral branches helps to mix "older" water with fresh, oxygen-replete water. Members of the genus *Cheilodipterus* and some of the larger *Apogon* species will eat ornamental shrimps and small fishes. More delicate crustaceans, like some of the tiny anemone shrimps (*Periclimenes* species), are also potential prey.

Provide cardinalfishes with plenty of hiding places. Many are nocturnal and will hide under a ledge or in a hole, or hang out near the entrance of a preferred shelter site when the aquarium lights are on. The smaller species rarely pick on heterospecifics, although they tend to be picked on by larger, crevice-dwelling fishes. They may defend a preferred hiding place from other secretive species.

Apogon cyanosoma Bleeker, 1853
Yellowstriped Cardinalfish

Maximum Length: 3.1 in. (8 cm).
Range: Western Pacific.
Minimum Aquarium Size: 15 gal. (57 L).
Foods & Feeding: Meaty foods, including chopped seafood, mysid shrimp, and frozen preparations for carnivores. Feed twice a day.
Aquarium Suitability/Reef Compatibility:
Aquarium Notes: This is a great reef aquarium cardinalfish and one of the more ubiquitous apogonids in the marine aquarium trade, in part because it is very colorful and hardy. It is a bolder species that spends much of its time in the open, but does not move far from cover. It is best kept singly, in pairs, or in small groups of five to seven individuals (all the members of a group should be introduced to the tank simultaneously and the aquarium should be 75 gallons [285 L] or more). It is not a great threat to small fishes and ornamental crustaceans, but it has been known to prey on more delicate ornamental shrimp (e.g., anemone shrimp, *Periclimenes* species). Several similar species from other parts of the Indo-Pacific are similar in their care requirements.

COURTING PAIR

Pterapogon kauderni Koumans, 1933
Banggai Cardinalfish (Highfin Cardinalfish)

Maximum Length: 3 in. (7.5 cm).
Range: Sulawesi, Indonesia.
Minimum Aquarium Size: 15 gal. (57 L).
Foods & Feeding: Meaty foods, including chopped seafood, mysid shrimp, and frozen preparations for carnivores. Feed twice a day.
Aquarium Suitability/Reef Compatibility:
Aquarium Notes: Exceptionally handsome and easily bred in the home reef, this is a hardy and commendable species, although captive-bred specimens may prove more durable than their wild-caught cousins. It is risky to keep these fish in groups in captivity, unless you have a large aquarium (100 gallons [380 L] or more). Although they may behave peacefully toward one another when first introduced, one fish or a pair will often start chasing and nipping their conspecific tankmates. This species is usually indifferent toward other fish species, except when they are tending eggs (they readily spawn, with the male mouthbrooding the eggs until hatching). After spawning, the pair, especially the female, will chase any fish that approaches too closely. Do not house Banggais with overly aggressive tankmates.

Sphaeramia nematoptera (Bleeker, 1856)
Pajama Cardinalfish

Maximum Length: 3.1 in. (8 cm).
Range: Western Pacific.
Minimum Aquarium Size: 15 gal. (57 L).
Foods & Feeding: Meaty foods, including chopped seafood, mysid shrimp, and frozen preparations for carnivores. Feed twice a day.
Aquarium Suitability/Reef Compatibility:
Aquarium Notes: This is a wonderful reef fish, chromatically bizarre, and one of the best species for beginning marine aquarists. It can be housed in small groups in the larger aquarium. Members of the group will set up a pecking order, with the largest individual being the most dominant, but aggressive exchanges usually are limited to the occasional chase or nudge, not all-out warfare. Individuals may communicate with each other by flicking their pelvic fins. This species should not be introduced into a tank that contains overly aggressive fishes, although once it acclimates, it will usually compete with any other fish for food and is usually ignored by all but the most pugnacious tankmates. This bold species will spend most of its time in full view. Aquarium spawning is not uncommon.

Schooling Cardinalfishes

Apogon flores
Bluebarred Cardinalfish
Max. Length: 1.9 in. (5 cm).

Apogon fragilis
Fragile Cardinalfish
Max. Length: 1.9 in. (5 cm).

Apogon gilberti
Gilbert's Cardinalfish
Max. Length: 1.9 in. (5 cm).

Apogon hoeveni
Frostfin Cardinalfish
Max. Length: 1.9 in. (5 cm).

Apogon leptacanthus
Bluestreak Cardinalfish
Max. Length: 2.5 in. (6.5 cm).

Archamia zosterophora
Girdled Cardinalfish
Max. Length: 3.1 in. (8 cm).

Reef Aquarium Cardinalfishes

Apogon angustatus
Broadstripe Cardinalfish
Max. Length: 3.9 in. (10 cm).

Apogon compressus
Ochrestriped Cardinalfish
Max. Length: 4.7 in. (12 cm).

Apogon hartzfeldii
Hartzfeld's Cardinalfish
Max. Length: 3.9 in. (10 cm).

Apogon maculatus
Flamefish
Max. Length: 4.3 in. (11 cm).

Apogon margaritophorus
Redstriped Cardinalfish
Max. Length: 2.7 in. (7 cm).

Apogon sealei
Seale's Cardinalfish
Max. Length: 3.1 in. (8 cm).

Fivelined Cardinalfish (*Cheilodipterus quinquelineatus*) juv.: this genus of torpedo-shaped cardinalfishes makes an uncommon addition to a reef community.

Toothed Cardinalfishes (Genus *Cheilodipterus*)

These sleek predators will do well in a reef aquarium. They are completely safe with corals and tridacnids, but will feed on small fishes, worms, and crustaceans. Larger species are a threat to a wider range of fish tankmates. They often float near coral crevices, in caves, or above stony corals during the day and move further afield to feed after dark. Although they prefer live baby guppies and live ghost shrimp, they will also eat frozen mysid shrimp and chopped seafoods. Feed them at least once a day. Most are solitary fishes that do best if not housed with conspecifics. Except for smaller fishes, which they will eat, they rarely bother other fish species. Pick your *Cheilodipterus* species carefully, as some get quite large and will need to be housed in a large reef tank with other large fishes. These fishes are more likely than other cardinalfishes to leap from an open aquarium. There are several species in this genus that uncannily mimic poison-fanged blennies (genus *Meiacanthus*). Examples include the Mimic Cardinalfish (*Cheilodipterus parazonatus)* and the Yellowbelly Cardinalfish (*Cheilodipterus zonatus).*

Flashing Tilefish (*Hoplolatilus chlupatyi*): this amazing species can change its colors in an instant. Unfortunately, this group poses husbandry challenges.

Torpedo Tilefishes (Genus *Hoplolatilus*)

Most members of this very appealing genus are, alas, not easy to keep, and a reef aquarium packed with live rock is not the optimal aquarium in which to house a tilefish. They often grow to 5 in. (13 cm) or more, and all species need to be housed in larger tanks (preferably over 100 gallons [380 L]) with plenty of swimming space. Provide them with a cave or a flat piece of live rock lying on a sand substrate with a depression beneath. They will also dig their own holes. Do not house them with invertebrates that have a potent sting (e.g., carpet sea anemones) as they are likely to swim into them when the lights are turned off. Most do not harm sessile invertebrates, but Fourmanoir's Tilefish (*Hoplolatilus fourmanoiri*) has been observed to bite and kill Elegance Corals (*Catalaphyllia jardinei*). Some tilefishes may also attack ornamental shrimps. They should be kept in pairs or trios—they can be kept with conspecifics or congeners. Most are less likely to acclimate if they are kept on their own.

Keeping them with peaceful dither fishes will aid acclimation. I

Golden Tilefish (*Hoplolatilus luteus*): the most durable of the genus and also the most pugnacious, having been observed to pick on small zooplanktivores.

have had an occasional tilefish chase or nip at small zooplankton feeders, but these interactions never ended with the recipient of the aggression being harmed. The Golden Tilefish (*Hoplolatilus luteus*) and Fourmanoir's Tilefish (*Hoplolatilus fourmanoiri*) are the most hardy and aggressive members of the genus. These two species are more likely to fight with conspecifics and congeners.

Some captive tilefishes will accept aquarium fare, but live food is often needed to initiate feeding. Feed them several times a day. They will often jump out of open aquariums, including through small holes in the tank lid, usually when the lights are extinguished or if they are being picked on. They may also hurl themselves against the aquarium top, causing themselves injury. A small night-light placed over the tank may help prevent both these behaviors.

Torpedo tilefishes often suffer from improper decompression during collection. Avoid purchasing individuals that swim with their heads down and their tails up, laboring to stay stationary in the water column. Individuals suffering from this malady rarely survive.

Hoplolatilus cuniculus
Green Tilefish, Pale Tilefish
Max. Length: 5.9 in. (15 cm).

Hoplolatilus fourmanoiri
Fourmanoir's Tilefish
Max. Length: 5.5 in. (14 cm).

Hoplolatilus fronticinctus
Stocky Tilefish
Max. Length: 7.9 in. (20 cm).

Hoplolatilus marcosi
Skunk, Marcos', Redstripe Tilefish
Max. Length: 4.7 in. (12 cm).

Hoplolatilus purpureus
Purple Tilefish
Max. Length: 5.1 in. (13 cm).

Hoplolatilus starcki
Bluehead Tilefish, Starck's Tilefish
Max. Length: 5.9 in. (15 cm).

Sea Bream (*Scolopsis bilineata*): this family of fishes is bold, active, and suitable for a larger reef aquarium. Inset: Whiptail (*Pentapodus emeryii*).

Whiptails & Spinecheeks (Family Nemipteridae)

Several members of this family appear in the aquarium trade and may catch the eye of the reefkeeper. They are bold, active fishes that will spend most of their time in the open. They are suitable for a larger reef aquarium, although they will feed on worms, chitons, snails, shrimps, crabs, copepods (both benthic and planktonic), serpent stars, and small fishes. Their feeding activities often attract the attention of opportunistic wrasses. It is important that they be housed in a tank with plenty of swimming room, and the base of the reef structure should cover less than one-third of the tank bottom. They need suitable hiding places to facilitate acclimation.

Feed whiptails or spinecheeks several times a day. In most cases, they accept finely chopped fresh or frozen shrimp, scallops, marine fish flesh, mysid shrimp, and prepared frozen foods for carnivores. While their feeding activities will deplete live substrate of beneficial micro-invertebrates, they will help turn over the upper layers of the sand surface. They are not nearly as effective at this task as some of the sifting gobies, but are not likely to disturb deep sand beds.

Spotted Drum (*Equetus punctatus*): while these lovely fish can be kept in the reef tank, they are very delicate. Inset: Jackknife Fish (*Equetus lanceolatus*).

Drums (Family Sciaenidae)

The drums get their name from their modified swim bladder that is used to make a drumming or croaking sound. The drums are beguiling as juveniles, but are delicate aquarium fishes. They often suffer from transport and handling stress. Even transferring a drum from one tank to another can lead to fasting or disease problems. Drums are often reluctant to feed when introduced to their new home. Live brine shrimp or ghost shrimp are often needed to initiate feeding. A productive refugium and live sand can also help to provide natural fare while you try and coax it to feed. Feed them at least twice a day. Provide overhangs, small caves or crevices in which they can shelter when threatened. They are rarely aggressive, but are prone to being picked on by more combative tankmates. They do well with peaceful tankmates. If the tank is large enough, with suitable shelter sites, it is possible to house a drum with moderately aggressive tankmates. The long dorsal filament of certain juveniles is a ready target for fin-nippers. In the reef tank, drums will eat small snails, polychaete worms, crabs, and shrimps.

Redspot Goatfish (*Parupeneus heptacanthus*): the larger individual darkens in color as it is cleaned by anemone shrimps.

Goatfishes (Family Mullidae)

Goatfishes are demanding aquarium residents, and suited only to larger reefs with open aquascaping. While they do not eat corals, larger individuals may flip over loose coral colonies with their barbels when hunting. They feed continuously throughout the day or night, depending on the species (especially true for younger fishes). It is important to feed them at least four or five times a day. Most goatfishes are very active, covering large areas of seafloor as they forage, so the aquarium should have plenty of open space, especially on the bottom. Goatfishes will quickly exhaust the supply of invertebrates (e.g., worms, crustaceans) in live substrate. Meeting their high metabolic needs, especially those of juvenile individuals, can be difficult. Many are also highly predatory, gobbling up smaller fishes and all kinds of motile invertebrates. For this reason, consider carefully before adding them to a reef aquarium. Because they often have intestinal worms, treat goatfishes with a food laced with a dewormer while in quarantine. Many also become quite large; an extra-large aquarium is required to keep them long-term.

Indian Goatfish (*Parupeneus indicus*): high metabolic needs and predatory habits make most goatfishes less than desirable for most home reef systems.

One goatfish upside is that most species will help stir the sand on the bottom of the tank. This can frustrate some aquarists because the clouds of detritus and sediment the goatfish creates can take away from the aquarium's attractiveness. One of the byproducts of detritus breakdown is phosphate, which is an important algal nutrient and could lead to the growth of undesirable algae. But this sand-stirring behavior serves a valuable purpose. If you have an external filter that will remove this debris when it is in suspension, it will reduce the amount of detritus available for bacteria to break down, and thus limit algal-promoting phosphate.

Aquarists who are attempting to encourage the growth of infaunal invertebrates in their live sand should be aware that goatfishes quickly decimate worm and crustacean populations. Small crustaceans (including ornamental shrimps, anemone crabs, and hermit crabs), small snails, small fishes, and polychaete worms are also potential prey for most goatfishes. One benefit to aquarists is that goatfishes also eat small Fireworms (*Hermodice carunculata*) and small mantis shrimps. Opportunistic fishes (like wrasses) often follow foraging goatfishes, which can be fascinating to watch.

Yellowfin Goatfish (*Mulloidichthys vanicolensis*): juvenile goatfishes graze constantly in the wild and need to be fed multiple times per day in captivity.

Slender Goatfishes (Genus *Mulloidichthys*)

Members of the *Mulloidichthys* genus have relatively slender bodies, hence their group name. They are found on coral reefs and in more protected inshore habitats—juveniles are often found grazing aggressively in seagrass meadows. Some regularly refuge in shoals, which form during the day and disband at night when these fishes go hunting. In the aquarium, they tend to become emaciated and perish unless fed very frequently (at least four times a day). Juveniles might do better if kept in small groups. These goatfishes will vigorously probe the sand with their barbels and mouths in search of infaunal prey. They feed on polychaetes, bivalves, sea slugs, snails, crabs, shrimps, smaller crustaceans, and echinoderms. Larger individuals will also eat smaller fish tankmates as they sleep at night. Most of these goatfishes become large (around 16 in. [41 cm]). Because of their size, they also need plenty of open bottom space and swimming room (a tank of 180 gallons [684 L] or more is necessary for most *Mulloidichthys* species). Most reefkeepers are well advised to think twice before acquiring a cute goatfish juvenile.

Dash-and-Dot Goatfish (*Parupeneus barberinus*): as it feeds, it is followed by wrasses and sea beams.

Stocky Goatfishes (Genus *Parupeneus*)

The members of the genus *Parupeneus* tend to be more heavy-bodied than the other goatfishes. They vary in their captive suitability. All are voracious, feeding on a variety of motile invertebrates as well as small fishes. Juveniles need to be fed often (at least four times a day). Keep them in a reef tank with plenty of open space but with hiding places in which they can take shelter when frightened. Suddenly turning on the light can startle these fish—they may dart about the tank and collide with the aquarium glass or aquascaping. They are also known to leap out of open aquariums. Most stocky goatfishes feed by stirring soft substrate with their barbels, but a couple of species (e.g., Yellowsaddle Goatfish [*Parupeneus cyclostomus*], Multibarred Goatfish [*Parupeneus multifasciatus*]) more often probe reef crevices and are not effective sand stirrers. These fishes will only forage in the top few centimeters of the aquarium substrate. This can be beneficial, as it will stir the upper layer of substrate, but will not affect the infaunal organisms that live deeper in the sediment.

Parupeneus barberinoides (Bleeker, 1852)
Bicolor Goatfish (Half-and-Half Goatfish, Swarthyheaded Goatfish)

Maximum Length: 9.8 in. (25 cm).
Range: Western Pacific.
Minimum Aquarium Size: 100 gal. (380 L).
Foods & Feeding: Feed a varied diet of meaty foods, including chopped seafood, mysid shrimp, and frozen preparations. Will also feed on infaunal organisms in live sand. Live black worms may be useful in getting newly acquired individuals to start feeding. Young fish should be fed four or five times a day.
Aquarium Suitability/Reef Compatibility:
Aquarium Notes: This is a handsome species and one of the better goatfishes for the reef tank because of its smaller size. Like others in the family, it will need plenty of swimming room. It will eat ornamental crustaceans. It should also be housed with nonaggressive tankmates. This species may become progressively thinner in captivity, even if well fed, often because of intestinal worm infections. One beneficial behavior is that it will grub in the substrate and help stir up detritus that has collected there. Longevity records for this species vary greatly.

ADULT

Parupeneus cyclostomus (Lacépède, 1801)
Yellowsaddle Goatfish (Yellow Goatfish)

Maximum Length: 19.7 in. (50 cm).
Range: Indo-Pacific.
Minimum Aquarium Size: 180 gal. (684 L).
Foods & Feeding: Feed a varied diet of meaty foods, including chopped seafood, mysid shrimp, and frozen preparations. Will also feed on infaunal organisms in live sand. Live black worms may be useful in getting newly acquired individuals to start feeding. Young fish should be fed four or five times a day.
Aquarium Suitability/Reef Compatibility:
Aquarium Notes: This is a nervous fish that grows very large and will need plenty of swimming space and several good hiding places. Juveniles will do best if kept with nonaggressive tankmates. Because it does not grub in the substrate, it is not a good fish for stirring substrate in a reef aquarium. Juveniles will spend much of their time swimming beneath their tankmates, especially long, slender fishes like wrasses and tilefishes. They often form hunting partnerships with wrasses in the wild and are also followed by groupers. This species feeds more on fishes than other goatfishes, but will also eat crabs, mantis shrimp, alpheid shrimps, and amphipods.

Silver Mono (*Monodactylus argenteus*): marine aquarists will find this family sold as brackish-water fishes, but they easily adapt to full saltwater environments.

Monos (Family Monodactylidae)

Monos are interesting additions to the reef tank as they spend most of their time actively swimming in the water column, producing bright silver flashes that some aquarists find very appealing. They feed on algae, small crustaceans, and zooplankton and are not usually a threat to corals. They can also be effective dither fishes. Monos should be started off as juveniles in a large tank that will be well-suited to their long-term care, as adults do not respond well to being moved. It is best to keep monos in groups of three, five, or more individuals. If kept singly, they are often very nervous and spend much of their time hiding. Kept in a group of five or more, any possible aggression will likely be distributed among the group members so no one fish is being picked on constantly. Be aware that larger Sebae Monos (*Monodactylus sebae*) have been known to ingest fishes that are small enough to swallow whole. Feed all monos a varied diet, adding food two or three times a day. When buying monos from a freshwater retail tank, they can easily be acclimated to full-strength saltwater over a period of several days in a quarantine tank.

Big Longnose Butterflyfish (*Forcipiger longirostris*): this species is one of a handful of chaetodontids that can be housed with corals.

Butterflyfishes (Family Chaetodontidae)

Despite their coral-nipping reputation, some butterflyfishes can actually be kept successfully in systems housing corals and other prized invertebrates. For example, the species that feed primarily on zooplankton present minimal risk in the reef tank, as long as the aquarist is willing to feed them several times daily. These include the Pyramid Butterflyfish (*Hemitaurichthys polylepis*) and the Schooling Bannerfish (*Heniochus diphreutes*). In the case of the latter species, be careful to avoid mistakenly introducing the closely related Longfin Bannerfish (*Heniochus acuminatus*), which will nip at large- and small-polyped stony corals. A number of other butterflyfish species can be added to a reef tank, although there is greater risk involved. The incidence of problems seems to be slightly less if the tank is larger and the fishes are fed more frequently. Burgess' Butterflyfish (*Chaetodon burgessi*), the Reef Butterflyfish (*Chaetodon sedentarius*), Tinker's Butterflyfish (*Chaetodon tinkeri*), Copperbanded Butterflyfish (*Chelmon rostratus*), Yellow Longnose Butterflyfish (*Forcipiger flavissimus*), Caribbean Longsnout Butter-

Saddled Butterflyfish (*Chaetodon ephippium*): larger polyphagous species, like this one, are a serious threat to many soft and stony corals.

flyfish (*Prognathodes aculeatus*), and Bank Butterflyfish (*Prognathodes aya*) are all species that have been successfully kept in reef tanks with certain coral species.

Most butterflyfishes are more likely to nip at stony corals (especially large-polyped varieties) than at soft corals, excluding xeniids (e.g., *Xenia* spp.) and gorgonians. Many of the other soft-coral varieties are armed with noxious chemicals that repel the attacks of all but the most specialized butterflyfishes (e.g., Spottail Butterflyfish [*Chaetodon ocellicaudus*]). Some of the best soft corals to keep with butterflyfishes are members of the genera *Lemnalia*, *Litophyton*, *Sinularia*, *Scleronephthya* and *Dendronephthya* (although the latter two genera are very difficult to keep alive).

If you add a butterflyfish to your reef tank, keep an eye on it, as well as on your corals. If an individual begins picking at the live corals, it should be removed. Butterflyfishes will decimate polychaete worm populations, including Christmas tree worms and fanworms, and may nip at the tube feet of sea urchins or sea stars. Some species will also eat sea anemones. **Remember, there is always some risk in adding a butterflyfish to a reef tank.**

Reef Aquarium Butterflyfishes

Chaetodon burgessi
Burgess' Butterflyfish
Max. Length: 5.5 in. (14 cm).

Chaetodon kleinii
Klein's Butterflyfish
Max. Length: 5.5 in. (14 cm).

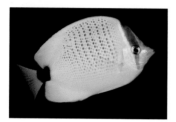

Chaetodon miliaris
Lemon Butterflyfish
Max. Length: 5.1 in. (13 cm).

Chelmon marginalis
Margined Butterflyfish
Max. Length: 7 in. (18 cm).

Prognathodes aculeatus
Caribbean Longnose Butterflyfish
Max. Length: 3.9 in. (10 cm).

Prognathodes brasilineatus
Brazilian Longsnout Butterflyfish
Max. Length: 3.9 in. (10 cm).

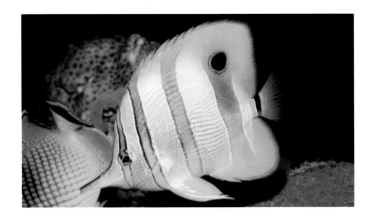

Chelmon rostratus (Linnaeus, 1758)
Copperbanded Butterflyfish (Beaked Coralfish)

Maximum Length: 7.1 in. (18 cm).
Range: East Indian and western Pacific.
Minimum Aquarium Size: 75 gal. (285 L).
Foods & Feeding: Feed meaty foods like frozen mysid shrimp, seafood shavings, and frozen preparations. Live foods, such as clams or black mussels that have had their shells broken open or live brine shrimp, may be needed to initiate feeding.
Aquarium Suitability/Reef Compatibility:
Aquarium Notes: This is a beauty coveted by reefkeepers, but a fish that varies in hardiness. Some specimens settle into their new homes within several days and begin eating, while others may refuse to feed, requiring live foods to initiate feeding. Some aquarists have suggested that smaller individuals (around 3 in. [7.6 cm] in length) fare better in captivity. Most individuals can be kept in a reef tank with soft corals and small-polyped stony corals, but some will nip at large-polyped stony corals, certain soft corals (including xeniids and clavulariids), and zoanthids (e.g., *Parazoanthus* species). Most individuals will eat glass anemones (*Aiptasia* species) and will decimate polychaete worm populations. Keep only one per tank.

YELLOW LONGNOSE BUTTERFLYFISH (*FORCIPIGER FLAVISSIMUS*)

Forcipiger spp.
Longnose Butterflyfishes

Maximum Length: 8.7 in. (22 cm).

Range: Indo-Pacific.

Minimum Aquarium Size: 75 gal. (285 L).

Foods & Feeding: Meaty foods, including chopped seafood, mysid shrimp, and frozen preparations for carnivores. Feed twice a day in a reef tank.

Aquarium Suitability/Reef Compatibility:

Aquarium Notes: The two species in this genus both have bright yellow bodies and extremely elongated snouts, which are used to pluck invertebrates from reef interstices. The Yellow Longnose Butterflyfish (*F. flavissimus*) is the easier to keep, but is also more of a threat to invertebrates (e.g., it uses its jaws to pull the feeding tentacles off fanworms and to amputate echinoderm tube feet). It rarely feeds on hard- and soft-coral polyps in the wild, but does pose some risk to corals in the reef aquarium, especially large-polyped stony corals. The Big Longnose Butterflyfish (*F. longirostris*) (see page 148) is not a threat to ornamental invertebrates, but can be difficult to feed. It has a pipette-like mouth and ingests tiny crustaceans. It tends to do better in a reef tank with well-established live substrate.

Hemitaurichthys polylepis (Bleeker, 1857)
Pyramid Butterflyfish

Maximum Length: 7.1 in. (18 cm).
Range: East Indo-Pacific.
Minimum Aquarium Size: 100 gal. (380 L).
Foods & Feeding: Feed meaty foods, like finely chopped seafood, mysid shrimp, vitamin-enriched brine shrimp, frozen preparations, and flake food. Feed at least three times a day.
Aquarium Suitability/Reef Compatibility:
Aquarium Notes: This a prized fish that can be housed in a reef tank if the aquarist is willing to feed it frequently (i.e., several times per day). It feeds mainly on zooplankton, although it may occasionally ingest benthic invertebrates, including soft coral polyps (in particular xeniid corals), especially if underfed. The optimal tank for the Pyramid Butterflyfish will have plenty of swimming space. It can be kept singly, in pairs, or if your aquarium is large enough, in small groups. It is more likely to acclimate to its new home if not pestered by its tankmates, although once it has fully adjusted to life in captivity, moderately aggressive fishes can be introduced. The captive longevity record for this species is 15 years.

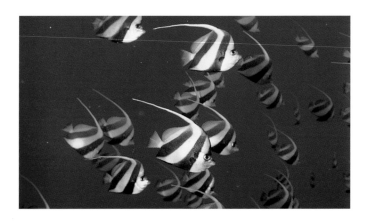

Heniochus diphreutes (Jordan, 1903)
Schooling Bannerfish

Maximum Length: 7.1 in. (18 cm).
Range: Indo-Pacific.
Minimum Aquarium Size: 100 gal. (380 L).
Foods & Feeding: Feed meaty foods, like finely chopped seafood, mysid shrimp, vitamin-enriched brine shrimp, and frozen preparations. Feed at least three times a day.
Aquarium Suitability/Reef Compatibility:
Aquarium Notes: This one of the more suitable butterflyfishes for the reef aquarium. It is less likely to bother invertebrates, but in order to maintain its health, it should be fed at least twice a day. Underfed individuals are more likely to pick at corals. It has been observed to pick at the dying tissue of large-polyped stony corals. Provide this species with plenty of swimming room. This species can be kept in groups if all individuals are added to the tank at the same time. Do not mistake this for the very similar Threadfin Bannerfish (*Heniochus acuminatus*), which *will* eat your corals. The safe species has a less protruding snout, a more rounded breast and, most tellingly, the second black band ends at the tip of the anal fin. In *H. acuminatus*, which you do not want, the anal fin tip is white.

Threespot or Flagfin Angelfish (*Apolemichthys trimaculatus*): although not particularly aggressive, members of this genus will nip at corals in the reef tank.

Apolemichthys Angelfishes (Genus *Apolemichthys*)

As a group, the marine angelfishes are among the most alluring and coveted species available to home aquarists. Keeping them successfully in a reef aquarium requires careful selection—and a measure of luck. Small angelfishes in this genus may do fine in the reef aquarium, larger individuals can be quite destructive. Adding one to a reef aquarium is a risky proposition if you have a collection of soft coral polyps and stony corals (especially large-polyped stony corals). They will also pick at zoanthids. This genus includes some of the hardiest members of the angelfish family, as well as two species that typically fare poorly in the aquarium: the Bandit Angelfish (*A. arcuatus*) and the Flagfin Angelfish (*A. trimaculatus*). The hardiest member of the genus is the Indian Yellowtail Angelfish (*A. xanthurus*).

All *Apolemichthys* species do better in a tank with live rock and/or live plant material on which to browse. Juveniles or subadults are more likely to accept captive foods. These fishes need plenty of a hiding places in which to retreat.

Boyle's Angelfish (*Paracentropyge boylei*): a deep-water treasure, this smaller angelfish is one of the less durable members of the family.

Pygmy Angelfishes (Genera *Centropyge* and *Paracentropyge*)

The reef tank is a perfect environment for pygmy angelfishes as these aquariums tend to be replete with hiding places and grazing opportunities. Most of these fishes feed on diatoms and detritus. While coral polyps are not their natural fare, they will ingest coral slime. The corals that most often serve as feeding substrate are the large-polyped stony corals. If your large-polyped stony corals are always closed and the tank contains a *Centropyge* species, there is a good chance the fish is bothering the coral. They have also been known to nip at the oral disc of anemones, feed on their feces, or even eat dying anemones or corals. They may also nip zoanthids and the feeding appendages of feather duster and Christmas tree worms.

There seem to be some consistent behaviors among the pygmy angelfish species, but there are no hard and fast rules. For example, the Cherubfish (*Centropyge argi*) can typically be kept with most stony and soft corals without inflicting damage. However, an occasional specimen will begin picking at the tissue of large-polyped

Japenese Pygmy Angelfish (*Centropyge interruptus*): this larger-than-average member of the genus is a rarity but typically well behaved in the reef aquarium.

stony corals, soft coral polyps, and even mushroom anemones. Whatever *Centropyge* species you are thinking of adding, introducing any angelfish to a reef aquarium always entails a degree of risk.

The corals that are least likely to be bothered by your pygmy angelfishes are those that are highly ichthyotoxic and distasteful. These species include some (*not all*) members of the genera *Lemnalia, Sinularia, Sarcophyton, Cladiella, Paralemnalia,* and *Efflatounaria.*

Pygmy angelfishes are notorious for nipping the mantles of tridacnid clams (the rich slime on these clams is a source of food). If you have a pygmy angelfish and your tridacnid clam stops opening fully, the fish may be picking at the clam's mantle. These fishes are less likely to cause serious problems if the tank is large and they are fed more frequently. Introduce pieces of romaine lettuce or sheets of freeze-dried algae (nori) to reduce the likelihood of coral/clam nipping. Pygmy angels will thrive in aquariums as small as 15 gallons (57 L), but are best kept in larger tanks unless they are being housed on their own. Some species can be very aggressive in a smaller tank, pestering more docile tankmates.

Centropyge argi Woods & Kanazawa, 1951
Cherub Angelfish (Atlantic Pygmy Angelfish)

Maximum Length: 3.1 in. (8 cm).
Range: Tropical West Atlantic.
Minimum Aquarium Size: 30 gal. (114 L).
Foods & Feeding: Feed frozen preparations that contain *Spirulina* algae, as well as mysid shrimp and/or finely shaved fresh or frozen shrimp. Feed at least three times a day, unless in an aquarium that has healthy microalgae growth.
Aquarium Suitability/Reef Compatibility:
Aquarium Notes: This is a gloriously pigmented, durable fish full of interesting behaviors—but beware: it can also be a tyrant once established in an aquarium. It will harass docile fishes and even kill other pygmy angelfishes, especially in a small tank. A male and female, or two or more females, can be kept together as long as the tank is large enough (135 gallons [513 L] or more) and the angelfish are introduced simultaneously. Males will fight, often to the death. This angelfish will occasionally nip at large-polyped stony corals and clam mantles. Certain individuals have also been known to eat soft corals (e.g., *Clavularia, Anthelia, Xenia*) and necrotic coral or anemone tissue. A rare individual may eat mushroom anemones.

Centropyge bispinosus (Günther, 1860)
Coral Beauty (Twospined Angelfish, Dusky Angelfish)

Maximum Length: 3.9 in. (10 cm).
Range: Indo-Pacific.
Minimum Aquarium Size: 30 gal. (114 L).
Foods & Feeding: Feed frozen preparations that contain *Spirulina* algae, as well as mysid shrimp and/or finely shaved fresh or frozen shrimp. Feed at least three times a day, unless in an aquarium that has healthy microalgae growth.
Aquarium Suitability/Reef Compatibility:
Aquarium Notes: This species is extremely attractive, radiating vibrant colors. In addition, it is readily available, usually quite hardy, and typically inexpensive. In most cases, it is not as aggressive as many of its congeners, but individuals may assert their dominance in a smaller aquarium, especially after they have been in the setting for a while. Although this angelfish is not as problematic as some when it comes to a propensity for nipping corals and clams, adding one to a reef aquarium does entail some risk. The larger the reef tank, the less likely the fish is to pick at any particular sessile invertebrate until it damages it irreparably.

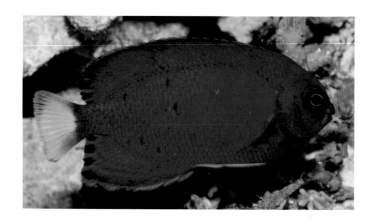

Centropyge flavicaudus Fraser-Brunner, 1933
Whitetail Pygmy Angelfish

Maximum Length: 3.1 in. (8 cm).
Range: Indo-Pacific.
Minimum Aquarium Size: 20 gal. (76 L).
Foods & Feeding: Feed frozen preparations that contain *Spirulina* algae, as well as mysid shrimp and/or finely shaved fresh or frozen shrimp. Feed at least three times a day, unless in an aquarium that has healthy microalgae growth.
Aquarium Suitability/Reef Compatibility:
Aquarium Notes: This is a hardy aquarium fish with subtle beauty whose diminutive size makes it a perfect candidate for small reef systems. However, it can be quite aggressive once established. This angelfish may nip at large-polyped stony corals and tridacnid clam mantles, although it is less of a threat than some of its larger congeners. It may also eat some soft coral polyps and nip at zoanthids. A recently published paper argues that *C. flavicaudus* is synonymous with Fisher's Angelfish (*C. fisheri*).

Centropyge loriculus (Günther, 1874)
Flame Angelfish

Maximum Length: 3.9 in. (10 cm).
Range: West, South, and Central Pacific.
Minimum Aquarium Size: 20 gal. (76 L).
Foods & Feeding: Feed frozen preparations that contain *Spirulina* algae, as well as mysid shrimp and/or finely shaved fresh or frozen shrimp. Feed at least three times a day, unless in an aquarium that has healthy microalgae growth.
Aquarium Suitability/Reef Compatibility:
Aquarium Notes: This a distinctive and traffic-stopping species much in demand by marine aquarists. It was once considered a durable aquarium fish, but in recent years individuals have been proving more difficult to keep long-term, perhaps traceable to their region of origin. It can be aggressive toward members of its own genus, as well as fishes with similar shape or behavior. If you plan to house it in a relatively peaceful community setting, it should be the last fish introduced.Like others in the genus, the Flame Angelfish may nip at large-polyped stony corals and tridacnid clam mantles. It may also eat some soft coral polyps and may nip at zoanthids.

Centropyge aurantius
Golden Angelfish
Max. Length: 3.9 in. (10 cm).

Centropyge bicolor
Bicolor Angelfish
Max. Length: 5.9 in. (15 cm).

Centropyge colini
Colin's Angelfish
Max. Length: 3.5 in. (9 cm).

Centropyge eibli
Eibl's Angelfish
Max. Length: 4.3 in. (11 cm).

Centropyge heraldi
Herald's Angelfish
Max. Length: 4.7 in. (12 cm).

Centropyge potteri
Potter's Angelfish
Max. Length: 3.9 in. (10 cm).

Black Velvet Angelfish (*Chaetodontoplus melanosoma*): juveniles are interesting and usually well-behaved in the reef aquarium, but adults can cause problems.

Velvet Angelfishes (Genus *Chaetodontoplus*)

For expert reefkeepers only, this genus has some of the most highly prized species in the marine aquarium universe. Although juveniles will often behave themselves in the reef aquarium, as they grow they will become more of a threat to sessile invertebrates. They usually do not bother more toxic soft corals (e.g., *Cladiella*, *Lemnalia*, *Lobophytum*, and *Sinularia*) and often ignore mushroom anemones, but large-polyped stony corals, the oral discs of sea anemones, and clam mantles are sometimes nipped by these grazers. Sponges comprise the bulk of their diet in the wild, so provide a varied captive menu that includes vegetable matter and frozen sponge rations. If they are well fed, they are less likely to begin picking on corals. Feed them three to five smaller portions each day. More delicate members of the genus acclimate more readily in a tank full of green filamentous algae or macroalgae. These fishes are susceptible to ich and velvet disease (these can be difficult to treat in the reef tank) and the viral infection *Lymphocystis*. Be sure to quarantine and condition new individuals before placing them into your reef tank.

JUVENILE

Chaetodontoplus melanosoma (Bleeker, 1853)
Black Velvet Angelfish (Gray Poma)

Maximum Length: 7.8 in. (20 cm).
Range: East Indian Ocean and West Pacific.
Minimum Aquarium Size: 55 gal. (209 L).
Foods & Feeding: Feed frozen preparations that contain *Spirulina* algae, as well as mysid shrimp and/or finely shaved fresh or frozen shrimp. Feed at least three times a day, unless in an aquarium that has healthy microalgae growth. It will browse on filamentous algae and diatoms growing on the aquarium decor.
Aquarium Suitability/Reef Compatibility:
Aquarium Notes: This is an affordable, easy-to-love species, but one that may nip at large-polyped stony corals, some soft coral polyps, zoanthids, and clam mantles. Adults are a greater threat than juveniles. This species will usually adapt to aquarium life if kept with nonaggressive tankmates and provided with plenty of hiding places. It is usually not an overly aggressive fish, but is likely to bully related species placed into a tank after it is established. If you are accumulating funds in hopes of one day acquiring one of the rare, staggeringly pricey members of this genus, here is a fish that will help teach the ways of this challenging genus.

Chaetodontoplus mesoleucus (Bleeker, 1853)
Singapore Angelfish (Vermiculated Angelfish)

Maximum Length: 6.7 in. (17 cm).
Range: West Pacific.
Minimum Aquarium Size: 55 gal. (209 L).
Foods & Feeding: Offer frozen preparations that contain *Spirulina* algae, as well as mysid shrimp and/or finely shaved fresh or frozen shrimp. Feed at least three times a day, unless in an aquarium that has healthy microalgae growth. It will browse on filamentous algae and diatoms growing on the aquarium decor.
Aquarium Suitability/Reef Compatibility:
Aquarium Notes: In captivity, this handsome, butterflylike species is somewhat of an enigma; some individuals adapt quickly to aquarium life, while others hide constantly and never feed. By keeping it in an aquarium with lots of hiding places in a quiet area of your home (where there is not a lot of activity around the aquarium) and with nonaggressive tankmates, you will increase your chances of success. A good crop of macroalgae (like *Caulerpa*) or microalgae may also facilitate acclimation. This species poses a moderate risk to large-polyped stony corals. It may also eat some soft coral polyps and nip at zoanthids and feather duster worms.

Chaetodontoplus caeruleopunctatus
Bluespotted Angelfish
Max. Length: 5.5 in. (14 cm).

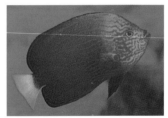

Chaetodontoplus cephalareticulatus
Maze Angelfish
Max. Length: 5.1 in. (13 cm).

Chaetodontoplus conspicillatus
Conspicuous Angelfish
Max. Length: 9.8 in. (25 cm).

Chaetodontoplus duboulayi
Scribbled Angelfish
Max. Length: 9.8 in. (25 cm).

Chaetodontoplus meredithi
Queensland Yellowtail Angelfish
Max. Length: 9.8 in. (25 cm).

Chaetodontoplus septentrionalis
Bluestripe Angelfish
Max. Length: 9.8 in. (25 cm).

Rock Beauty Angelfish (*Holacanthus tricolor*): often show-stoppingly beautiful, member of this genus all pose undeniable risks to sessile invertebrates.

Holacanthus Angelfishes (Genus *Holacanthus*)

Some of the most spectacular fishes on the world's coral reefs, these larger angelfishes are not ideal candidates for the average reef aquarium. While juveniles members of this genus may be endearing, adults are prone to picking at sessile invertebrates (they feed on sponges and tunicates in the wild). Large-polyped stony corals, gorgonians, and stoloniferan soft corals (e.g., *Xenia, Clavularia*) are especially prone to being picked at. Some adults may feed on small-polyped stony corals. Sea anemones and zoanthids might also be picked at, as well as feather dusters, Christmas tree worms, and tridacnid clam mantles. Adults will cause less damage in a reef tank with more toxic "treelike" soft corals (e.g., Alcyoniidae). The likelihood they will bite desirable inverts is in part a function of how much they are fed (if hungry, they are more likely to nip). They rarely bother ornamental crustaceans. Remember, these fishes grow rapidly, are large as adults, and need plenty of swimming room. They are prone to ich and occasionally suffer from flukes, *Lymphocystis,* and head and lateral line erosion.

Holacanthus Angelfishes

Holacanthus bermudensis (juv.)
Blue Angelfish
Max. Length: 14.8 in. (38 cm).

Holacanthus bermudensis
Blue Angelfish
Max. Length: 14.8 in. (38 cm).

Holacanthus ciliaris
Queen Angelfish
Max. Length: 17.5 in. (45 cm).

Holacanthus clarionensis (juv.)
Clarion Angelfish
Max. Length: 7.8 in. (20 cm).

Holacanthus passer (juv.)
King Angelfish, Passer Angelfish
Max. Length: 14.1 in. (36 cm).

Holacanthus tricolor
Rock Beauty Angelfish
Max. Length: 7.8 in. (20 cm).

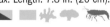

Lamarck's Angelfish (*Genicanthus lamarck*) male: this genus feeds mainly on algae and zooplankton, making them ideal smaller angelfishes for the reef tank.

Swallowtail Angelfishes (Genus *Genicanthus*)

These are, very simply, the best angelfishes for the reef aquarium: elegant, fascinating to watch, and almost entirely safe with corals and ornamental invertebrates. They feed primarily on algae and zooplankton, although they do eat benthic organisms on occasion (including sponges, polychaete worms, and bryozoans). Rarely, captive individuals may feed on soft coral polyps (especially when not fed enough). When buying *Genicanthus* angelfish species, avoid any that have difficulty maintaining their position in the water column or that wedge themselves in reef crevices with the lights on—this behavior is symptomatic of swim bladder injuries. Feed at least twice daily (preferably more often) with a varied diet that includes finely shaved fresh or frozen shrimp, frozen brine shrimp, mysid shrimp, and frozen preparations containing *Spirulina* algae. Swallowtail angelfishes tend not to be overly aggressive, but males and larger females may chase smaller, more docile planktivores. Keep only one male per tank. Most species seem to prefer a more dimly lit aquarium, but they can be acclimated to a brightly lit tank.

Swallowtail Angelfishes

Genicanthus bellus (female)
Ornate Angelfish
Max. Length: 7.1 in. (18 cm).

Genicanthus bellus (male)
Ornate Angelfish
Max. Length: 7.1 in. (18 cm).

Genicanthus caudovittatus (juv.)
Zebra Angelfish
Max. Length: 7.8 in. (20 cm).

Genicanthus lamarck (female)
Lamarck's Angelfish
Max. Length: 9 in. (23 cm).

Genicanthus melanospilos (male)
Blackspot Angelfish
Max. Length: 7.1 in. (18 cm).

Genicanthus semifasciatus
Japanese Swallowtail Angelfish
Max. Length: 8.2 in. (21 cm).

Blueface Angelfish (*Pomacanthus xanthometopon*): adults can be kept with some soft corals, but are a threat to clams and stony corals.

Pomacanthus Angelfishes (Genus *Pomacanthus*)

These eyecatching members of the angelfish family can be kept in a very large reef tank, but it is a calculated risk. They may nip large-polyped stony corals, certain soft corals (e.g., gorgonians, *Xenia, Anthelia*), and zoanthids. They will occasionally pick at and some will even eat small-polyped stony corals. That said, I have seen these fishes living in harmony with small-polyped stony corals in large reef tanks. It pays to remember that there is an inherent risk anytime you add a large angel to a tankful of stony corals. They can be successfully kept with some soft corals, like *Sinularia, Cladiella, Lemnalia,* and *Litophyton.* Large individuals may occasionally pick at mushroom and sea anemones and are especially prone to bothering tridacnid clams. Adults may even eat sea stars. Be aware that adult members of this genus are more likely to damage sessile invertebrates than juveniles are. *Pomacanthus* species are also less likely to do harm if well fed and kept in a larger tank. If you keep them in a reef tank, be sure to provide plenty of swimming room. They can be aggressive, but are usually not as feisty as the *Holacanthus* angels.

Pomacanthus Angelfishes

Pomacanthus asfur
Asfur Angelfish
Max. Length: 15.6 in. (40 cm).

Pomacanthus imperator (juv.)
Emperor Angelfish
Max. Length: 14.8 in. (38 cm).

Pomacanthus imperator (adult)
Emperor Angelfish
Max. Length: 14.8 in. (38 cm).

Pomacanthus navarchus
Bluegirdled, Majestic Angelfish
Max. Length: 9.8 in. (25 cm).

Pomacanthus paru
French Angelfish
Max. Length: 14.8 in. (38 cm).

Pomacanthus semicirculatus
Koran Angelfish
Max. Length: 13.7 in. (35 cm).

Indo-Pacific Sergeant (*Abudefduf vaigiensis*): members of this widespread dam-selfish genus are very hardy but can become pugnacious in aquarium confines.

Sergeants (Genus *Abudefduf*)

This bulletproof genus is represented on reefs around the world. Although they are some of the most durable of the aquarium fishes, none of the sergeants are particularly popular with aquarists. In fact, most wholesalers sell these fishes under the moniker "assort-ed damsels." Adults sport dark bars on a silver, white, or light blue background, while a few species have yellow highlights. They tend to occur singly or in loose aggregations when feeding near the reef, but when they enter the water column, at least some of the species form foraging schools. The diet of most members of the genus con-sists of zooplankton, small benthic crustaceans, and algae.

Most of these fishes get quite large (over 8 inches [20 cm] in length) and very belligerent. While juveniles are interesting—even cute, in some respects, the larger adolescents and adults can be true hellions. They should never be housed with less passive tankmates, and are best kept with larger angelfishes, surgeonfishes, and trigger-fishes. They can be kept in reef tanks, although one Atlantic species has been reported to eat zoanthids.

Clown Anemonefish (*Amphiprion percula*): while wild-caught specimens have poor survival rates, tank-raised individuals are excellent reef aquarium inhabitants.

Anemonefishes (Genera *Amphiprion* & *Premnas*)

Anemonefishes make wonderful additions to the reef aquarium. The only threat they pose to invertebrates is that an occasional individual may eat an ornamental shrimp (or shove it into its host sea anemone), feed on tubeworms, or adopt a coral as a surrogate host. This latter behavior may prove detrimental to the health of large-polyped stony corals if the fish constantly wallows among the coral polyps, causing them to contract and impede the coral's feeding behavior. Anemonefishes occasionally nip at the polyps of large-polyped stony corals, but are less likely to do this if a host sea anemone is present. For the most part, however, they are trouble-free members of a reef community and will eat most foods.

Although a host sea anemone is not necessary to the keeping of an anemonefish, many aquarists want to establish this symbiotic relationship in captivity. Be aware that some host sea anemones are difficult to keep, will sting sessile invertebrates, and may be prone to moving around the tank. Do your research carefully before purchasing a host sea anemone.

Clark's Anemonefish (*Amphiprion clarkii*): a pair tending their eggs, which are deposited on a hard surface near the base of their host sea anemone.

Most anemonefishes can fend for themselves with other fishes. The larger species can be very aggressive, harassing and even causing the death of more docile tankmates. The more diminutive species are occasionally picked on by larger tankmates, especially if they are kept without a host anemone. When keeping conspecifics, it is best to acquire a pair. These fishes are protandric hermaphrodites (transforming from males into females). If you acquire two juveniles, the most dominant will develop into a female, while the subordinate will become a male. When a group of conspecifics is added to a tank, a dominance hierarchy will form with the largest being most dominant, followed by the next largest and so on. In groups, it is not uncommon for the most subordinate individual to be picked on until it either wastes away or ends up hiding in the corner of the tank. If you mix different anemonefish species in a larger tank, be aware that some species are more aggressive than others. Behavioral problems are more likely to occur if the various species are kept with a single host anemone. A word of caution: quarantine your anemonefishes before adding them to your display tank. *Brooklynella* or *Amyloodinium* is difficult to treat in the reef aquarium.

False Clownfish or Ocellaris Clownfish (*Amphiprion ocellaris*): captive-raised individuals tend to be hardier than wild-caught individuals.

Percula Anemonefishes (Subgenus *Actinicola*)

There are two species in the subgenus *Actinicola*—the False or Ocellaris Clownfish (*Amphiprion ocellaris*) and the Percula Clownfish (*A. percula*). The beautiful coloration and endearing personality of *A. ocellaris* has made it a favorite of aquarists. Some individuals acclimate readily and are long-lived in captivity, while others last only as long as a good cricket match (a few days). Captive-raised individuals are always your best bet. They are very dependent on an anemone in the wild, although they do just fine without a protective host in captivity. Although they can be kept in groups, typically one individual will dominate and pick on the other members of the group. They are rarely aggressive toward other anemonefish species (except for other members of this subgenus).

Amphiprion percula tends to be more aggressive toward members of its own species than *A. ocellaris*. It should only be housed singly or in pairs. The sexes usually differ in size, with the female member of the pair being larger than the male (also true for *A. ocellaris*). They tend to be more aggressive when an anemone is present.

Orangefinned or Bluestriped Anemonefish (*Amphiprion chrysopterus*): this beautiful species tends to be less hardy than most in the *A.clarkii* species complex.

Clark's Anemonefishes (Subgenus *Amphiprion*)

If you want a species that is more likely to adopt a sea anemone host, Clark's Anemonefish (*Amphiprion clarkii*), perhaps the hardiest and most adaptable of this group, is the best choice—it has even been known to live in Atlantic anemones. Most individuals will adopt a resident sea anemone within hours after being introduced to the tank. This complex of anemonefishes contains at least 11 species. These species are less reliant on their host anemone for protection, sometimes wandering many meters from their cnidarian sanctuary. At least some are known to emigrate to other anemones to fill a vacancy in an existing social unit or to oust a current pair member. They can be very aggressive, especially toward other members of the genus, and should be housed singly or in mated pairs. Many reach larger sizes (5 in. [13 cm] or more). If a pair happens to lay eggs they will attempt to chase off other species (including the aquarist) incessantly. The bubbletip sea anemone (*Entacmaea quadricolor*) is readily paired with all Clark's anemonefishes, and captive-propagated *E. quadricolor* are readily available.

Clark's Anemonefishes

Amphiprion akindynos
Barrier Reef Anemonefish
Max. Length: 4.7 in. (12 cm).

Amphiprion allardi
Allard's Anemonefish
Max. Length: 5.5 in. (15 cm).

Amphiprion bicinctus
Twobanded Anemonefish
Max. Length: 5.5 in. (14 cm).

Amphiprion clarkii (juv.)
Clark's Anemonefish
Max. Length: 5.5 in. (14 cm).

Amphiprion clarkii
Clark's Anemonefish
Max. Length: 5.5 in. (14 cm).

Amphiprion tricinctus
Threeband Anemonefish
Max. Length: 4.7 in. (12 cm).

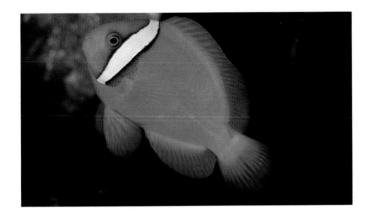

Tomato Anemonefish (*Amphiprion frenatus*): members of this group of five related species are stunning fishes that can become aggressive in a smaller reef tank.

Tomato Anemonefishes (Subgenus *Amphiprion*)

Tomato anemonefishes have vibrant colors and typically fare well in captivity. The only drawback is their size, with deep bodies compared to many smaller clownfishes, and their aggressiveness, especially in smaller aquariums. They will punish other anemonefishes and smaller, more passive tankmates. They will also fight among themselves, unless you can acquire a known pair. You should keep only one of these fishes per tank, and only keep them with larger or more pugnacious species. Although they are usually found close to their host sea anemones in the wild, they do fine without them in the aquarium. Tomato clownfishes have been know to settle into Atlantic anemones (*Condylactis* spp.). All but one of the five species in this group are reddish overall, and adults have a single bar behind the eye. Most ichthyologists accept the current taxonomic status of the various anemonefish forms, but some in this group could simply be color forms of a single species. Although not as vulnerable as some of their relatives, the members of this complex sometimes succumb to clownfish disease (*Brooklynella hostilis*).

Tomato Anemonefishes

Amphiprion ephippium (juv.)
Red Saddleback Anemonefish
Max. Length: 4.7 in. (12 cm).

Amphiprion ephippium
Red Saddleback Anemonefish
Max. Length: 4.7 in. (12 cm).

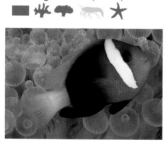

Amphiprion frenatus (female)
Tomato Anemonefish
Max. Length: 5.5 in. (14 cm).

Amphiprion mccullochi
McCulloch's Anemonefish
Max. Length: 4.7 in. (12 cm).

Amphiprion melanopus
Red and Black Anemonefish
Max. Length: 4.7 in. (12 cm).

Amphiprion rubrocinctus
Australian Anemonefish
Max. Length: 4.7 in. (12 cm).

Saddleback Anemonefish (*Amphiprion polymnus*): not as durable as others in the subfamily, these fishes are best acquired as captive-bred rather than wild.

Saddleback Anemonefishes
(Subgenus *Paramphiprion*)

Eminently placid, these anemonefishes are more peaceful toward heterospecifics than many other anemonefishes. While they rarely bother other fishes, they may fight with members of their own kind. In the aquarium, they have a reputation of being less than hardy. Wild-caught individuals often don't fare well during the shipping process and are susceptible to various parasites. Captive-raised individuals are always hardier and much more likely to survive and thrive. The three species in the saddleback group are elongated with scales between the eyes. Members of this complex will often do better in the presence of a host sea anemone, with Haddon's Sea Anemone (*Stichodactyla haddoni*) a prime choice. Most live in solitary anemones that occur at very low densities, and they rarely move far from their hosts. Pair formation, therefore, is likely to occur not by immigration but when individuals within the social unit change sex. At least one species in this subgenus (*A. latezonatus*) prefers cooler water (less than 74°F [23°C]).

Saddleback Anemonefishes

Amphiprion latezonatus (juv.)
Wideband Anemonefish
Max. Length: 5.5 in. (14 cm).

Amphiprion latezonatus
Wideband Anemonefish
Max. Length: 5.5 in. (14 cm).

Amphiprion polymnus (juv.)
Saddleback Anemonefish
Max. Length: 4.7 in. (12 cm)

Amphiprion polymnus (orange variant)
Saddleback Anemonefish
Max. Length: 4.7 in. (12 cm).

Amphiprion polymnus (Sulawesi variant)
Saddleback Anemonefish
Max. Length: 4.7 in. (12 cm).

Amphiprion sebae
Sebae Anemonefish
Max. Length: 5.5 in. (14 cm).

Whitebonnet Anemonefish (*Amphiprion leucokranos*): a bit of a mystery fish, possibly a hybrid between *Amphiprion chrysopterus* and *Amphiprion sandaracinos*.

Skunk Anemonefishes (Subgenus *Phalerebus*)

The beautiful, somewhat delicate, anemonefishes in this subgenus are strongly attached to their sea anemone hosts, rarely move far from them, and spend much of their time bathing in the tentacles. Unlike some of the more mobile anemonefishes, they rarely if ever emigrate to other social units (pairs are almost always the result of sex change). They can be a challenge to keep, as they tend to ship poorly and often succumb to parasites if stressed. Captive-raised individuals are much more durable than wild-caught fishes, which are very susceptible to *Brooklynella*. Skunk anemonefishes tend to be less aggressive than some of their kin and are more likely to be picked on by pugnacious tankmates. That said, dominant individuals may relentlessly pick on subordinate conspecifics. Some authors suggest that these fishes do much better if housed with a host sea anemone —they tend to be less nervous if a host is present. They have spawned in tanks that lack a host anemone, although overall they tend to be more difficult to spawn than some other *Amphiprion* species. The eggs are pink or orange in color.

ANEMONEFISHES

Skunk Anemonefishes

Amphiprion akallopisos
Indian Ocean Skunk Anemonefish
Max. Length: 4.3 in. (11 cm).

Amphiprion leucokranos
Whitebonnet Anemonefish
Max. Length: 3.5 in. (9 cm).

Amphiprion nigripes
Maldive Anemonefish
Max. Length: 4.3 in. (11 cm).

Amphiprion perideraion
Pink Skunk Anemonefish
Max. Length: 4.3 in. (11 cm).

Amphiprion perideraion (variant)
Pink Skunk Anemonefish
Max. Length: 4.3 in. (11 cm).

Amphiprion sandaracinos
Orange Skunk Anemonefish
Max. Length: 5.5 in. (14 cm).

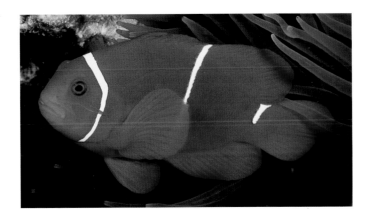

Maroon Anemonefish (*Premnas biaculeatus*): females of this spectacular species get large and can be very aggressive.

Maroon Anemonefish (Genus *Premnas*)

This genus contains just one species, with a prominent spine on the cheek similar to many large angelfishes. There are two color variants—one has white markings, the other (so-called "golden" form) has yellowish bars. It is one of the largest anemonefishes (maximum length 6.7 in. [17 cm]) and is highly sexually dimorphic (females can attain over 6 times the length of males). They readily acclimate and accept a wide array of aquarium fare. Some wild-caught individuals will suffer from parasitic infections soon after they arrive, but they usually respond well to immediate treatment. The biggest drawback with this species is that it can become terribly aggressive. They should never be housed with other anemonefishes, and care should be exercised if you plan on keeping them with more peaceful fish species. A large individual can wreak havoc in a small to medium-sized tank, especially in the presence of a host sea anemone. They can be kept in mated pairs, but the smaller males will be constantly chastised and should be provided with a Bubbletip Sea Anemone or other shelter for when the female is feeling feisty.

Green Chromis (*Chromis viridis*): excellent shoaling fish for the reef aquarium, colorful, harmless to desirable invertebrates and beneficial to branching corals.

Chromises (Genus *Chromis*)

This is the largest damselfish genus with over 80 species—all great for the reef aquarium, as chromises are mild-mannered with other fishes and never a threat to ornamental invertebrates. In the wild, many form large shoals that swim above the reef to capture passing zooplankton in the water column. It is possible to keep them in groups in a moderate-sized tank (e.g., 70 gal. [266 L]). They will form a dominance hierarchy, with subordinate members often receiving an unequal share of mistreatment from their conspecifics. If the group is large enough, the aggression will be spread out so that no one fish gets too much abuse. They spend most of their time in the open and in the upper layers of the aquarium and can act as dither fishes. Chromises tend to be less durable than some other damselfishes, are more susceptible to disease, and are more likely to be abused by aggressive tankmates. Some can be quite nervous, dashing about the aquarium or hiding most of the time. They tend to lose their vibrant colors if not fed a color-enhancing food. Juveniles tend to acclimate more readily than adults.

Chromis atripectoralis Welander & Schultz, 1951
Blackaxil Chromis (Green Chromis)

Maximum Length: 4.3 in. (11 cm).
Range: Indo-Pacific.
Minimum Aquarium Size: 30 gal. (114 L).
Foods & Feeding: Meaty foods, including finely shredded frozen seafood, mysid shrimp, frozen preparations, pigment-enriched flake food, and Cyclop-eeze. Feed twice per day.
Aquarium Suitability/Reef Compatibility:
Aquarium Notes: This is a wonderful reef aquarium fish. It often does best when kept in groups of six or more. The quality of this fish varies greatly, depending on how it is treated from the time it is collected until it gets to your local aquarium store. If mishandled between reef and retail store, it will usually break down quickly upon arriving at the local shop. This fish rarely quarrels with congeners, but it is often the target of more aggressive fishes, such as dottybacks, pygmy angelfishes, and other damselfishes (e.g., *Dascyllus* species). It might also be intimidated by larger fishes, even if the larger fishes are not piscivorous. Once this species is established, it makes an excellent dither fish.

Chromis cyanea (Poey, 1860)
Blue Chromis

Maximum Length: 5.1 in. (13 cm).
Range: Tropical Western Atlantic.
Minimum Aquarium Size: 30 gal. (114 L).
Foods & Feeding: Meaty foods, including finely shredded frozen seafood, mysid shrimp, frozen preparations, pigment-enriched flake food, and Cyclop-eeze. Feed twice per day.
Aquarium Suitability/Reef Compatibility:
Aquarium Notes: This beautiful Caribbean fish makes an interesting community member in the reef aquarium. When first introduced or when stressed, its color can be disappointingly dull. But once acclimated, it should adopt the pleasing blue chromatic attire it usually sports in the wild. If not provided with a varied diet, however, this color may fade over time. It may also turn pale in a brightly lit tank. Juveniles acclimate more readily than adults. They often do best in groups, but dominance hierarchies will develop among individuals (a linear pecking order based on size). Because of this, it is best to keep this chromis in groups of six or more. If the group is smaller, those individuals at the bottom of the pecking order may literally get harassed to death.

ADULT

Chromis insolata (Cuvier, 1830)
Sunshine Chromis (Olive Chromis)

Maximum Length: 6.3 in. (16 cm).
Range: Tropical Western Atlantic.
Minimum Aquarium Size: 55 gal. (209 L).
Foods & Feeding: Meaty foods, including finely shredded frozen seafood, mysid shrimp, frozen preparations, pigment-enriched flake food, and Cyclop-eeze. Feed twice per day.
Aquarium Suitability/Reef Compatibility:
Aquarium Notes: This lovely fish is sometimes collected by Florida fish suppliers. Juvenile *C. insolata* can be kept in groups, while adults are likely to quarrel unless you house them in a large tank. They are rarely aggressive toward heterospecifics, although adults may bother congeners. This species often acclimates more rapidly in a more dimly lit aquarium. It is possible that its colors may fade in an intensely lit shallow-water reef aquarium. As with others in the genus (and other zooplankton feeders), make sure it is fed frequently. At a length of 1.5 to 2 in. (3.8 to 5 cm) the juveniles change to the adult coloration, which is dull green above and silvery gray below, with blue on the head.

Chromis iomelas Jordan & Seale, 1906
Half-and-Half Chromis

Maximum Length: 3.5 in. (9 cm).
Range: Indo-Pacific.
Minimum Aquarium Size: 20 gal. (76 L).
Foods & Feeding: Meaty foods, including finely shredded frozen seafood, mysid shrimp, frozen preparations, pigment-enriched flake food, and Cyclop-eeze. Feed twice per day.
Aquarium Suitability/Reef Compatibility:
Aquarium Notes: This is a durable aquarium fish with distinctive black-and-white coloration. It should be kept singly or in groups of five or more in a larger tank (two or three may fight until only the dominant individual remains alive). These are zooplanktivores that will spend much of their time in the water column. In groups, they can be effective dither fishes. Do not keep them with overly aggressive tankmates, unless the aquarium is very large. This fish is very similar to the Twotone Chromis (*Chromis dimidiata*) and the Bicolor Chromis (*C. margaritifer*). In the Twotone Chromis, the first two anal spines are brown.

Chromis retrofasciata Weber, 1913
Blackbar Chromis

Maximum Length: 2 in. (5 cm).
Range: Western Pacific.
Minimum Aquarium Size: 10 gal. (38 L).
Foods & Feeding: Meaty foods, including finely shredded frozen seafood, mysid shrimp, frozen preparations, pigment-enriched flake food, and Cyclop-eeze. Feed twice per day.
Aquarium Suitability/Reef Compatibility:
Aquarium Notes: This is a terrific aquarium fish—colorful, durable and not very aggressive toward heterospecifics. It will fight with conspecifics if the tank is too small, so keep just one per tank unless your aquarium is of moderate size (e.g., 75 gal. [285 L]), in which case you can keep a pair or a small group, although this species does not form large shoals like some of the other chromises. It is prone to being picked on by more aggressive damselfishes and other pugnacious tankmates (e.g., dottybacks). Feed it frequently. This species will spend most of its time hovering near the substrate.

Chromis amboinensis
Ambon Chromis
Max. Length: 3.1 in. (8 cm).

Chromis flavomaculata
Yellowspotted Chromis
Max. Length: 5.9 in. (15 cm).

Chromis lineata
Lined Chromis
Max. Length: 2 in. (5 cm).

Chromis limbaughii
Limbaugh's Chromis
Max. Length: 4.7 in. (12 cm).

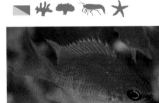

Chromis scotti
Purple Chromis
Max. Length: 3.9 in. (10 cm).

Chromis xanthura (juv.)
Paletail Chromis
Max. Length: 5.9 in. (15 cm).

Milne Bay Demoiselle (*Chrysiptera cymatilis*): this is one of many lovely species in a genus whose members are ideally suited for the reef tank.

Demoiselles (Genus *Chrysiptera*)

This genus contains about 25 species, including some of the most desirable of all the damselfishes for the reef aquarium, including the nano-reef. The genus also includes some of the smallest damsels (they average about 3 inches [8 cm] in length). They are not a threat to ornamental invertebrates. Demoiselles are very disease-resistant and tend not to be as pugnacious as other damsels (or at least are not as great a threat because of their smaller size). Many can be kept in small groups in a moderate-sized tank. They are also less likely to cause problems with unrelated tankmates, and can even be kept with more docile species if the tank is roomy. There are exceptions to the rule. The South Seas Devil (*Chrysiptera taupou*) is a very aggressive fish. Larger Blue Devils (*Chrysiptera cyanea*) can also be belligerent, especially in smaller tanks.

The true pacifists of the genus include the Azure (*Chrysiptera hemicyanea*), Goldtail (*C. parasema*), and Talbot's Demoiselle (*C. talboti*). These three can be trusted with most fish tankmates, although an occasional fish may get feisty in a small aquarium.

MALE

Chrysiptera cyanea (Quoy & Gaimard, 1825)
Blue Devil (Blue Damselfish, Orangetail Damselfish)

Maximum Length: 3.1 in. (8 cm).
Range: Western Pacific.
Minimum Aquarium Size: 10 gal. (38 L).
Foods & Feeding: Meaty foods, including finely shredded frozen seafood, mysid shrimp, frozen preparations, pigment-enriched flake food, and Cyclop-eeze. Feed twice a day.
Aquarium Suitability/Reef Compatibility:
Aquarium Notes: Gloriously pigmented, this is an inexpensive and hardy fish. Juveniles and females are usually not overly aggressive, although larger males can be quite pugnacious, picking on more peaceful tankmates. A male and female can be kept in a smaller tank together, while one male and several females or a group of females and/or juveniles can be kept in a medium-sized aquarium with plenty of hiding places. It will readily spawn in captivity. Ideal for the reef aquarium, it will not harm invertebrates and will eat some algae. In the Philippines, males have blue fins with dark margins; those of the female are clear. In the rest of the range, males have an orange ventral surface and bright orange or yellow tail; females have a black spot near the rear base of the dorsal fin.

Chrysiptera galba (Allen & Randall, 1974)
Canary Demoiselle

Maximum Length: 3.5 in. (9 cm).
Range: Central Pacific.
Minimum Aquarium Size: 20 gal. (76 L).
Foods & Feeding: Meaty foods, including finely shredded frozen seafood, mysid shrimp, frozen preparations, pigment-enriched flake food, and Cyclop-eeze. Feed twice a day.
Aquarium Suitability/Reef Compatibility:
Aquarium Notes: This is a great display fish because of its boldness and brilliant coloration and is ideally suited to the reef aquarium. It is rarely seen in most marine shops, but is occasionally exported from the Cook Islands. It often suffers from shipping stress and as a result often has trouble acclimating to its new aquarium home. Professional fishkeeper Jim Walters suggests keeping this species in the dark for a couple of days, which seems to facilitate acclimation. It can be quite aggressive toward more passive tankmates, including small anthias, more passive demoiselles and chromises, and dart gobies. Once acclimated, it will hold its own with moderately aggressive tankmates. Keep only one per tank unless your aquarium is extra large, in which case you might try a pair.

Chrysiptera hemicyanea (Weber, 1913)
Azure Demoiselle

Maximum Length: 2.4 in. (6 cm).
Range: Western Pacific.
Minimum Aquarium Size: 10 gal. (38 L).
Foods & Feeding: Meaty foods, including finely shredded frozen seafood, mysid shrimp, frozen preparations, pigment-enriched flake food, and Cyclop-eeze. Feed twice a day.
Aquarium Suitability/Reef Compatibility:

Aquarium Notes: This is one of the most desirable of all the damselfishes for the home aquarium. It is a small, peaceful fish that rarely causes problems in a community tank. However, other damselfishes, dottybacks, pygmy angels, and other potential bullies are likely to pick on it. The Azure Demoiselle tends to maintain its brilliant colors if given a varied diet, including vegetable matter. More than one *C. hemicyanea* can be kept in the same aquarium, although it is best to introduce them simultaneously. One curious behavior it brings in from the wild: this species will eat fish feces in the aquarium. Like others in the genus, it is not a threat to invertebrates and is a near-perfect reef aquarium fish.

Chrysiptera parasema (Fowler, 1918)
Goldtail Demoiselle (Yellowtail Blue Damsel)

Maximum Length: 2.8 in. (7 cm).
Range: Western Pacific.
Minimum Aquarium Size: 10 gal. (38 L).
Foods & Feeding: Meaty foods, including finely shredded frozen seafood, mysid shrimp, frozen preparations, pigment-enriched flake food, and Cyclop-eeze. Feed twice a day.
Aquarium Suitability/Reef Compatibility:
Aquarium Notes: Its electric coloration, ready availability and price make this damselfish a staple in the marine aquarium world. It combines beauty and good personality, being one of the less aggressive members of this genus. It can be kept in small groups in a medium-sized tank with plenty of hiding places. A male-female pair can be kept in a smaller tank and will often spawn. The Goldtail Demoiselle should not be kept with highly aggressive species, including more pugnacious damselfishes. This species is ideal for the reef aquarium, never harming desirable invertebrate tankmates and providing some algae-grazing services.

Chrysiptera rex (Snyder, 1909)
King Demoiselle (Pink Demoiselle)

Maximum Length: 2.8 in. (7 cm).
Range: Western Pacific.
Minimum Aquarium Size: 10 gal. (38 L).
Foods & Feeding: Meaty foods, including finely shredded frozen seafood, mysid shrimp, frozen preparations, pigment-enriched flake food, and Cyclop-eeze. Feed twice a day.
Aquarium Suitability/Reef Compatibility:
Aquarium Notes: This species has subtle beauty and is relatively docile, usually doing well in a reef aquarium with a peaceful fish community. If housed in smaller tanks, *C. rex* may pick on smaller tankmates. In contrast, this fish is likely to be picked on by dottybacks, other damselfishes, large wrasses, sand perches, and triggerfishes. Provide it with plenty of hideouts. In a larger tank, pairs or small groups can be housed together. The color of the King Demoiselle is somewhat variable. Those in the population around Palau have a white body with a bluish head. In other locations, the head is gray to purple, while the rest of the body and fins are orangish.

Chrysiptera springeri (Allen & Lubbock, 1976)
Springer's Demoiselle

Maximum Length: 2.2 in. (5.5 cm).
Range: Indonesia and the Philippines.
Minimum Aquarium Size: 10 gal. (38 L).
Foods & Feeding: Meaty foods, including finely shredded frozen seafood, mysid shrimp, frozen preparations, pigment-enriched flake food, and Cyclop-eeze. Feed twice a day.
Aquarium Suitability/Reef Compatibility:
Aquarium Notes: This is a peaceful, highly desirable damselfish. It is likely to be picked on by more belligerent damselfishes, including congeners *C. cyanea* and *C. taupou*. For this reason, it is best kept in a tank that does not house other members of the damselfish family, unless the aquarium is large and has a numerous refuging places. It can be kept in small groups if there are enough hiding nooks and crannies to go around. When this species is stressed, its overall color darkens and the blue becomes less apparent.

Chrysiptera starcki (Allen, 1973)
Starck's Demoiselle

Maximum Length: 3.9 in. (10 cm).
Range: Indo-Pacific.
Minimum Aquarium Size: 20 gal. (76 L).
Foods & Feeding: Meaty foods, including finely shredded frozen seafood, mysid shrimp, frozen preparations, pigment-enriched flake food, and Cyclop-eeze. Feed twice a day.
Aquarium Suitability/Reef Compatibility:
Aquarium Notes: This is highly desirable aquarium fish. It is an excellent choice for the reef aquarium and will maintain its amazing colors if fed a nutritious diet. It was once rarely available and thus very expensive, but with more collecting efforts in the Coral Sea, the price has come down. It tends to be quite peaceable for a damselfish, with young and adolescent individuals rarely causing problems in captivity. However, as it grows larger, it may become more pugnacious, especially toward small, more passive tankmates. *Chrysiptera starcki* is likely to chastise some of its less aggressive congeners. This species may appear somewhat pale in shallow-water reef tanks with intense lighting.

Chrysiptera taupou (Jordan & Seale, 1906)
South Sea Devil (Fiji Blue Devil)

Maximum Length: 3.1 in. (8 cm).
Range: Western Pacific.
Minimum Aquarium Size: 10 gal. (38 L).
Foods & Feeding: Meaty foods, including finely shredded frozen seafood, mysid shrimp, frozen preparations, pigment-enriched flake food, and Cyclop-eeze. Feed twice a day.
Aquarium Suitability/Reef Compatibility:
Aquarium Notes: Here is a fish that is both beauty and beast. It is the most aggressive in its genus and may be ounce-for-ounce one of the most belligerent pomacentrids. Keep only one per tank unless you can acquire a male-female pair (the species is sexually dichromatic—mature males, as above, have blue on the front of the dorsal fin; in adult females this same area is yellow). While it is incredibly durable and will not harm invertebrates, placing one in a reef tank will limit the other fishes you can acquire (unless the aquarium is large and replete with hiding places). Do not keep it with docile species, including other damselfishes, unless they match it in belligerence. It is best kept in a moderately aggressive community tank with fishes like larger dottybacks, angelfishes, tangs, and pufferfishes.

Chrysiptera caeruleolineata
Blueline Demoiselle
Max. Length: 2.4 in. (6 cm).

Chrysiptera cyanea (female)
Blue Devil
Max. Length: 3.1 in. (8 cm).

Chrysiptera flavipinnis
Yellowfin Demoiselle
Max. Length: 2.4 in. (6 cm).

Chrysiptera rollandi
Rolland's Demoiselle
Max. Length: 2.4 in. (6 cm).

Chrysiptera rollandi (variant)
Rolland's Demoiselle
Max. Length: 2.4 in. (6 cm).

Chrysiptera talboti
Talbot's Demoiselle
Max. Length: 2.4 in. (6 cm).

Red Sea Dascyllus (*Dascyllus marginatus*): their movement among stony coral branches and the nutrients in their waste increase the coral's growth rate.

Dascyllus (Genus *Dascyllus*)

This genus is comprised of nine species of deep-bodied dam-selfishes—all very hardy but not always desirable community members when they move past the cute juvenile stage. They often occur in groups that hang over and duck into stony coral heads. Both the damsels and the coral benefit. The coral colonies grow more rapidly because of the nutrients (including nitrogen) excreted in the damsels' waste and the increased water circulation caused by the damsels' movements among the coral branches. Two *Dascyllus* species also live in sea anemones. They mainly feed on zooplankton. As juveniles they exhibit dramatic color patterns and are inexpensive beginners' fishes. Juveniles make an interesting display if housed in a small group with stony coral colonies. As they get larger, most become more and more aggressive. While a male and female may pair up, group unity usually breaks down and serious squabbles occur as they mature. They will terrorize less aggressive tankmates and can easily disrupt the balance of a confined community. They are, however, no threat to invertebrates.

Dascyllus aruanus (Linnaeus, 1758)
Humbug Dascyllus (Threestriped Damselfish)

Maximum Length: 3.1 in. (8 cm).
Range: Indo-Pacific.
Minimum Aquarium Size: 20 gal. (76 L).
Foods & Feeding: Meaty foods, including finely shredded frozen seafood, mysid shrimp, frozen preparations, pigment-enriched flake food, and Cyclop-eeze. Feed twice a day if algae is in short supply.
Aquarium Suitability/Reef Compatibility: ■ ⚜ 🐗 🦐 ⚊ ★
Aquarium Notes: While the juvenile Humbug is often sold to new marine aquarists as cute and hard-to-kill, it typically becomes quite belligerent as it matures into a fish that can easily take over a tank. As a result, it is best not to house this species with passive tankmates unless the aquarium is large and the Humbug is added after the docile tankmates have become acclimated. In nature, it feeds heavily on filamentous algae, algal fronds, and planktonic copepods. If microalgae is present in the tank, feed *D. aruanus* several times a week, but if algae is in short supply, feed it twice a day. This is not a recommended fish for most reef communities with smaller, less confrontational species.

Dascyllus auripinnis Randall & Randall, 2001
Yellow Threespot Dascyllus (Yellow Domino Damselfish)

Maximum Length: 5.7 in. (14.5 cm).
Range: Central and South Pacific.
Minimum Aquarium Size: 55 gal. (209 L).
Foods & Feeding: Meaty foods, including finely shredded frozen seafood, mysid shrimp, frozen preparations, pigment-enriched flake food, and Cyclop-eeze. Feed twice a day if algae is in short supply.
Aquarium Suitability/Reef Compatibility:
Aquarium Notes: This is an eyecatching fish and one of the more highly sought after _Dascyllus_ species. It is similar in behavior to the closely related _Dascyllus trimaculatus_ (page 208). While juveniles may be amiable in a variety of fish communities, as they grow, they become quite aggressive and will need to be housed with other scrappy species. It is not an appropriate tankmate for many desirable smaller, less belligerent reef aquarium fishes. Juveniles can be kept in small groups, but adults are likely to fight, unless you house a male-female pair together or have a very large aquarium. It is a durable species that will eat most prepared foods.

Dascyllus melanurus Bleeker, 1854
Blacktailed Dascyllus (Fourstriped Damselfish)

Maximum Length: 3.1 in. (8 cm).
Range: Western Pacific.
Minimum Aquarium Size: 20 gal. (76 L).
Foods & Feeding: Meaty foods, including finely shredded frozen seafood, mysid shrimp, frozen preparations, pigment-enriched flake food, and Cyclop-eeze. Feed twice a day if algae is in short supply.
Aquarium Suitability/Reef Compatibility: ◼ ✳ 🐢 🦐 ★
Aquarium Notes: This handsome little damselfish is found in the wild among the branches of small-polyped stony corals. Its movements among the branches and the nitrogen it produces encourage the growth of its host coral. Groups of these dascyllus hover over the colony and feed on planktonic crustaceans. They will also eat some filamentous algae. Its husbandry is similar to that of *D. aruanus* (page 204). While the juveniles tend to be relatively peaceful, the adults can be hellions, although they will not harm invertebrate tankmates. A group of juveniles makes a striking display, but adults will fight if hiding spaces (i.e., branching stony corals) are in short supply. Unlike the similar *D. aruanus*, this fish has a black margin on its caudal (tail) fin.

Dascyllus reticulatus (Richardson, 1846)
Reticulate Dascyllus

Maximum Length: 3.1 in. (8 cm).
Range: Eastern Indo-Pacific.
Minimum Aquarium Size: 20 gal. (76 L).
Foods & Feeding: Meaty foods, including finely shredded frozen seafood, mysid shrimp, frozen preparations, pigment-enriched flake food, and Cyclop-eeze. Feed twice a day if algae is in short supply.
Aquarium Suitability/Reef Compatibility:
Aquarium Notes: This is one of the smaller, more sociable dascyllus species, and one with an alluring appearance and character. It can be kept with more passive fishes in a large aquarium, but it should not be housed with peaceful species in small tanks. While juveniles do well in groups, as they get larger they may quarrel. This is especially true if appropriate microhabitat (e.g., stony coral colonies) is limited. This species is very similar to the Indian Dascyllus (*D. carneus*). It differs in having less black on the dorsal fin and lacks blue highlights on the scales (these are present in *D. carneus*).

Dascyllus trimaculatus (Rüppell, 1829)
Threespot Dascyllus (Domino Damselfish)

Maximum Length: 5.5 in. (14 cm).
Range: Indo-Pacific.
Minimum Aquarium Size: 55 gal. (209 L).
Foods & Feeding: Meaty foods, including finely shredded frozen seafood, mysid shrimp, frozen preparations, pigment-enriched flake food, and Cyclop-eeze. Feed twice a day if algae is in short supply.
Aquarium Suitability/Reef Compatibility:
Aquarium Notes: *Dascyllus trimaculatus* is a mainstay in the aquarium trade. It is very hardy, and the bold color pattern of the juveniles is very attractive. However, as this fish grows, it can become very belligerent, attacking more peaceful species. Keeping it in a community tank can lead to injuries and death of tankmates that are not themselves very large or pugnacious. This species does, however, have some interesting behaviors as a juvenile. In one case, I had a juvenile *D. trimaculatus* "clean" or groom an ich-infested Copper-banded Butterflyfish (*Chelmon rostratus*). The juveniles are often found sharing sea anemones with anemonefishes (*Amphiprion* species). Some adults will hover near these anemones as well, but tend to prefer to hide in branching corals or coral crevices.

Yellowtail Damselfish (*Microspathodon chrysurus*) juv.: exquisitely attractive juveniles sometimes tempt reef aquarists, but this a temptation to be resisted.

Jewel Damselfishes (Genus *Microspathodon*)

Think of these fishes, typified by the species above, as simply "beautiful to belligerent"—and worthy of a serious second thought before you bring one home. This is a small genus of damselfishes that includes four species that are limited to the Tropical Atlantic and Eastern Pacific. The only species regularly seen in the aquarium trade is the pictured Yellowtail Damselfish (*Microspathodon chrysurus*). (This species should not be confused with the Goldtail Demoiselle, *Chrysiptera parasema*, which is a diminutive darling.) The juveniles are exquisite: dark blue overall with neon blue spots on the body and fins. Adults are less attractive: brown overall, with fewer blue spots and a bright yellow tail. The Yellowtail Damselfish is a handful of aggression—especially toward its own kind—when small, then grows into a truly nasty fish. They get larger (over 8 in. [20 cm] in total length) than many of their relatives, which means they can abuse and injure a wider range of tankmates. If you have a very large tank, you may be able to keep a pair of adults, but it is risky business. They rarely harm invertebrates.

Barhead Damselfish (*Neoglyphidodon thoracotaeniatus*) juvenile: although lovely as juveniles, adults in this genus are often unattractive and unruly in captivity.

Dark Damselfishes (Genus *Neoglyphidodon*)

Need a fish that is a drab dark brown or black overall and that will terrorize or kill your other fishes? This genus contains eight species that fill the bill, all coming from the Indo-Pacific. The juveniles of most of the species are temptingly attractive, but as they grow, many change from dramatic to dull. They are also known for their bellicose dispositions. The adults will raise cain in a smaller reef tank or in an aquarium with more docile species. If you want to keep one, place them in a tank with moderately belligerent species, such as larger hawkfishes, angelfishes, sand perches, large wrasses, and more placid triggerfishes. Keep only one per tank. As far as your reef tank is concerned, be aware that Black Damselfish (*Neoglyphidodon melas*) is reported to feed on soft coral polyps, sea anemones, and zoanthids. This species has also been reported to associate with tridacnid clams and may feed on the clam's feces. The rest are reported to feed on zooplankton, some algae, and tiny, benthic crustaceans, but it is possible that some of these other species may feed on coral polyps.

Neoglyphidodon crossi (juv.)
Cross' Damselfish
Max. Length: 5.1 (13 cm).

Neoglyphidodon crossi
Cross' Damselfish
Max. Length: 5.1 (13 cm).

Neoglyphidodon melas (juv.)
Black Damselfish
Max. Length: 6.3 in.(16 cm).

Neoglyphidodon nigroris (juv.)
Behn's Damselfish
Max. Length: 5.1 in. (13 cm).

Neoglyphidodon nigroris
Behn's Damselfish
Max. Length: 5.1 in. (13 cm).

Neoglyphidodon oxyodon (juv.)
Javanese, Neon Damselfish
Max. Length: 5.9 in. (15 cm).

Yellowtail Demoiselle (*Neopomacentrus azysron*): this attractive species spends much of its time in the water column feeding on zooplankton.

Lyretail Demoiselles (Genus *Neopomacentrus*)

The lyretail demoiselles are great additions to the reef aquarium. They are members of a unique group of pomacentrids that have elongated bodes and forked tails. Completely safe with reef aquarium corals and ornamental invertebrates, they are zooplankton feeders that swim well into the water column where they pick off passing zooplankters. They have no interest in sessile invertebrates and will spend much of their time in the open, acting as dither fishes. They are a hardy, relatively nonaggressive group of aquarium inhabitants. More than one adult can be kept in a medium-sized aquarium, although all individuals should be introduced simultaneously. While they are less likely to harass their tankmates, diminutive, peaceful species may be in some danger of being picked on in smaller tanks. Lyretail demoiselles may be harassed by more aggressive tankmates, including other damselfishes. Provide members of this genus with plenty of hiding places.

Jewel Damselfish (*Plectroglyphidodon lacrymatus*): this handsome species, along with others in the genus, is prone to eating small-polyped stony corals.

Coral-eating Damsels (Genus *Plectroglyphidodon*)

The nine species in this genus live at relatively shallow depths, often in areas exposed to surge. At least two of these damsels feed on small-polyped stony corals. Others graze on algae and small invertebrates; at least one species is know to "farm" algae. For example, the most-commonly collected species is the Jewel Damselfish (*Plectroglyphidodon lacrymatus*), a solitary, very territorial fish that feeds mainly on algae (filamentous algae, diatoms, and macroalgae fronds) and the small invertebrates associated with the algal mat. It will remove polyps from the *Acropora* that it inhabits to facilitate algae growth, a behavior called algae farming. It, along with others in the genus, is belligerent: keep only one per tank and only with aggressive tankmates. The Jewel Damselfish should not be housed in a reef tank with small-polyped stony corals, unless it is a large system and the aquarist wants to observe algae farming firsthand. It can be housed with soft corals. *Plectroglyphidodon lacrymatus* is not to be confused with the Yellowtail Damselfish (*Microspathodon chrysurus*) the juveniles of which are often called Jeweled Damsels.

Sulphur Damselfish (*Pomacentrus sulfureus*): the members of this genus vary greatly in their disposition—some are docile while others are quite aggressive.

Common Damselfishes (Genus *Pomacentrus*)

With about 54 species, this genus is one of the largest in the damselfish family and all are suitable for the reef tank, many eminently desirable. Some are small (under 2 in. [5 cm] in length) and can be relatively peaceful. Others get larger (some over 3.9 in. [10 cm] in length) and are very scrappy. Some are colorful throughout their lives, while others may be colorful as juveniles but drab as adults. In the wild, *Pomacentrus* fishes tend to be highly territorial. They will not only chase members of their own kind, but also drive away food competitors. Some feed on zooplankton, others are omnivorous, feeding on algae and associated tiny invertebrates.

Better choices are the zooplankton-eaters in this group, and these can successfully be kept in groups if they are added together into a larger aquarium. These *Pomacentrus* species are more likely to be picked on by tankmates and are less likely to be belligerent toward heterospecifics. On the other hand, the omnivorous *Pomacentrus* species are territorial and do best if only one is kept per tank. They tend to pick on smaller, more passive tankmates.

Peaceful *Pomacentrus* Species

Pomacentrus alleni
Allen's Damselfish
Max. Length: 2.4 in. (6 cm).

Pomacentrus auriventris
Goldbelly Damselfish
Max. Length: 2.8 in. (7 cm).

Pomacentrus caeruleus
Caerulean Damselfish
Max. Length: 3.1 in. (8 cm).

Pomacentrus coelestis
Neon Damselfish
Max. Length: 3.5 in. (9 cm).

Pomacentrus moluccensis
Lemon Damselfish
Max. Length: 2.8 in. (7 cm).

Pomacentrus pavo
Pavo or Blue Damselfish
Max. Length: 4.3 in. (11 cm).

Belligerent *Pomacentrus* Species

Pomacentrus amboinensis
Ambon Damselfish
Max. Length: 3.9 in. (10 cm).

Pomacentrus bankanensis (juv.)
Speckled Damselfish
Max. Length: 3.5 in. (9 cm).

Pomacentrus nigromarginatus
Blackmargined Damselfish
Max. Length: 3.5 in. (9 cm).

Pomacentrus simsiang (juv.)
Blueback Damselfish
Max. Length: 3.5 in. (9 cm).

Pomacentrus vaiuli (juv.)
Princess Damselfish
Max. Length: 3.5 in. (9 cm).

Pomacentrus vaiuli
Princess Damselfish
Max. Length: 3.5 in. (9 cm).

Longfin Gregory (*Stegastes diencaeus*) juv.: although young fish in this genus are quite attractive, the adults turn brown overall and are highly aggressive.

Gregories (Genus *Stegastes*)

Gregories are some of the most aggressive damselfishes. They are very territorial, not only attacking members of their own kind but also other herbivores that enter their feeding territory. The 33 species in this genus are hardy to the point of being called "bullet-proof," but are best avoided because of their scrappy nature. The juveniles are quite attractive, while adults are often varying shades of brown or are black overall. They reach relatively large sizes (all attain at least 4 in. [3.9 cm] in length. Adults feed mostly on algae, while juveniles will also consume animal matter (e.g., forams, minute crustaceans, and other benthic invertebrates). In the aquarium, they are less selective about which territorial "intruders" they will chastise and should not be housed with peaceful species.

Some gregories "farm" algae by killing small-polyped stony corals in their territories—killing the corals provides more substrate for the algae on which they feed to grow. It is not advisable to introduce these fishes to a reef tank that contains stony corals unless it is a system large enough to accommodate some damaging behaviors.

217

Yellowbreasted Wrasse (*Anampses twistii*): a beautiful fish with special husbandry requirements. Keep one male per covered tank.

Tamarin Wrasses (Genus *Anampses*)

Theoretically near-perfect as reef aquarium inhabitants, these wrasses are drop-dead gorgeous, peaceable and harmless to corals and most invertebrates. Alas, they are a challenge to maintain and are only recommended for the most advanced aquarist. These wrasses tend to ship poorly and usually refuse food when first introduced to the tank. Live black worms and enriched live brine shrimp can be used to induce a feeding response. Live rock and a tank with a healthy amphipod population can help to maintain their weight while they adjust to the more popular aquarium foods. In time, some of the *Anampses* species may accept frozen mysid shrimp, frozen brine shrimp, or finely chopped fresh or frozen table shrimp, while others will eat only live foods. All need a thick sand bed in which they can refuge at night. Smaller females (approximately 3 in. [8 cm] in length) may be more likely to acclimate to captivity, while Juveniles have higher metabolic needs and must be fed accordingly. Some of the larger species will eat small bivalves, worms, ornamental shrimps, serpent stars, and small sea urchins.

Anampses caeruleopunctatus
Bluespotted Tamarin Wrasse
Max. Length: 16.5 in. (42 cm).

Anampses chrysocephalus
Redtail, Psychedelic Tamarin Wrasse
Max. Length: 6.7 in. (17 cm).

Anampses femininus
Feminine Tamarin Wrasse
Max. Length: 9.4 in. (24 cm).

Anampses lineatus
Lined Tamarin Wrasse
Max. Length: 4.7 in. (12 cm).

Anampses meleagrides
Yellowtail Tamarin Wrasse
Max. Length: 8.7 in. (22 cm).

Anampses neoguinaicus
New Guinea Tamarin Wrasse
Max. Length: 5.9 in. (15 cm).

Lyretail Hogfish (*Bodianus anthioides*): while juveniles are good reef tank inhabitants, adults can decimate populations of motile invertebrates.

Hogfishes (Genus *Bodianus*)

The hogfishes are some of the hardiest members of the wrasse family. As a whole, they are durable aquarium fish that readily accept most aquarium fare, while ignoring all live corals. Most can be kept in reef aquariums as juveniles, but as they grow they will eat worms, snails, small clams, and crustaceans. The size of the aquarium needed to harbor a hogfish will depend on the species—most small to medium-sized members of the family (i.e., those species that attain a maximum length of less than 10 in. [25 cm]) can be kept in tanks ranging from 20 to 75 gallons (76 to 285 L), while more robust species require a tank of 135 gallons (513 L) or larger once they reach adult size. They need hiding places as well as ample swimming room.

Hogfishes, unlike certain other wrasses, do not bury in the substrate, so the depth of sand in your tank is of little concern. However, several of these fishes will hunt buried prey items by blowing jets of water at the finer substrate. This predatory behavior is fascinating to watch and will also stir the upper layers of the substrate.

Spanish Hogfish (*Bodianus rufus*): a graphic warning about hogfish feeding habits—motile invertebrates, such as brittle stars, are likely to meet this fate.

Many hogfishes will not tolerate the presence of members of their own species in the same tank, but they can be kept with other members of their genus. One caution: avoid placing two similarly colored species in the same tank.

As far as unrelated species are concerned, hogfishes can be belligerent toward smaller fishes, more docile species, or those fishes introduced after the hogfish has become an established resident of the tank. The moderate- to large-sized hogfishes should be kept with fish species that can hold their own, like lionfishes, squirrelfishes, soldierfishes, smaller groupers, goatfishes, angelfishes, hawkfishes, medium-sized damselfishes, sand perches, and less aggressive triggerfishes. Adding a hogfish to an established community of aggressive fishes, however, can cause the hogfish to remain hidden most of the time and never acclimate. Of course, large frogfishes, scorpionfishes, and groupers will eat any hogfish that they can swallow whole. While the larger hogfish species simply won't fit into the average reef tank community, some of the smaller members of this group are worthy of consideration. Choose carefully, based on size and feeding habits.

Bodianus bimaculatus Allen, 1973
Twinspot Hogfish (Twospot Hogfish, Candy Hogfish)

Maximum Length: 3.9 in. (10 cm).
Range: Indo-west-Pacific.
Minimum Aquarium Size: 20 gal. (76 L).
Foods & Feeding: Meaty foods, including finely shredded frozen seafood, mysid shrimp, frozen preparations, and pigment-enriched flake food. Feed at least twice a day.
Aquarium Suitability/Reef Compatibility:
Aquarium Notes: This one of the best reef aquarium hogfishes—small in size and with a clear preference for small prey items. It does not feed on most desirable invertebrates, although larger individuals will harass delicate shrimps or larger shrimps that have just molted. The Twinspot Hogfish prefers deep-water habitats, but will readily acclimate to more intense illumination. It does get more aggressive toward other fishes as it gets larger, and big adults are especially prone to picking on other wrasses (e.g., flasher and fairy wrasses). Keep only one per tank. It is prone to jumping out of an open aquarium or into overflow boxes. This species has been observed to clean other fishes both in the wild and in the aquarium.

Bodianus sepiacaudus Gomon, 2006
Crescenttail Hogfish (Pacific Redstriped Hogfish, Inktail Hogfish)

Maximum Length: 3.9 in. (10 cm).
Range: West, South and Central Pacific.
Minimum Aquarium Size: 20 gal. (76 L).
Foods & Feeding: Meaty foods, including finely shredded frozen seafood, mysid shrimp, frozen preparations, and pigment-enriched flake food. Feed at least twice a day.
Aquarium Suitability/Reef Compatibility:
Aquarium Notes: Once rare, this beautiful species is now readily available to reef aquarists. It is generally safe in most reef systems, but larger individuals may become a threat to small bivalves and crustaceans. I've kept it with cleaner and pistol shrimps without a problem, but I did have a larger individual that attacked a molting Banded Coral Shrimp (*Stenopus hispidus*). It may chase similarly shaped wrasses incessantly. Keep only one per tank as they are likely to quarrel. This hogfish is a great jumper, so the tank must be kept covered. It will readily adapt to brightly lit reef aquariums even though it is normally found in deep water.

Bodianus bilunulatus
Saddleback Hogfish
Max. Length: 22 in. (55 cm).

Bodianus diana
Diana's Hogfish
Max. Length: 9.8 in. (25 cm).

Bodianus izuensis
Izu Hogfish
Max. Length: 4.3 in. (11 cm).

Bodianus mesothorax (juv.)
Mesothorax Hogfish
Max. Length: 7.5 in. (19 cm).

Bodianus mesothorax
Mesothorax Hogfish
Max. Length: 7.5 in. (19 cm).

Bodianus perditio
Goldspot Hogfish
Max. Length: 31.5 in. (80 cm).

Cheeklined Maori Wrasse (*Oxycheilinus diagrammus*): although very personable, these wrasses get large and are a choice for big, predatory reef tanks only.

Maori Wrasses (Genera *Cheilinus* & *Oxycheilinus*)

Their large size, formidable teeth, and predatory nature makes most members of these genera a greater threat in the reef aquarium than many other wrasses. This group includes the largest of all the wrasses, the Napoleon Wrasse (*Cheilinus undulatus*). Many Maori wrasses get over 20 in. (50 cm) in length, so they require a larger tank with plenty of swimming space. Initially they are often shy, skulking behind reef structures, sometimes for days, before making an appearance. However, they usually become bold, then aggressive, members of the aquarium community.

These wrasses eat snails, tubeworms, ornamental shrimps, small crabs, brittle stars, sea stars, sea urchins, and small fishes. Their diet makes them less than desirable selections for most reef aquariums. They will eat pests like fireworms and mantis shrimps, so you could house one with your live rock and then remove it before adding your chosen reef invertebrates.

Unfortunately, the Maori wrasse will also eat, with gusto, any desirable motile invertebrate it finds, including prized shrimps.

Cheilinus chlorurus
Floral Maori Wrasse
Max. Length: 17.7 in. (45 cm).

Cheilinus fasciatus
Redbreasted Maori Wrasse
Max. Length: 15 in. (38 cm).

Cheilinus oxycephalus
Redbreasted Maori Wrasse
Max. Length: 6.7 in. (17 cm).

Oxycheilinus bimaculatus
Twinspot Maori Wrasse
Max. Length: 5.9 in. (15 cm).

Oxycheilinus celebicus
Celebes Maori Wrasse
Max. Length: 9.8 in. (24 cm).

Oxycheilinus diagrammus
Cheeklined Maori Wrasse
Max. Length: 11.8 in. (30 cm).

Whitebanded Tuskfish (*Choerodon zosterophorus*): this is not an ideal reef genus, but smaller tuskfish species such as this one can be kept in a larger system.

Tuskfishes (Genus *Choerodon*)

Although best known by the more readily available Harlequin Tuskfish (see following page), this genus contains a few species of tuskfishes occasionally encountered in the fish trade. While most are very durable aquarium residents, they are not well suited to most reef tanks because they get too large, need plenty of swimming room, and have very eclectic diets.

Tuskfishes feed on mollusks, crustaceans, worms, echinoderms, and small fishes. While they do not eat coral, they may well disturb coral colonies when looking for hidden prey. It is possible to house some of the smaller species in the reef aquarium if you are not concerned about keeping snails, small clams, ornamental shrimps, serpent stars, urchins, or sea stars in your reef tank.

Like many of the larger wrasses, tuskfishes are much less destructive as juveniles than they are as adults. They are also more likely to attack and eat tankmates added to the tank after they have attained some size and become fully acclimated.

Choerodon fasciatus (Günther, 1867)
Harlequin Tuskfish

Maximum Length: 9.8 in. (25 cm).

Range: Indo-west-Pacific.

Minimum Aquarium Size: 55 gal. (209 L).

Foods & Feeding: Meaty foods, including finely shredded frozen seafood, mysid shrimp, frozen preparations, and pigment-enriched flake food. Feed at least twice a day (and preferably more).

Aquarium Suitability/Reef Compatibility:

Aquarium Notes: A boldly pigmented icon of the coral reef, this predatory species is not likely to bother captive corals of any kind. However, like its congeners, it is a threat to a range of motile invertebrates, including shrimps, crabs, mollusks, sea stars and the like. Juveniles are not as bold, spend more time hiding among caves and crevices, and are less of a predatory threat. Adults can be quite aggressive, picking on smaller and more docile tankmates (especially those added after the tuskfish is established in the aquarium).

Larger individuals tend to ship more poorly than young specimens or subadults. Those collected from the Great Barrier Reef tend to be slightly more intense in color and are usually hardier, probably because of better collection and shipping techniques.

Redmargin Fairy Wrasse (*Cirrhilabrus rubromarginatus*) male: fairy wrasses are among the most beautiful fishes for a peaceful reef aquarium community.

Fairy Wrasses (Genus *Cirrhilabrus*)

The fairy wrasses can offer both breathtaking beauty with astonishing color patterns and eminently peaceable dispositions, making them ideally suited to the reef aquarium. The smaller fairy wrasses are a good choice for the beginning hobbyist, while larger individuals more often succumb to the rigors of capture and shipping stress. With the possible exception of small, delicate shrimp species (e.g., *Periclimenes*), they do not harm invertebrates. They do best in a peaceful community tank, but some can be kept with moderately aggressive fishes, but should be added to the tank before the aggressors.

Fairy wrasses are shy when initially introduced to the aquarium, often hiding for several days. If a peaceful acclimation period is provided, they usually become quite brazen, even to the point of nipping or lying on the aquarist's hand or forearm as he or she cleans the aquarium. If they are introduced to a tank already harboring belligerent or territorial fishes, they typically stay hidden and end up starving to death or succumbing to disease.

Coral Sea Fairy Wrasse (*Cirrhilabrus bathyphilus*) male: this species is a deep-water beauty well-suited to the reef tank.

Male fairy wrasses will fight each other and may display toward, but rarely kill, other fish species added after the wrasses are acclimated. They are most likely to behave aggressively toward closely related species like flasher wrasses (*Paracheilinus*) or small, docile species.

If you are keeping male *Cirrhilabrus* species with more passive zooplanktivores, the fairy wrasses should be the last fishes introduced. If, on the other hand, you plan to keep them with potentially pugnacious tankmates, they should be the first fishes in the aquarium. If you want to keep more than one *Cirrhilabrus*, add a harem consisting of one male and several females. It is important to introduce all harem members simultaneously or to add the females first. After the females have adjusted to the tank, add the more aggressive male. (Do not wait too long to do this or one of the females may change sex.) Groups will have to be kept in a larger aquarium (100 gallons [380 L] or more). In small tanks, even females may not get along, or males may pester females to death.

Male fairy wrasses often change colors in captivity if they are not housed with conspecifics (the male's color [and possibly his gender]

Finespotted Fairy Wrasse (*Cirrhilabrus punctatus*): a male from Papua New Guinea sporting nuptial coloration.

will begin to revert back to that of the female). They appreciate good water movement, numerous hiding places and plenty of swimming room. The shallow-water species will have no problems adjusting to the high light levels characteristic of small-polyped stony coral aquariums, while deep-water species adapt more quickly if placed in tanks with less intense illumination. Note: deep-water forms can be kept successfully in high light conditions, but may take longer to acclimate.

Fairy wrasses are very good jumpers. Be careful when working in the tank or when extinguishing the lights—times when nervous fishes tend to flee upward. Ambient light levels should be reduced gradually so that you do not frighten them. They are fairly disease-resistant. Feed two or three times a day to ensure they do not become emaciated and subsequently perish, and offer a varied diet that includes color-enhancing foods. If the fish's stomach or back begins to look pinched, feed more often.

Carpet anemones (*Stichodactyla* species) are a threat to fairy wrasses, as these invertebrates have been known to capture and consume smaller wrasses such as these at night.

MALE

Cirrhilabrus cyanopleura Ishikawa, 1904
Yellowflanked Fairy Wrasse (Blueheaded Fairy Wrasse)

Maximum Length: 5.1 in. (13 cm).
Range: Eastern Indian and Western Pacific.
Minimum Aquarium Size: 55 gal. (209 L).
Foods & Feeding: Meaty foods, including finely shredded frozen seafood, mysid shrimp, frozen preparations, pigment-enriched flake food, and Cyclop-eeze. Feed at least twice a day.
Aquarium Suitability/Reef Compatibility:
Aquarium Notes: Handsome and disease-resistant, this brightly pigmented fairy wrasse is a great addition to the reef aquarium. The more highly sought after males sport a yellow blotch on the side, hence the common name. It can be kept in harems in large aquariums, but it is advisable to introduce just one male per tank, except in very large systems. It may also quarrel with congeners (especially those that are similar in color). Although it often mixes with other fairy wrasses (*Cirrhilabrus* species) and flasher wrasses (*Paracheilinus* species) in the wild, it is likely to pick on the latter if space is limited. This species is synomous with *Cirrhilabrus lyukyuensis*. Some sources believe them to be color morphs of the same species.

MALE (INDIAN OCEAN FORM)

Cirrhilabrus exquisitus Smith, 1957
Exquisite Fairy Wrasse

Maximum Length: 4.7 in. (12 cm).
Range: Indo-west-Pacific.
Minimum Aquarium Size: 55 gal. (209 L).
Foods & Feeding: Meaty foods, including finely shredded frozen seafood, mysid shrimp, frozen preparations, pigment-enriched flake food, and Cyclop-eeze. Feed at least twice a day.
Aquarium Suitability/Reef Compatibility:
Aquarium Notes: This is a dramatic fish that flashes metallic blue when displaying and is a great choice for the reef aquarium. Like all others in this group, it will thrive only in a relatively peaceful reef community. Males are especially prone to leaping from open aquariums, as are others in this genus. Only one male should be housed per tank, although a male and several females will thrive in a large aquarium. I have had this species chase and nip at smaller zooplanktivores (e.g., chromises and firefishes), but it seldom does real harm. The Pacific form of this fish may represent a different, undescribed species (see photograph, page 11).

MALE (FOREGROUND); FEMALE (BACKGROUND)

Cirrhilabrus flavidorsalis Randall & Carpenter, 1980
Yellowfin Fairy Wrasse

Maximum Length: 2.6 in. (6.5 cm).

Range: Philippines and Indonesia.

Minimum Aquarium Size: 30 gal. (114 L).

Foods & Feeding: Meaty foods, including finely shredded frozen seafood, mysid shrimp, frozen preparations, pigment-enriched flake food, and Cyclop-eeze. Feed at least twice a day.

Aquarium Suitability/Reef Compatibility:

Aquarium Notes: This is a great reef aquarium inhabitant that will not harm invertebrates and has begun to show up occasionally in aquarium stores in the last several years. It is, like others in this genus, a near-perfect candidate for the peaceful reef community, while also being very disease-resistant. Keep only one male per tank and only house a male with conspecifics or similar fairy wrasses in a large tank (135 gallons [513 L] or larger). I have had males that picked on other fishes, in particular very gentle flasher wrasses (*Paracheilinus* species) and longray shrimp gobies (*Stonogobiops* species). In one case, a male had to be removed because of its relative aggressiveness.

MALE

Cirrhilabrus lineatus Randall & Lubbock, 1982
Lined Fairy Wrasse

Maximum Length: 4.3 in. (11 cm).
Range: Great Barrier Reef and Coral Sea.
Minimum Aquarium Size: 55 gal. (209 L).
Foods & Feeding: Meaty foods, including finely shredded frozen seafood, mysid shrimp, frozen preparations, pigment-enriched flake food, and Cyclop-eeze. Feed at least twice a day.
Aquarium Suitability/Reef Compatibility:
Aquarium Notes: This is a showcase fish and a spectacular addition to the reef aquarium. It will not thrive with rambunctious and highly competitive tankmates, but will do fine with relatively mild-mannered tankmates. Although the flamboyant males often ship poorly, once they acclimate, they usually do quite well in captivity. Juveniles and females will acclimate more readily than the more colorful males. Acclimation is less likely to occur if they are harassed by resident tankmates or overzealous aquarists (leave the fish alone even if it hides constantly). The large males are very prone to jumping from an open tank, even when the cover is opened only during cleaning activities.

MALE

Cirrhilabrus lubbocki Randall & Carpenter, 1980
Lubbock's Fairy Wrasse

Maximum Length: 3.5 in. (9 cm).

Range: Philippines and Indonesia.

Minimum Aquarium Size: 30 gal. (114 L).

Foods & Feeding: Meaty foods, including finely shredded frozen seafood, mysid shrimp, frozen preparations, pigment-enriched flake food, and Cyclop-eeze. Feed at least twice a day.

Aquarium Suitability/Reef Compatibility:

Aquarium Notes: This is one of the smaller and more durable members of the *Cirrhilabrus* clan. It can be kept singly in small reefs or in groups in tanks as small as 135 gallons (513 L). It will not harm corals or other invertebrates. Although the females are not commonly collected, when they do show up, they are usually improperly labeled as "Red Fairy Wrasse" or even "Red Parrot Wrasse." The females are similar to the Redfinned Fairy Wrasse (*Cirrhilabrus rubripinnis*), which is also sold under these common names.

The male *C. lubbocki* exhibits several different color forms and phases; during courtship, it takes on a silvery blue coloration.

MALE

Cirrhilabrus rubripinnis Randall & Carpenter, 1980
Redfinned Fairy Wrasse

Maximum Length: 3.1 in. (8 cm).
Range: Philippines and Indonesia .
Minimum Aquarium Size: 30 gal. (114 L).
Foods & Feeding: Meaty foods, including finely shredded frozen seafood, mysid shrimp, frozen preparations, pigment-enriched flake food, and Cyclop-eeze. Feed at least twice a day or preferably more often.
Aquarium Suitability/Reef Compatibility:
Aquarium Notes: The males of this species are spectacular, having oversized pelvic fins and blue on the ventrum. With a long history of collection for the aquarium trade, this is a great reef candidate. The females are red overall with a lighter belly and are similar to the females of several other species. A durable species, it can be long-lived, but it is an accomplished jumper that will leap through relatively small openings.

Keep only one male per tank, and avoid placing it in a community with highly competitive feeders or overtly aggressive fishes. In a smaller reef,it may harass other red fishes in its own size range.

MALE

Cirrhilabrus rubriventralis Springer & Randall, 1974
Longfinned Fairy Wrasse (Social Wrasse)

Maximum Length: 2.9 in. (7.5 cm).
Range: Red Sea and Western Indian Ocean.
Minimum Aquarium Size: 30 gal. (114 L).
Foods & Feeding: Meaty foods, including finely shredded frozen seafood, mysid shrimp, frozen preparations, pigment-enriched flake food, and Cyclop-eeze. Feed at least twice a day, preferably more often.
Aquarium Suitability/Reef Compatibility:
Aquarium Notes: This appealing fairy wrasse is a good, durable selection for the reef tank. As with all fairy wrasses, it does best with relatively passive tankmates, and may fail to thrive in highly competitive communities where it is driven away from available food. Keep only one male per tank, unless the aquarium is very large (i.e., 135 gallons [513 L] or more). Males have been known to change back to females if picked on by consexuals. Once they have fully acclimated to their aquarium home, males may exhibit aggression toward smaller tankmates (especially those introduced after it is established). Keep it in a covered tank, as this species is an accomplished jumper.

MALE

Cirrhilabrus scottorum Randall & Pyle, 1989
Scott's Fairy Wrasse

Maximum Length: 5.1 in. (13 cm).
Range: West, South and Central Pacific.
Minimum Aquarium Size: 55 gal. (209 L).
Foods & Feeding: Meaty foods, including finely shredded frozen seafood, mysid shrimp, frozen preparations, pigment-enriched flake food, and Cyclop-eeze. Feed at least twice a day or preferably more often.
Aquarium Suitability/Reef Compatibility:
Aquarium Notes: Easily one of the most-coveted species for a reef aquarium, this species has both personality and beauty to spare. While the males are spectacular, they sometimes suffer from shipping stress and will have a difficult time acclimating to a tank that already contains aggressive fishes. That said, they often do better than some of the other larger members of this genus. They will also acclimate more quickly if you keep your hands out of the tank and make sure the tank is located in a relatively quite spot. Be sure to provide this wrasse with plenty of hiding places. Keep only one male per tank, and only attempt to keep a male with females in a large aquarium. The male's color often fades if females are not present.

MALE

Cirrhilabrus solorensis Bleeker, 1853
Redhead Fairy Wrasse (Solar Fairy Wrasse)

Maximum Length: 5.1 in. (13 cm).
Range: Western Pacific.
Minimum Aquarium Size: 55 gal. (209 L).
Foods & Feeding: Meaty foods, including finely shredded frozen seafood, mysid shrimp, frozen preparations, pigment-enriched flake food, and Cyclop-eeze. Feed at least twice a day or preferably more often.
Aquarium Suitability/Reef Compatibility:
Aquarium Notes: Once a rare sensation, this stunning species has become relatively common in reef aquariums in recent years. The large males are brilliantly hued, and females and small males readily acclimate to captivity. Larger males are a bit more prone to shipping maladies, but they are more durable than some of the larger *Cirrhilabrus* species. Keep only one male per tank. Harems (one male, several females) can be accommodated in larger tanks (180 gallons [684 L] or larger). While they typically ignore unrelated species and are of no threat to most invertebrates, these fairy wrasses may pick on other zooplanktivores.

MALE

Cirrhilabrus tonozukai Allen & Kuiter, 1999
Tono's Fairy Wrasse

Maximum Length: 3 in. (7.5 cm).
Range: Indonesia.
Minimum Aquarium Size: 30 gal. (114 L).
Foods & Feeding: Meaty foods, including finely shredded frozen seafood, mysid shrimp, frozen preparations, pigment-enriched flake food, and Cyclop-eeze. Feed at least twice a day.
Aquarium Suitability/Reef Compatibility:
Aquarium Notes: Like others in the genus, this species is ideal for the reef aquarium. Keep one male per tank (the males have a long dorsal filament—females are quite different in appearance). If you keep a group, it is best to have four or five females and a single male. Males are more likely to flare their fins in display if kept with females. Placing a mirror on the end of the tank can also elicit displaying. This species is a smaller member of the genus that may be picked on by larger congeners. It is a good choice to house with flasher (*Paracheilinus*) wrasses (add males of both species simultaneously). Like others in the *Cirrhilabrus* genus, it is an adept jumper. It is very similar to the Whipfin Fairy Wrasse (*Cirrhilabrus filamentosus*) (page 242).

Cirrhilabrus aurantidorsalis (male)
Goldback Fairy Wrasse
Max. Length: 3.5 in. (9 cm).

Cirrhilabrus condei (male)
Conde's Fairy Wrasse
Max. Length: 3.1 in. (8 cm).

Cirrhilabrus cyanopleura (male)
Bluehead Fairy Wrasse
Max. Length: 4.3 in. (11 cm).

Cirrhilabrus filamentous (male)
Whipfin Fairy Wrasse
Max. Length: 3.1 in. (8 cm).

Cirrhilabrus joanallenae (male)
Joan's Fairy Wrasse
Max. Length: 3.3 in. (8.5 cm).

Cirrhilabrus jordani (male)
Jordan's or Flame Fairy Wrasse
Max. Length: 3 in. (7.5 cm).

Cirrhilabrus laboutei (male)
Laboute's Fairy Wrasse
Max. Length: 3.9 in. (10 cm).

Cirrhilabrus luteovittatus (male)
Yellowstreaked Fairy Wrasse
Max. Length: 3.9 in. (10 cm).

Cirrhilabrus pylei (female)
Pyle's Fairy Wrasse
Max. Length: 3.5 in. (9 cm).

Cirrhilabrus rubromarginatus (female)
Redmargined Fairy Wrasse
Max. Length: 4.3 in. (11 cm).

Cirrhilabrus rubrisquamis (male)
Redscaled Fairy Wrasse
Max. Length: 2.6 in. (6.5 cm).

Cirrhilabrus temminckii (male)
Temminck's Fairy Wrasse
Max. Length: 3.9 in. (10 cm).

Creole Wrasse (*Clepticus parrae*) male: this is a large, active species from the Caribbean and tropical Western Atlantic that feeds primarily on zooplankton.

Creole Wrasses (Genus *Clepticus*)

The Atlantic wrasse in this genus, *Clepticus parrae*, can make a colorful addition to the larger reef aquarium. It is by nature a zooplankton feeder and thus is less of a threat to sessile invertebrates. Larger individuals, however, may try to consume delicate shrimps and the like, especially if the crustaceans are added after the wrasse is established. *Clepticus parrae* needs to be fed frequently—at least a couple of times per day—with prepared foods for carnivores, shredded seafood, and/or mysid shrimp. It also gets rather large and will need to be housed in a reef tank of at least 135 gallons (513 L) with plenty of open swimming space and hiding places. It spends most of its time swimming and bobbing about the water column and is a capable jumper, so a tank cover is a must. While the Creole Wrasse is unlikely to pester larger or more aggressive fishes, adults may bully smaller zooplanktivores (e.g., smaller fairy wrasses, flasher wrasses, dartfishes). Although juveniles can be kept in small groups, adults often fight among themselves. It is a protogynous hermaphrodite; males are more colorful than females.

Yellowtail Coris (*Coris gaimard*): these wrasses can become quite destructive in the reef aquarium, flipping corals over and eating motile invertebrates.

Coris Wrasses (Genus *Coris*)

The members of this genus tend to be durable fishes that do well in many captive venues. However, they regularly flip pieces of rubble or coral over to expose concealed prey items, which can tumble an aquascape and cause damage to coral colonies. Subadult and adults prey on snails, small clams, tubeworms, ornamental crustaceans, sea stars, sea urchins, and sea cucumbers. Large individuals may also attack smaller fishes, especially benthic species (e.g., gobies). Adults sometimes ship poorly and have greater difficulty acclimating than juveniles or subadults. Tiny juveniles can be difficult to keep because of their high caloric requirements (individuals greater than 2 in. [5 cm] are preferable). A layer of fine sand (at least 2 in. [5 cm] in depth) will aid acclimation. When they bury, coris wrasses will shove their heads in the sand, turn on their sides, and vigorously beat their tails. This behavior will help put some detritus into suspension where it can be removed by external filters or provide food for certain suspension feeders. This digging will also prevent substrate from compacting.

Coris aygula
Twinspot Coris, Clown Coris
Max. Length: 21.7 in. (55 cm).

Coris batuensis
Dapple Coris
Max. Length: 6.7 in. (17 cm).

Coris caudimacula
Tailspot Coris
Max. Length: 7.9 in. (20 cm).

Coris dorsomacula
Spotfin Coris
Max. Length: 7.9 in. (20 cm).

Coris frerei
Formosan Coris
Max. Length: 23.6 in. (60 cm).

Coris gaimard (juvenile)
Yellowtail Coris, Red Coris
Max. Length: 13.7 in. (35 cm).

Pavo's Razorfish (*Iniistius pavo*): while juveniles are attractive, these fishes require special biotope aquascaping that most reef aquariums cannot provide.

Razorfishes (Genera *Cymolutes, Hemipteronotus, Iniistius & Xyrichtys*)

These fascinating fishes live in the sand flats and slopes adjacent to coral reefs. They are well known for their ability to burrow and even "swim" under the sand. As juveniles, many mimic plant debris as they hover above the substrate. They are not well-suited to most reef tanks because they require a substantial portion of the tank bottom to be open sand. If you are able to provide this, however, you can successfully keep these fishes. They need a fine sand substrate at least 3 in. (8 cm) in depth, which they will help aerate and turn. One downside is that they will eat ornamental crustaceans, some beneficial worms, snails, and serpent stars (especially true of adult razorfishes). Large adults will even eat small fishes. Some razorfishes are quite large and will need to be housed in an extra-large aquarium (check the fish's maximum length before you buy). Some of the best aquarium razorfishes come from the tropical Atlantic. The Pavo Razorfish (*Iniistius pavo*), a common Pacific species, gets too large for most home reef aquariums.

Hemipteronotus splendens Bean, 1891
Green Razorfish

Maximum Length: 5.9 in. (15 cm).
Range: Eastern Atlantic.
Minimum Aquarium Size: 75 gal. (285 L).
Foods & Feeding: Meaty foods, including finely shredded frozen seafood, mysid shrimp, frozen preparations, and pigment-enriched flake food. Feed at least once a day, unless you have a healthy stock of crustaceans and worms for it to feed on, in which case you can feed every other day.
Aquarium Suitability/Reef Compatibility:
Aquarium Notes: This attractive razorfish is one of the best for the reef tank, as it does not attain a large size and readily adapts to captive life. As with other razorfishes, it needs an open, deep sand bed in which it can bury. It will feed on smaller prey than other razorfishes of similar size. It is primarily a zooplanktivore (e.g., copepod feeder). That said, larger individuals may eat newly introduced ornamental shrimps. It can be aggressive toward other labrids (wrasses) and may pick on more docile species in a smaller tank.

FEMALE

Xyrichtys martinicensis Valenciennes, 1840
Rosy Razorfish

Maximum Length: 5.9 in. (15 cm).
Range: Eastern Atlantic.
Minimum Aquarium Size: 75 gal. (285 L).
Foods & Feeding: Meaty foods, including shredded frozen seafood, mysid shrimp, frozen preparations, and pigment-enriched flake food. Feed at least once a day, unless you have a healthy stock of crustaceans and worms for it to feed on, in which case you can feed every other day.
Aquarium Suitability/Reef Compatibility:
Aquarium Notes: This Atlantic razorfish is found in sand flats and sea-grass beds, where it feeds on small, benthic invertebrates. It is likely to feed on worms, small snails, ornamental shrimps, and juvenile serpent stars—although it is entirely safe with corals. Keep one male per tank. If the reef tank is large enough (180 gallons [684 L] or more), a male and one or more females may be included. As with other razorfishes, provide an open, deep sand bed in which it can bury. This species is sexually dichromatic.

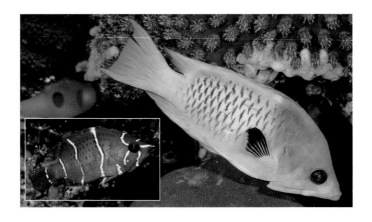

Dwarf Slingjaw Wrasse (*Epibulus* sp.) female: a highly predatory labrid for the large reef tank. Inset: juvenile *E. insidiator*.

Slingjaw Wrasses (Genus *Epibulus*)

The common member of this genus, the Slingjaw Wrasse (*Epibulus insidiator*), makes an interesting aquarium resident. Juveniles or small adults do well in robust reef aquariums, but they are a threat to crustaceans and small fishes. This species will use its protrusible jaws to wrest its prey from coral branches or reef crevices. While it prefers live foods (e.g., ghost shrimp) it can be switched to frozen preparations or chopped seafood. If fed ghost shrimp, gut-pack them beforehand with a nutritious frozen or flake food. An adult slingjaw should be kept in a large aquarium (135 gallons [513 L] or larger) with plenty of hiding places. It will be reclusive and nervous when first introduced, although this will change once it learns to recognize the aquarist as a food provider. While juveniles acclimate more quickly than adults, youngsters tend to spend most of their time slinking from crevice to crevice. Keep only one per tank. Although it is not usually aggressive toward other fish species in the aquarium, I have seen it chase heterospecifics in the wild. These fish are capable of jumping out of open aquariums.

Indian Ocean Bird Wrasse (*Gomphosus caeruleus*) female: this durable species will eat a variety of motile invertebrates. Inset: *Gomphosus varius* (male).

Bird Wrasses (Genus *Gomphosus*)

There are two equally spectacular species in this genus: the Indian Ocean Bird Wrasse (*Gomphosus caeruleus*) and the Green Bird Wrasse (*Gomphosus varius*). The latter is common in the aquarium trade. I hate to dissuade people from keeping these wrasses because they are so hardy; on a number of occasions, I have seen large Green Bird Wrasses survive almost total wipeouts. The problem is that they are very predatory, feeding on a wide range of invertebrates and even small fishes. Their diet can include small tridacnid clams and other bivalves, snails, feather duster worms, and a wide range of crustaceans. The upside is that they will also eat fireworms and mantis shrimps. If you keep them, keep only one male per tank. You can house a male and female together (they are sexually dichromatic) in a larger tank (135 gallons [513 L] or larger), but introduced them at the same time. Feed them two times a day, unless natural fare (e.g., worms and crustaceans) is available in the tank. Both species are active, prolific jumpers and need a covered tank and lots of swimming room. They do not bury under the substrate.

Richmond's Wrasse (*Halichoeres richmondi*) male: among the most strikingly beautiful of reef fishes, members of this genus vary in their reef suitability.

Halichoeres Wrasses (Genus *Halichoeres*)

Bold, beautiful and generally all-around great aquarium fishes, this large genus contains more than 75 species, many of them spectacular but varying in their suitability for the reef aquarium. Smaller species are generally safe with corals and many ornamental invertebrates, although even these species are a potential threat to fanworms, small snails, and more diminutive shrimps. Larger species have a greater dietary breadth and are potentially dangerous to a wider range of motile invertebrates. They will ignore coral polyps but will flip over loose pieces of live rock and coral when hunting hidden prey. Most species will feed on fireworms and pyramidellid snails, and some also eat flatworms.

Because these wrasses bury in the substrate at night or when threatened, it is important to have a minimum of 2 in. (5 cm) of fine coral sand on the aquarium bottom. A coarse coral gravel will damage their jaws, fins, and scales, which can lead to skin infections. Larger specimens may not tolerate collection and shipping very well, but these wrasses tend to be durable and not picky about food.

Halichoeres chrysurus Randall, 1981
Golden Wrasse (Canary Wrasse, Yellow Coris)

Maximum Length: 4.7 in. (12 cm).
Range: Eastern Indian Ocean to Central Pacific.
Minimum Aquarium Size: 30 gal. (114 L).
Foods & Feeding: Meaty foods, including finely shredded frozen seafood, mysid shrimp, frozen preparations, and pigment-enriched flake food. Feed at least twice a day.
Aquarium Suitability/Reef Compatibility:
Aquarium Notes: This is one of the best wrasses for the reef aquarium—brightly colored, active, and with an amenable disposition. Although the adult may prey on ornamental crustaceans or worms, its more diminutive size makes it a minimal threat to motile invertebrates. It is not a coral flipper.

In a larger tank (135 gallons [513 L] or larger), it can be housed in small groups (be sure that all members of the group are females and that they are added all at once). This species has been known to clean other fishes in the aquarium. Small groups of these wrasses often follow foraging goatfishes. The Canary Top Wrasse (_Halichoeres leucoxanthus_) is a similar species.

FEMALE

Halichoeres chloropterus (Bloch, 1791)
Pastel Green Wrasse (Green Coris)

Maximum Length: 7.4 in. (19 cm).
Range: Western Pacific.
Minimum Aquarium Size: 55 gal. (209 L).
Foods & Feeding: Meaty foods, including finely shredded frozen seafood, mysid shrimp, frozen preparations, and pigment-enriched flake food. Feed at least twice a day.
Aquarium Suitability/Reef Compatibility:
Aquarium Notes: This is one of the more common members of the *Halichoeres* genus and a very attractive fish. It will not harm sessile invertebrates, but it is a threat to worms, small snails, and crustaceans. It has been reported to eat flatworms and pyramidellid snails.

In the wild, this fish will often swim among the tentacles of less lethal sea anemones and associate closely with the longtentacled plate coral (*Heliofungia actiniformis*), a relationship that might be fostered in the aquarium. Keep only one per tank (although if you have a large tank, you may be able to house two females together or a male and female).

MALE

Halichoeres melanurus (Bleeker, 1851)
Pinstriped Wrasse (Tailspot Wrasse)

Maximum Length: 4.7 in. (12 cm).
Range: Western Pacific.
Minimum Aquarium Size: 30 gal. (114 L).
Foods & Feeding: Meaty foods, including finely shredded frozen seafood, mysid shrimp, frozen preparations, and pigment-enriched flake food. Feed at least twice a day.
Aquarium Suitability/Reef Compatibility:
Aquarium Notes: This is a colorful, welcome addition to the reef aquarium. It is a modestly sized version of larger cousins that can only be trusted in fish-only marine communities, and its smaller size makes it less of a threat to motile invertebrates.

It will eat bristleworms (both nuisance and beneficial species) and pyramidellid snails. Keep only one male per tank, unless you have a huge system. Females can be housed together, or a harem of females and one male can be kept in a large tank (135 gallons [513 L] or more).

Females have alternating blue and orange longitudinal stripes and two eyespots (one on the dorsal fin and one just before the tail).

MALE

Halichoeres ornatissimus (Garrett, 1863)
Ornate Wrasse (Christmas Wrasse)

Maximum Length: 6.7 in. (17 cm).
Range: Hawaiian Islands.
Minimum Aquarium Size: 55 gal. (209 L).
Foods & Feeding: Meaty foods, including finely shredded frozen seafood, mysid shrimp, frozen preparations, and pigment-enriched flake food. Feed at least twice a day.
Aquarium Suitability/Reef Compatibility:
Aquarium Notes: This a Hawaiian endemic and not uncommon in the North American aquarium trade. It is exceptionally colorful, does not grow very large, and is a suitable reef aquarium wrasse.

Like others in the genus, larger individuals are a threat to ornamental crustaceans. It is best to add these animals to the tank before the wrasse is introduced; this will make them less likely to be attacked and eaten. A well-fed labrid is also less likely to eat shrimp or crab tankmates.

It may fit best in a more aggressive reef community, and will tend to intimidate smaller, less muscular species, including the flasher and fairy wrasses.

Halichoeres argus (male)
Argus Wrasse
Max. Length: 4.3 in. (11 cm).

Halichoeres biocellatus (female)
Twospot Wrasse
Max. Length: 4.7 in. (12 cm).

Halichoeres cosmetus (female)
Adorned Wrasse
Max. Length: 5.1 in. (13 cm).

Halichoeres cyanocephalus (female)
Lightning Wrasse
Max. Length: 11.8 in. (30 cm).

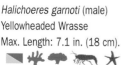

Halichoeres garnoti (male)
Yellowheaded Wrasse
Max. Length: 7.1 in. (18 cm).

Halichoeres hortulanus (female)
Checkerboard Wrasse
Max. Length: 10.6 in. (27 cm).

Halichoeres leucurus (male)
Grayhead Wrasse
Max. Length: 7.4 in. (19 cm).

Halichoeres melasmapomus (male)
Blackear Wrasse
Max. Length: 9.4 in. (24 cm).

Halichoeres prosopeion (male)
Twotone Wrasse, Halfgray Wrasse
Max. Length: 5.1 in. (13 cm).

Halichoeres scapularis (male)
Zigzag Wrasse
Max. Length: 7.9 in. (20 cm).

Halichoeres zeylonicus (female)
Goldstripe Wrasse
Max. Length: 7.9 in. (20 cm).

Halichoeres zeylonicus (male)
Goldstripe Wrasse
Max. Length: 7.9 in. (20 cm).

Banded Thicklip Wrasse (*Hemigymnus fasciatus*): interesting, but presents husbandry challenges. Inset: juvenile Blackedge Thicklip Wrasse (*H. melapterus*).

Thicklip Wrasses (Genus *Hemigymnus*)

For the adventuresome reefkeeper only, the three species in this genus of solitary wrasses have rubbery lips that are used to scavenge live prey from the seafloor. Juveniles feed mainly on zooplankton (e.g., copepods) that live near the bottom, while adults eat larger invertebrates (including worms, snails, clams, crustaceans, sea urchins, and serpent stars). They have strong dentition that can even masticate hard-shelled invertebrates (snails and larger crustaceans). When they feed on sand-dwelling prey, they take up mouthfuls of substrate, sorting out the edible then purging the inedible through the gill openings and the mouth. This helps keep the substrate detritus-free, putting sediment into suspension where it can be removed by external filters. It also helps feed certain soft corals. The falling debris, however, may settle on and damage certain soft and stony corals. Thicklip wrasses will quickly decimate the animal fauna in live sand. They get too large for most reef tanks (18 in. [45 cm] or longer) and must be fed at least three times a day. They often waste away even if fed frequently.

Candycane Wrasse (*Hologymnosus doliatus*) male: a large voracious predator that needs lots of swimming space.

Ring Wrasses (Genus *Hologymnosus*)

The four species in this very appealing, chromatically endowed genus are large and active and will need more swimming room than provided in most home reef aquariums. Juveniles typically ship better and make the transition to a captive lifestyle more readily than adults. *Hologymnosus* species bury in the substrate at night or when threatened. When initially introduced to the aquarium, they may hide for several days before coming out to search for food.

Ring wrasses will eat any fish tankmates that can be swallowed whole and will also make short work of ornamental shrimps and small crabs, which they render into bite-sized morsels by bashing them against rocks or coral. Snails are also not immune from these attacks—I have seen them knock these invertebrates off the glass and wrest the foot and organs from their shells. They will also flip pieces of rubble over with their mouths when searching for prey. They may disturb smaller pieces of live coral when hunting in this manner. If you have a system that might accept (and survive) a ring wrasse, the accepted rule is to keep only one per aquarium.

Bluestreak Cleaner Wrasse (*Labroides dimidiatus*): two specimens preen a parrotfish, exhibiting behavior not easily sustained in an aquarium setting.

Cleaner Wrasses (Genus *Labroides*)

These wrasses are engaging fishes, but conscientious reef aquarists should refuse to purchase them. As obligatory cleaners, these wrasses feed on ectoparasites, fish slime, and scales. Although they vary somewhat in aquarium suitability, all species are difficult to maintain long-term in the home aquarium. They will fare poorly unless kept with a large community of fishes from which to browse mucus and parasites. The most common species, the Bluestreak Cleaner Wrasse (*Labroides dimidiatus*), does slightly better than its congeners. It is more likely to ingest other foods, although it rarely does so with gusto. It may graze the substrate, and has been known to pick at the mantles of tridacnid clams (irritating them and causing them to close). The cleaner wrasses are protogynous hermaphrodites, and most exhibit a haremic mating system. The male defends a large area from consexuals; within his domain are three to six subordinate females. If you are looking to keep a cleaner fish, choose instead one of the cleaner gobies or some of the other wrasses that are facultative cleaners (e.g., juvenile hogfishes).

Tubelip Wrasse (*Labropsis australis*): adults feed almost entirely on small-polyped stony corals. Inset: Red Sea Cleaner Wrasse (*Larabicus quadrilineatus*).

Tubelip Wrasses (Genera *Labropsis* & *Larabicus*)

Although not common, some of the six species in the genus *Labropsis* occasionally make their way into the aquarium hobby. They tend to do poorly in the reef tank because of their specialized diets. Many in this genus feed exclusively on the polyps of small-polyped stony corals when they reach adulthood. As juveniles, at least some are cleaners (one species also cleans as an adult). As is the case with a number of obligatory corallivores, switching them to an artificial diet is difficult. Of course, aquarists who keep the corals that these wrasses normally eat (e.g., *Acropora* species) will probably want to avoid adding them to their tank. The more advanced aquarist who wants to attempt housing these fishes should keep in mind that members of the same species are likely to fight and congeners might also quarrel.

Larabicus quadrilineatus (Red Sea Cleaner Wrasse) is more likely to acclimate to aquarium life than other *Labropsis* species, but it is by no means easy to keep. As a juvenile, it is a cleaner, and as an adult it is a coral-polyp feeder.

Vermiculate Leopard Wrasse (*Macropharyngodon bipartitus*): a genus of coveted, incredibly patterned wrasses, this group demands expert care and feeding.

Leopard Wrasses (Genus *Macropharyngodon*)

The 10 species in this genus are undeniably beautiful but delicate and often difficult to keep. They typically suffer during the shipping process and also present feeding challenges. They do best in a reef tank with an attached refugium. This venue should provide a steady supply of the foraminiferans (shelled protozoans), minute snails, and tiny crustaceans that they normally prey upon. Although leopard wrasses may eventually accept prepared and introduced live foods, the presence of well-established live rock and live sand will provide foraging opportunities. In many respects, their husbandry is similar to that of the Green Mandarinfish (*Synchiropus splendidus*). Even if it seems as though your leopard wrasse is getting enough to eat, it sometimes gets thinner and suddenly dies—possibly from intestinal worms. Fenbendazole and piperazine (e.g., *Pipzine* by Aquatronics) can be used to deworm them. Other than being a challenge to keep, these wrasses are great additions to the reef aquarium as they will not harm desirable invertebrates. Provide them with a sand bed (at least 2 in. [5 cm] deep) in which to bury.

MALE

Macropharyngodon ornatus (Randall, 1978)
Ornate Leopard Wrasse

Maximum Length: 5.1 in. (13 cm).
Range: East Indian to West Pacific.
Minimum Aquarium Size: 30 gal. (114 L).
Foods & Feeding: Keep in a tank with live rock. Although it should be fed a variety of prepared and live foods once a day, the presence of live rock will enable it to forage continually on the associated micro-invertebrate fauna (e.g., foraminiferans). It is a good practice to replace an old piece of live rock from time to time with a new one to replenish the natural stocks of food.
Aquarium Suitability/Reef Compatibility:
Aquarium Notes: This strikingly patterned wrasse is not a threat to most ornamental invertebrates and will aid the reef aquarist in controlling pyramidellid snails and commensal flatworms. It is easily intimidated by aggressive fishes and will perish in competitive situations. A 2-in. (5-cm) layer of fine sand will increase your chances of success. This fish is rarely aggressive toward other species or even members of its own species. If you want to keep more than one *M. ornatus* in your tank, however, it is advisable to add them all at the same time and to keep only one male per tank.

Macropharyngodon bipartitus (female)
Vermiculate Leopard Wrasse
Max. Length: 5.1 in. (13 cm).

Macropharyngodon choati (male)
Choat's Leopard Wrasse
Max. Length: 3.9 in. (10 cm).

Macropharyngodon geoffroyi (male)
Potter's Leopard Wrasse
Max. Length: 6.2 in. (16 cm).

Macropharyngodon meleagris (juv.)
Leopard Wrasse
Max. Length: 5.5 in. (14 cm).

Macropharyngodon meleagris (male)
Leopard Wrasse
Max. Length: 5.5 in. (14 cm).

Macropharyngodon negrosenses
Black Leopard Wrasse
Max. Length: 4.7 in. (12 cm).

Rockmover or Dragon Wrasse (*Novaculichthys taeniourus*): juveniles can make a stunning addition to the reef aquarium, but adults will become a real nuisance.

Rockmover Wrasses (Genus *Novaculichthys*)

The two species in this genus are incredible, fascinating fishes, but not suitable for most reef aquariums because of their habit of flipping rubble and corals (hence their common name) and their proclivity toward eating all kinds of motile invertebrates. They will eat snails, bivalves, polychaete worms, crabs, shrimps, serpent stars, sea stars, and sea urchins. They also flip fungiid corals and large-polyped stony coral colonies when hunting, and have been known to jump from uncovered aquariums.

The most common member in the genus, the Rockmover or Dragon Wrasse (*Novaculichthys taeniourus*) is not only a threat to invertebrates, it can be very aggressive toward any fish tankmates. Although ornate, interesting, and relatively well-behaved as a juvenile, *N. taeniourus* will become a destructive and uncontrollable aquarium inhabitant as it matures. *Novaculichthys* species do best in a fish-only tank with aggressive tankmates. These wrasses bury and will require a fine sand bed (2 to 4 in. [5 to 10 cm] deep) in which to hide at night. They eat virtually any meaty food offered.

Filamented Flasher Wrasse (*Paracheilinus filamentosus*) male: this stunning wrasse is an ideal addition to the invertebrate aquarium.

Flasher Wrasses (Genus *Paracheilinus*)

Flasher wrasses are ideal candidates for most reef aquariums. They will not bother invertebrates (although larger individuals may eat smaller anemone shrimps, like *Periclimenes* species). They spend most of their time in the water column and serve as dither fish, encouraging shy fishes to spend more time in the open. They readily adapt to captivity, especially if housed with other peaceful fishes. They are best kept in small groups, but add all at the same time to a larger tank (180 gallons [684 L] or more) or put the females in first. Keeping more than one male can be tricky, and males of different species may quarrel. With the possible exception of close relatives (e.g., fairy wrasses) or other small planktivores, flasher wrasses are rarely aggressive toward tankmates. Feed them at least twice a day. They are more likely to "flash" (flare their fins) if kept in groups or if the wrasse can see its reflection (a mirror on the side of the tank works, although if it is kept there all the time, the flasher will become habituated). Flashers form a mucus cocoon at night. Beware, they will jump out of an open aquarium.

MALE

Paracheilinus angulatus Randall & Lubbock, 1981
Lyretail Flasher Wrasse (Royal Flasher Wrasse)

Maximum Length: 3 in. (7.5 cm).
Range: Western Pacific.
Minimum Aquarium Size: 20 gal. (76 L).
Foods & Feeding: Meaty foods, including finely shredded frozen seafood, mysid shrimp, frozen preparations, pigment-enriched flake food, and Cyclop-eeze. Feed at least twice a day—preferably more often.
Aquarium Suitability/Reef Compatibility:
Aquarium Notes: This vibrant flasher wrasse makes a fascinating display animal. Males will behave aggressively toward consexuals and larger individuals will chase congeners that are smaller or introduced after the flasher has become established. Ideal tankmates for this and other flasher wrasses include more passive anthias, assessors (*Assessor* species), gobies, dartfishes, blennies, small fairy wrasses, and other smaller, more peaceful labrid species. They have been known to fall victim to predatory crustaceans (e.g., large hermit crabs, cancrid crabs), elephant ear polyps (*Amplexidiscus fenestrafer*), and carpet anemones (*Stichodactyla* species).

MALE

Paracheilinus carpenteri Randall & Lubbock, 1981
Carpenter's Flasher Wrasse (Redfin Flasher Wrasse)

Maximum Length: 3 in. (7.5 cm).
Range: Western Pacific.
Minimum Aquarium Size: 20 gal. (76 L).
Foods & Feeding: Meaty foods, including finely shredded frozen seafood, mysid shrimp, frozen preparations, pigment-enriched flake food, and Cyclop-eeze. Feed at least twice a day or preferably more often.
Aquarium Suitability/Reef Compatibility:
Aquarium Notes: Vibrant in appearance when properly cared for, this is one of the more common members of the genus and it usually does very well in the reef aquarium. It may take a day or two before it starts spending most of its time in the open. Be sure to provide it with a peaceful community in which to acclimate. Once settled in, adult males may behave aggressively toward conspecifics and male congeners. Like others in the genus, an aquarium cover of some form is required to keep them from jumping out of the tank—or into overflow boxes.

Paracheilinus cyaneus (male)
Blue Flasher Wrasse
Max. Length: 3.3 in. (8.5 cm).

Paracheilinus filamentosus (male)
Filamented Flasher Wrasse
Max. Length: 3.9 in. (10 cm).

Paracheilinus flavianalis (male)
Yellowfin Flasher Wrasse
Max. Length: 3.3 in. (8.5 cm).

Paracheilinus lineopunctatus (male)
Dot and Dash Flasher Wrasse
Max. Length: 2.8 in. (7 cm).

Paracheilinus mccoskeri (male)
McCosker's Flasher Wrasse
Max. Length: 2.6 in. (6.5 cm).

Paracheilinus octotaenia (male)
Eightline Flasher Wrasse
Max. Length: 3.5 in. (9 cm).

Paracheilinus angulatus x
Paracheilinus carpenteri (male)

Paracheilinus angulatus x
Paracheilinus cyaneus (male)

Paracheilinus angulatus x
Paracheilinus lineopunctatus (male)

Paracheilinus flavianalis x
Paracheilinus filamentosus (male)

Flasher Mutts (hybrids)

In the wild, it is not uncommon to see mixed groups of flasher wrasses. Not only do these fishes aggregate together, they sometimes cross-spawn. This can make identifying some of the flasher wrasses coming into the aquarium trade vexatious—if not impossible. As illustrated by the photographs above, you can see elements of the two species involved in the cross. For example, some of the individuals have the lunate tail that is indicative of *Paracheilinus angulatus.* The resulting offspring can be more like one parent or the other. It is not known if these hybrids are fertile and capable of successful reproduction.

Whitebarred Wrasse (*Pseudocheilinus ocellatus*) juv.: this species and its congeners are wonderful reef aquarium inhabitants with fascinating behaviors.

Lined Wrasses (Genera *Pseudocheilinus* & *Pseudocheilinops*)

These relatively diminutive fishes are undeniably appealing and are, in fact, excellent reef fishes and a minimal threat to all but the smallest mollusks or crustaceans. Because of their reclusive dispositions, they actually do best in a reef aquascape. In the wild and in the aquarium, they sneak among coral branches or between reef nooks and crannies. They will need to be provided with plenty of holes and crevices in which to hide. Larger species may thin out stocks of small shrimps and crabs. They will occasionally leap out of an open reef aquarium when the lights are extinguished or when they are harassed by other fishes.

One advantage to housing these fishes with tridacnid clams is that they can help control populations of parasitic pyramidellid snails and may also eat noxious flatworms. Some can be quite aggressive to tankmates once they have become established, so if you plan a more passive fish community, add the *Pseudocheilinus* species last, and only if the reef tank is large.

Pseudocheilinus hexataenia (Bleeker, 1857)
Sixline Wrasse

Maximum Length: 3 in. (7.5 cm).
Range: Indo-Pacific.
Minimum Aquarium Size: 10 gal. (38 L).
Foods & Feeding: Meaty foods, including finely shredded frozen seafood, mysid shrimp, frozen preparations, and pigment-enriched flake food. Feed at least once a day, unless you have a healthy stock of crustaceans and worms for it to feed on, in which case you can feed every other day.
Aquarium Suitability/Reef Compatibility:
Aquarium Notes: Bold for its size, this species will thrive in the reef aquarium once established. It is better suited to the community tank than larger congeners. Even so, it can become aggressive toward more docile wrasses and other shy, docile species. More than one can be housed in a larger aquarium (135 gallons [513 L] or more) if added simultaneously. It is best to select smaller individuals. Like many smaller fishes, it does best in a rocky, complex aquascape with numerous hiding places. I have known larger adults to consume ornamental shrimps. It will occassionaly clean ectoparasites from other fishes.

273

ADULT

Pseudocheilinus ocellatus Randall, 1999
Whitebarred Wrasse (Mystery Wrasse)

Maximum Length: 3.1 in. (8 cm).
Range: Indo-Pacific.
Minimum Aquarium Size: 15 gal. (57 L).
Foods & Feeding: Meaty foods, including finely shredded frozen seafood, mysid shrimp, frozen preparations, and pigment-enriched flake food. Feed at least once a day, unless you have a healthy stock of crustaceans and worms for it to feed on, in which case you can feed every other day.
Aquarium Suitability/Reef Compatibility:
Aquarium Notes: This species is both magnificent in appearance and a hardy addition to the fish-only or reef aquarium. When first introduced, it will spend most of its time lurking among rockwork. Once it acclimates (relatively quickly if there are no larger, more aggressive fishes present), it will make frequent forays into the open. It may leap from an open aquarium. I have kept it with a range of fish species without incident, but it gets more aggressive as it gets larger. Juveniles are a minimal threat to ornamental invertebrates, but larger *P. ocellatus* are a threat to ornamental shrimps and crabs.

Pseudocheilinus octotaenia Jenkins, 1900
Eightline Wrasse

Maximum Length: 5.3 in. (13.5 cm).
Range: Indo-Pacific.
Minimum Aquarium Size: 30 gal. (114 L).
Foods & Feeding: Meaty foods, including finely shredded frozen seafood, mysid shrimp, frozen preparations, and pigment-enriched flake food. Feed at least once a day, unless you have a healthy stock of crustaceans and worms for it to feed on, in which case you can feed every other day.
Aquarium Suitability/Reef Compatibility:
Aquarium Notes: This species gets too large for the small reef tank and is aggressively inclined. It frequently assaults tankmates (including firefishes, dart gobies, other wrasses, reef basslets, and tobies) shredding fins and removing scales with its large canine teeth. Do not keep more than one in the same aquarium. It will also fight with congeners. It is shy initially, hiding most of the time, but after acclimating it will become quite bold. Larger *P. octotaenia* will eat ornamental shrimps, as well as bristle worms, capturing and consuming polychaetes up to 3 in. (7.6 cm) in length. It will also eat small sea urchins that have tests (shells) about the size of a marble.

Pseudocheilinus tetrataenia Schultz, 1960
Fourline Wrasse

Maximum Length: 2.9 in. (7.3 cm).
Range: Western and Central Pacific.
Minimum Aquarium Size: 10 gal. (38 L).
Foods & Feeding: Meaty foods, including finely shredded frozen seafood, mysid shrimp, frozen preparations, and pigment-enriched flake food. Feed at least once a day, unless you have a healthy stock of crustaceans and worms for it to feed on, in which case you can feed every other day.
Aquarium Suitability/Reef Compatibility:
Aquarium Notes: This diminutive wrasse is an interesting choice both for a nano-reef or larger reef aquarium. Although small, it can become belligerent when space is limited, so it is not safe to keep with docile species in a small tank. Groups can be kept in large aquariums (180 gallons [684 L] or more), although there is always a risk of fighting among males (because they are not sexually dichromatic, it will not be possible to ensure that a group does not have one or more males). I have had it harass gobies, assessors, and other wrasses in small reef tanks. Like others in the genus, this species is secretive when first added to the aquarium.

MALE

Pseudocheilinops ataenia Schultz, 1960
Pinkstreaked Wrasse

Maximum Length: 2.6 in. (6.5 cm).
Range: Western Pacific.
Minimum Aquarium Size: 10 gal. (38 L).
Foods & Feeding: Meaty foods, including finely shredded frozen seafood, mysid shrimp, frozen preparations, and pigment-enriched flake food. Feed at least once a day, unless you have a healthy stock of crustaceans and worms for it to feed on, in which case you can feed every other day.

Aquarium Suitability/Reef Compatibility:

Aquarium Notes: This small, colorful fish is ideal for the reef aquarium and nano-reef. It is very shy initially, but gradually becomes quite bold and spends a considerable amount of time in the open. It is ignored by most of its tankmates, although I have seen the related *Pseudocheilinus* species chase it. If the tank is large with plenty of hiding places, *P. ataenia* will simply hide between the branches of corals. It is rarely aggressively toward any other fishes. It is sexually dichromatic, with males sporting more pronounced yellow lines down the body and bluish gray markings on the gill cover. It typically occurs in small, loose groups in the wild.

Torpedo Wrasse (*Pseudocoris heteroptera*) terminal phase. Inset: Redspot Wrasse (*Pseudocoris yamashiroi*) initial phase. Active swimmers for larger reefs.

False Corises (Genus *Pseudocoris*)

Active swimmers, the five species in this genus are occasionally available and make good community members for larger reef systems. All get about 5.9 in. (15 cm) in length and need plenty of open swimming space. They feed on zooplankton and spend much of their time in the water column. They tend to form small to medium-sized shoals and often form mixed groups with other zooplanktivores. They tend not to be overly aggressive, although males may pester other zooplankton-feeding wrasses. Keep only one male per tank. Juveniles and females can be housed in small groups and may do best if kept in shoals or with other zooplankton-feeding wrasses (e.g., *Paracheilinus*). *Pseudocoris* wrasses (especially males) will jump out of open aquariums . New individuals may hide for a day or two, but typically become bolder with time. If harassed by tankmates, they usually do not survive. The most common in the aquarium trade is the Redspot Wrasse (*Pseudocoris yamashiroi*), which can be kept in groups—but only one male per tank, the general rule with virtually all wrasse species.

Chiseltooth Wrasse (*Pseudodax moluccanus*): adults and juveniles (inset) make an attractive addition to the large reef tank where adult size is not a concern.

Chiseltooth Wrasse (Genus *Pseudodax*)

This genus has a single species that sometimes shows up in aquarium stores, usually labeled an "assorted wrasse." It is not harmful to sessile invertebrates, but adults may eat ornamental shrimps, a variety of worms, and small clams and snails. Note well: it reaches a length of 9.8 in. (25 cm). Juveniles are facultative cleaners and will engage in this activity in captivity (they will also take introduced foods). It tends to ship poorly, but once settled in to its new home, it usually does quite well. Young fish are more likely to survive and bounce back from shipping than larger adults, and they generally do much better than full-time cleaner wrasses. This species needs a sand bed at least 2 in. [5 cm] in depth in which to bury. Keep only one per tank, as juveniles will squabble with each other as will adult males. Juveniles are likely to quarrel with other cleaner wrasses, especially those of similar color (e.g., *Labroides* and *Labropsis* species). Offer meaty foods, including frozen preparations, mysid shrimps, and finely chopped seafood. Feed at least twice a day in a reef tank (more often in a tank without live substrate).

Smalltail Wrasse (*Pseudojuloides cerasinus*) male: the pencil wrasses can be strikingly beautiful, but they are difficult to obtain and even harder to keep.

Pencil Wrasses (Genus *Pseudojuloides*)

There are more than 10 species in this genus, but only a couple are regularly seen in the aquarium trade. Although they would seem to be ideally suited for the reef aquarium, *Pseudojuloides* wrasses tend to be very challenging to keep. Food-habit studies do not indicate that they have specialized diets, but they tend to become emaciated and perish in the aquarium. Like the leopard wrasses, they do better in a well-established reef tank than in a more sterile aquarium that lacks live substrate. In a reef tank, they will find some natural fodder. The pencil wrasses may feed on frozen mysid shrimp and will usually take live foods (e.g., brine shrimp), but even then they often pine away. Feed them at least twice a day. They should not be housed with aggressive tankmates. You can keep a male and female in the same tank (most of the species are sexually dichromatic). They are also proficient jumpers that will leap from open tanks. Provide a layer of fine sand (at least 2 in. [5 cm] deep) under which they can bury. They are very poor shippers.

Cockerel Wrasse (*Pteragogus enneacanthus*): true to the common name for this group, these medium-sized wrasses tend to hide among corals and live rock.

Secretive Wrasses (Genus *Pteragogus*)

These wrasses, none of which exceed 8 in. (20 cm) in length, are ideal for the medium to large reef aquarium. They will not harm corals, but may feed on some motile invertebrates, including ornamental crustaceans. They usually spend most of their time slinking between live rock and among corals. They will even rest among the polyps of soft corals, although this not typically a problem. They are usually not a threat to fishes of equal size or larger, but they might feed on small piscine tankmates that can be swallowed whole. They are particularly shy when first added to the aquarium, but with time and if not bothered, they will become more brazen. Live food (ghost shrimps, live-bearing fishes) can be useful to initiate a feeding response. Feed them at least once a day. Keep only one member of the genus per tank, as aggressive interactions are likely to occur between conspecifics and congeners. In the wild, they tend to be solitary. They do not bury at night.

Belted Ribbon Wrasse (*Stethojulis balteata*) male: these are very active fishes, often flamboyantly colored, but demanding of expert husbandry.

Ribbon Wrasses (Genus *Stethojulis*)

These attractive wrasses are very active and are usually seen dashing about the reef. They often form groups, with initial-phase individuals greatly outnumbering males in these shoals. They can be kept in reef tanks, but for some unknown reason they fare poorly in captivity. The best longevity records for these fishes have been for individuals placed in well-established reef tanks or aquariums with lush filamentous algae growth, with associated minute crustacean fauna. Their natural diet typically consists of minute benthic invertebrates and planktonic organisms that live on or near the seafloor. Some of the larger species feed on tiny snails and minute crustaceans, which they swallow whole. A captive diet should include tiny, protein-rich food items: smaller individuals will eat Cyclopeeze, while mysid shrimps are a good choice for larger fishes. Live vitamin-enriched brine shrimp can help induce a feeding response. Feed them several times a day, even in a reef tank. They bury under the sand so will need a sand bed at least 2 in. (5 cm) in depth.

Pseudojuloides cerasinus (female)
Smalltail Wrasse
Max. Length: 4.7 in. (12 cm).

Pseudojuloides severnsi (male)
Royal Pencil Wrasse
Max. Length: 5.9 in. (15 cm).

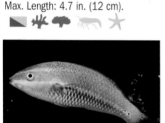

Stethojulis bandanensis (male)
Redspot Ribbon Wrasse
Max. Length: 6.3 in. (16 cm).

Stethojulis interrupta (male)
Cut Ribbon Wrasse
Max. Length: 5.1 in. (13 cm).

Stethojulis interrupta (female)
Cut Ribbon Wrasse
Max. Length: 5.1 in. (13 cm).

Stethojulis *trilineata* (male)
Threelined Ribbon Wrasse
Max. Length: 5.5 in. (14 cm).

Moon Wrasse (*Thalassoma lunare*) top: handsome, durable fishes but predatory on motile invertebrates. Note cooperative hunting behavior with a goatfish.

Banana Wrasses (Genus *Thalassoma*)

The members of this genus are active wrasses that often grow large and are quite hardy aquarium inhabitants. They will ignore all corals but are a definite threat to a variety of motile invertebrates. Some desirable invertebrates that are on their bill of fare are snails, bivalves, worms, urchins, serpent stars, and sea stars. Larger individuals will also eat smaller fishes, especially slender species (e.g., dartfishes). They do not bury under the substrate and need plenty of swimming room as they tend to pace back and forth constantly, from one end of the tank to the other. They can be rather bellicose, harassing new piscine introductions to the aquarium, especially if they are smaller or similar in shape. Congeners are likely to quarrel. Keep them in a tank with more belligerent or larger fishes. You can add a male and a female(s), or juveniles, to the same tank if it is larger. At night or when threatened, they hide among rockwork. They are proficient jumpers that will leap out of open aquariums. These are protogynous hermaphrodites, with initial-phase and secondary-phase individuals.

TERMINAL PHASE (FOREGROUND); INITIAL PHASE (BACKGROUND)

Thalassoma bifasciatum (Bloch, 1791)
Bluehead Wrasse

Maximum Length: 7.1 in. (18 cm).

Range: Tropical Western Atlantic.

Minimum Aquarium Size: 30 gal. (114 L).

Foods & Feeding: Meaty foods, including finely shredded frozen seafood, mysid shrimp, frozen preparations, and pigment-enriched flake food. Feed at least twice a day.

Aquarium Suitability/Reef Compatibility:

Aquarium Notes: The supermale of this Caribbean species is gorgeous. It is also one of the few members of this genus that feeds mostly on zooplankton. However, it will also eat small, benthic invertebrates (including polychaete worms, tiny snails, crustaceans, and small serpent stars) and will pick parasites off other fishes (this is done by initial-phase [yellow] individuals). If it is not well fed, it may also turn its attention to ornamental shrimps and crabs. You can keep a male with several initial-phase individuals if the aquarium is larger (preferably 135 gallons [513 L] or larger). This species may pick on more passive fishes introduced after it is settled in. It is an able jumper that will leap from an open tank.

INITIAL PHASE

Thalassoma lucasanum (Gill, 1862)
Cortez Rainbow Wrasse

Maximum Length: 3.9 in. (10 cm).
Range: Tropical Eastern Pacific.
Minimum Aquarium Size: 30 gal. (114 L).
Foods & Feeding: Meaty foods, including finely shredded frozen seafood, mysid shrimp, frozen preparations, and pigment-enriched flake food. Feed at least twice a day.
Aquarium Suitability/Reef Compatibility:
Aquarium Notes: Although not as common as its Atlantic congener (*Thalassoma bifasciatum*), this species is smaller and equally colorful. Unfortunately, supermales are prone to color loss if they are not fed a varied diet and kept with conspecific females. It feeds mostly on zooplankton, but will eat small benthic invertebrates. Initial-phase individuals are also facultative cleaners. You can keep a male with several initial-phase individuals if the aquarium is larger (preferably 135 gallons [513 L] or more). This species is likely to leap from an open aquarium.

Thalassoma amblycephalum (male)
Twotone Wrasse
Max. Length: 5.5 in. (14 cm).

Thalassoma hardwicke (male)
Hardwick's Wrasse
Max. Length: 7.9 in. (20 cm).

Thalassoma jansenii (male)
Jansen's Wrasse
Max. Length: 7.9 in. (20 cm).

Thalassoma klunzingeri (male)
Klunzinger's Wrasse
Max. Length: 7.9 in. (20 cm).

Thalassoma lutescens (juv.)
Sunset Wrasse
Max. Length: 11.8 in. (30 cm).

Thalassoma lutescens (initial phase)
Sunset Wrasse
Max. Length: 11.8 in. (30 cm).

Yellowbanded Possum Wrasse (*Wetmorella nigropinnata*): these tiny wrasses are ideal for a docile reef community, but do poorly with big, competitive tankmates.

Possum Wrasses (Genus *Wetmorella*)

These diminutive wrasses reach lengths of 2 to 2.6 in. (5 to 6.5 cm). They can be kept in nano-reef tanks, but need to be fed frequently as there will not be enough natural fodder in a small tank to sustain them. You may not see them that frequently if there is a lot of live rock present in the tank, because *Wetmorella* species are quite reclusive. They spend most of their time moving among the rockwork but are more likely to spend time in the open if kept in relatively quiet surroundings.

They are also potential targets of tank bullies, and it is best to avoid keeping them with more pugnacious species that may pick on them or prevent them from getting enough to eat. I have seen larger *Wetmorella* wrasses bother smaller conspecifics in smaller tanks. If you plan on keeping more than one individual of the same species or even congeners in the same tank, make sure the tank is large enough (e.g., 70 gallons [266 L] or larger) and that it is replete with places for them to hide. They seem to really appreciate caves and ledges. When there are aggression problems amongst the possum

Pygmy Possum Wrasse (*Wetmorella trilineata*): these wrasses are lurkers that move about under ledges and in caves, foraging for tiny crustaceans and worms.

wrasses, the largest *Wetmorella* in the tank is likely to be the bully, no matter what species it is.

They feed on tiny worms and crustaceans that associate with live rock. They also readily take aquarium foods, like mysid shrimp, frozen preparations, and flake food. They love Cyclop-eeze, which they pick out of the water column.

Even though they will eat introduced fodder, it is still best to house them in a tank with established live rock and live sand substrate because they are so reclusive (especially when first added to a tank) and prone to being dominated by tankmates. This will enable them to feed throughout the day on the minute prey living on the rock. A productive refugium can also help ensure that they have access to a steady supply of live foods. They are not prone to parasitic infection. I believe the most likely cause of death would be malnutrition resulting from infrequent feeding and an impoverished microinvertebrate population in their tank. They might also be intimidated—and thus not get enough to eat—if their tankmates are too boisterous at feeding time. They may tend to suffer from shipping stress, so choose a new specimen carefully.

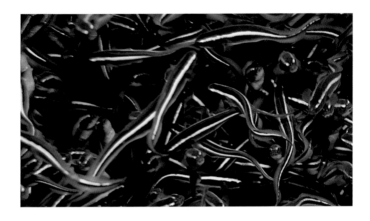

Convict Blenny (*Pholidichthys leucotaenia*): gregarious as juveniles, secretive and pair-forming as adults, these fish dig tunnels under aquarium rockwork.

Convict Blenny (Family Pholidichthyidae)

This family contains two unusual species (only one enters the aquarium trade). Although suitable for the reef tank, it is a prodigious digger that will create tunnels and holes under the reef structure (its other common name is Engineer Goby). This can cause serious cave-ins if precautions are not taken (i.e., place rock on the tank bottom first to ensure stability, then add sand). Although not a threat to corals, a large Convict Blenny will eat ornamental shrimps. It is great for stirring up debris that has formed in places that are often hard for other displacers to get to. It will make a mess when introduced to a tank that has been set up for awhile, as it will suspend much debris in the water column for some time. Adults are very secretive and will spend much of their time hiding. Studies indicate they may care for their young when they hatch out of eggs deposited in their burrows. Disease-resistant and rarely bother other fish tankmates. Best kept singly or in pairs. Feed meaty foods (finely chopped seafood, mysid shrimp, prepared frozen preparations) once per day in a reef tank, keep this fish in at least a 20-gallon aquarium.

Threadfin Sand Diver (*Trichonotus elegans*): these amazing fish have special needs that can be more difficult to provide in the reef aquarium.

Sand Divers (Family Trichonotidae)

This family of sand dwellers is suitable only for a specially planned reef aquarium. They need to be housed in a tank with lots of surface area and plenty of open bottom space. There should also be a thick layer of sand substrate (at least 2 in. [5 cm] in depth). The sand divers, as the name implies, will dive head first under the sand and actually move from one spot to another while buried (it is essential that the sand be a fine grade or they will damage their skin and fins when burying). These fishes prey mainly on zooplankton, so they will need to be fed several times a day in the aquarium. The sand divers typically occur in shoals, consisting of fewer males than females. While you can house more than one female per tank, it is best not to house males in the same tank. (Males of most species are more colorful and have more filamentous dorsal fins.) If housed with aggressive fishes, the sand divers may hide constantly or jump out of an open aquarium if they are picked on. They are also potential prey for a number of piscivores (e.g., frogfishes, scorpionfishes).

291

Bluelined Sand Perch (*Parapercis pulchella*): hardy, predatory fishes that will eat small fishes and motile invertebrates and dominate the bottom reaches of a tank.

Sand Perches (Family Pinguipedidae)

Although not a threat to corals in the reef tank, the members of this group can be aggressive toward other bottom-dwelling fishes. Avoid housing them with passive species. Unlike some benthic carnivores (e.g., frogfishes, scorpionfishes) they are much less likely to perch on corals and irritate them. Most live on open sand or rubble bottoms—some open sand bottom will be appreciated. Larger sand perches feed heavily on small fishes—keeping them with any fish that they can swallow whole will have a predictable conclusion. Many small invertebrates are also at risk. Sand perches will eat bristleworms, small mantis shrimps, and hairy xanthid crabs, but more desirable invertebrates may also be in peril. Small sand perches have also been known to eat feather duster worms and Christmas tree worms, while larger individuals may consume small bivalves, anemone crabs, cleaner shrimps, anemone shrimps, pistol shrimps, small boxer shrimps, and juvenile brittle and serpent stars. They will jump out of an open tank. It is prudent to house only one per tank, as they are likely to fight (especially males).

Parapercis schauinslandi (Steindachner, 1900)
Schauinsland's Sand Perch (Redspotted Sand Perch, Red Grubfish)

Maximum Length: 5 in. (13 cm).
Range: Indo-Pacific.
Minimum Aquarium Size: 20 gal. (76 L).
Foods & Feeding: Meaty foods, including chopped seafood, mysid shrimp, and frozen preparations for carnivores. Feed every other day in the reef tank (once or twice a day in a tank without live substrate).
Aquarium Suitability/Reef Compatibility:
Aquarium Notes: This is one of the best sand perch species for the reef tank as it does not get as large many in its clan and is thus less of a threat to invertebrates. It is also less aggressive toward fish tankmates than many of its congeners. It can become more of a bully as it gets larger. Even small specimens may harass other bottom-dwelling fishes introduced to the tank after the sand perch is established, especially in a smaller aquarium.

A small aggregation of these fish can be kept in a larger reef tank, but be sure to introduce all individuals to the aquarium simultaneously.

Parapercis clathrata
Latticed Sand Perch
Max. Length: 7 in. (18 cm).

Parapercis hexophthalma
Speckled Sand Perch
Max. Length: 11 in. (28 cm).

Parapercis signata
Blackflag Sand Perch
Max. Length: 5.1 in. (13 cm).

Parapercis snyderi
Blackfin Sand Perch
Max. Length: 3.9 in. (10 cm).

Parapercis xanthozona
Whitestripe Sand Perch
Max. Length: 9.1 in. (23 cm).

Parapercis sp.
Yellowtail Sand Perch
Max. Length: 5.5 in. (14 cm).

Japanese Fringehead (*Neoclinus toshimaensis*): there are several families of small blenny allies that are ideal for the reef aquarium, including the nano-reef.

Tube & Pike Blennies (Family Chaenopsidae)

Although these fishes are only occasionally offered in aquarium stores, they often have dramatic saillike dorsal fins and make interesting and durable aquarium inhabitants, especially in a smaller tank. They are great for the reef aquarium, although larger pike blennies (*Chaenopsis* species) will eat shrimps and fishes small enough to be swallowed. Tube blennies are elongate and compressed, with a long, continuous dorsal fin that can be saillike in some species. Most live in empty calcareous tubes constructed by serpulid worms. They back into the opening of the tube and dart out to capture passing plankton. The pike blennies are eellike in form and are often seen in repose on sand and hard substrates. They are also more voracious. The pike blennies are also the largest members of the family, the biggest measuring 6.3 in. (16 cm) in length. Most of the other chaenopsid blennies attain less than 2.4 in. (6 cm). These blennies can be kept together in medium-sized tanks, as long as all individuals have proper hiding places. Pike blennies will jump from open aquariums.

Weed Blennies or Labrisomid Blennies
(Family Labrisomidae)

These diminutive fishes enter the aquarium trade and are good candidates both for fish-only tanks and reef aquariums. Larger individuals may eat ornamental shrimps and small, benthic fishes. The weed blennies have an elongate body, with cirri (filament-like projections) present on the nape, near the nostril, and near the eye, and there are more spines than soft rays in the dorsal fin. Most species are quite small, which means they are suitable for the nano-reef. Some shelter in the tentacles of sea anemones, barrel sponges and/or among sea urchin spines.

Triplefins (Family Tripterygiidae)

These small blennylike fishes are a perfect selection for the more peaceful reef aquarium community and ideal for the nano-reef. Members of this family of small fishes (most are under 2 in. [5 cm] in length) are elongate, with a dorsal fin divided into three parts (hence, the name triplefins). They feed on small benthic invertebrates and will not harm corals. They may be hard to locate once added to a large reef tank full of live rock. Only one individual should be housed in a small tank, although you could house congeners, or even pairs together in a larger aquarium. Some species are sexually dichromatic, so acquiring a male-female pair is a practical option. They are likely to be picked on by more aggressive, substrate-bound fishes (e.g., hawkfishes, sand perches) and their small size makes them a potential target for a number of piscivorous fishes. Other enemies include carpet anemones, elephant ear anemones, crabs, reef lobsters, and even larger shrimps.

Acanthemblemaria spinosa
Spinyhead Blenny
Max. Length: 1.1 in. (2.8 cm).

Chaenopsis alepidota
Orangethroat Pike Blenny
Max. Length: 4.9 in. (12.5 cm).

Labrisomus nuchipinnis
Hairy Blenny
Max. Length: 6 in. (15 cm).

Malacoctenus boehlkei
Diamond Blenny
Max. Length: 2.6 in. (6.5 cm).

Helcogramma rhinoceros
Rhinoceros Triplefin
Max. Length: 1.6 in. (4 cm).

Helcogramma striatum
Striped Triplefin
Max. Length: 2 in. (5 cm).

Bluestriped Fang Blenny (*Plagiotremus rhinorhynchus*): this odd blenny swims in the water column and bites mucus and scales from passing fishes.

Fang Blennies (Genera *Aspidontus, Plagiotremus & Petroscirtes*)

These are the "bad boys" of the blenny world. To varying degrees, they all feed on the mucus and scales of other fishes. A number of them mimic other piscine neighbors (e.g., cleaner wrasses or other blennies), which enables them to get closer to potential victims. They are not sought after community fishes because of their undesirable feeding mode. Of these three genera, the members of *Petroscirtes* depend less on fish scales and mucus (they feed more on filamentous algae, diatoms, and small crustaceans). These blennies have well-developed fangs that are used more for self-defense than for feeding. The members of *Plagiotremus* depend on mucus and scales the most. However, if kept on their own, they will accept mysid and brine shrimp and some frozen preparations. They will have to be fed often (two or three times a day). While the species in these three genera will not harm corals, at least some (e.g., *Aspidontus* species) eat fanworm feeding tentacles. Many of these fishes fight with conspecifics, so keep only one per tank.

Aspidontus dussumieri
Slender Sabertooth Blenny
Max. Length: 4.7 in. (12 cm).

Aspidontus taeniatus
False Cleaner Blenny
Max. Length: 4.5 in. (11.5 cm).

Petroscirtes breviceps
Shorthead Fang Blenny
Max. Length: 5.1 in. (13 cm).

Petroscirtes mitratus
Highfin Fang Blenny
Max. Length: 5.9 in. (15 cm).

Petroscirtes variabilis
Variable Fang Blenny
Max. Length: 3 in. (7.5 cm).

Plagiotremus sp.
Tongan Imposter Blenny
Max. Length: 3.1 in. (8 cm).

Highfin Blenny (*Atrosalarias fuscus*) adult [Inset: juvenile]: a curious-looking algae grazer with prominent eyes that may reside among branching corals.

Highfin Blennies (Genus *Atrosalarias*)

This genus contains just two species: the Highfin Blenny (*Atrosalarias fuscus*) and the Hosokawa Blenny (*A. hosokawai*)—the former is more often seen in the aquarium trade. The juvenile *A. fuscus* is bright yellow over the head, body, and fins, while adults are dark brown to black. It has big eyes and looks like a specter when it swims from one spot to another. It attains a length of about 5.5 in. (14 cm). It usually lives among branching corals and ingests filamentous algae, foraminiferans (shelled protozoans), detritus, and sand. It also consumes sponges, fish eggs, minute crustaceans, small snails, insects, and small worms. It is thought that many of these organisms are ingested incidentally as the fish feeds on algae. It will occasionally nip coral polyps in the aquarium. In captivity it should be offered frozen foods that contain the blue-green algae *Spirulina*. It will also do better if kept in a tank with a crop of microalgae for it to graze upon. It is best to keep only one Highfin Blenny per tank, unless you can acquire a male-female pair or your tank is very large.

Red Rockskipper (*Blenniella chrysospilos*) and (inset) Lined Rockskipper (*Istiblennius lineatus*): may nip corals if the algae and detritus they prefer are lacking.

Rockskippers (Genera *Blenniella* & *Istiblennius*)

The rockskippers are often found in habitats with high wave energy in the intertidal zone. They regularly flip (or "skip") from one tide pool to the next, often leaving the water for short periods of time when they make these migrations. Although they are not known coral eaters, on rare occasions they have been known to nip at corals or clam mantles. Usually this does not cause irreparable damage to these sessile invertebrates. Rockskippers principally feed on algae and detritus, which they rasp from hard substrates. They also incidentally ingest fine sand, minute crustaceans, and tiny snails. Algae is important to ensure their survival—they often starve in a newly set up aquarium—so it is best to add them to an established tank. They are more likely to nip at corals when they are starving. Feed them frozen preparations and flake foods for herbivores (if algae is not present in the tank feed them several times a day). These fishes may skip out of an uncovered tank and may quarrel if more than one is placed in a smaller aquarium, but they can be kept together in a larger tank.

Redstreaked Blenny (*Cirripectes stigmaticus*): a bit larger and less commonly seen than related genera, these algae-grazers are generally reef-safe.

Combtooth Blennies (Genus *Cirripectes*)

Droll in appearance, combtooth blennies are herbivores, grazing on algae that grows on hard surfaces, but they also ingest occasional minute invertebrates that associates with the algae (e.g., foraminiferans, ostracods, gastropods). Less commonly collected than others in their family, they can be housed in the reef tank, but an occasional specimen may nip at both small- and large-polyped stony corals. Many of these blennies live among small-polyped stony coral branches (like *Acropora* and *Pocillopora* species). Their movement between the coral branches can help move oxygen-enriched water into the coral colony. Keep only one per tank, unless you can acquire a pair; many are sexually dichromatic, which makes this feasible. Combtooths can be kept with other blennies in a larger aquarium (135 gallons [513 L] or more). They may chase other herbivores out of their territories and will occasionally bite the flanks or fins of intruders. Offer them a herbivore diet (e.g., frozen preparations and flake foods that include *Spirulina* algae), especially if algae in the tank is in short supply.

Blackspot Blenny (*Ecsenius lividanalis*) variant: one of an interesting group, well-suited to certain reef tanks, although some may nip at coral polyps and clams.

Comical Blennies (Genus *Ecsenius*)

Among the most colorful of their family, the so-called comical blennies are not regularly collected and are a bit of a rare find for the aquarist alert for incoming "oddball" fishes. They are often kept in reef aquariums, where most of them will spend the majority of their time in repose on the substrate or rasping algae off hard surfaces. Because of their small sizes, they can be kept in smaller aquariums. Be aware that some of these fishes will nip at corals and clam mantles. A rare individual may eat small-polyped stony corals or rasp slime off large-polyped stony corals. This can cause the polyps to retract. They can be somewhat aggressive, especially toward other blennies and fishes that may invade their favorite hiding places, but they rarely cause real problems in the aquarium. On occasion, they may nip at and wound a fish tankmate. Keep only one per tank, unless the aquarium is large. It is important to feed them vegetable matter, like frozen foods that contain the blue-green algae *Spirulina*. They will also do better if some microalgae is present in the aquarium.

Ecsenius bicolor (Day, 1888)
Bicolor Blenny

Maximum Length: 4 in. (10 cm).
Range: Indo-Pacific.
Minimum Aquarium Size: 20 gal. (76 L).
Foods & Feeding: Vegetable matter, including frozen and dried foods containing marine algae and the blue-green algae *Spirulina*. Usually will not thrive unless some microalgae (its natural source of food) is present. Feed at least once a day or more, depending on the abundance of microalgae.

Aquarium Suitability/Reef Compatibility:

Aquarium Notes: This is a chromatically variable member of the so-called "comical blenny" genus, exhibiting four distinct color phases. It has been known to nip large-polyped stony corals and clam mantles, but it usually does little harm in a large reef aquarium. It is usually ignored by its tankmates but may behave aggressively toward members of its own species or smaller, bottom-dwelling species. I have seen it pick on gobies and firefishes. This heterospecific aggression is usually not a cause for concern in a larger tank. Keep only per tank, unless you can acquire a male-female pair. It will occasionally jump out of an uncovered aquarium.

Ecsenius midas Starck, 1969
Midas Blenny

Maximum Length: 5.1 in. (13 cm).
Range: Indo-Pacific.
Minimum Aquarium Size: 20 gal. (76 L).
Foods & Feeding: Varied diet, including finely chopped seafood, mysid shrimp, vitamin-enriched brine shrimp, as well as frozen preparations for herbivores. Feed at least twice a day.
Aquarium Suitability/Reef Compatibility:
Aquarium Notes: This is one of the best *Ecsenius* species for the reef tank. It rarely bothers corals as it feeds primarily on zooplankton. It spends much of its time tucked in small holes with only its head protruding or swimming in the water column. While it tends to ignore unrelated species, it will sometimes pick on small plankti-vores (I have seen a Midas Blenny bite the fins of a firefish and dart gobies). It is more likely to become a behavioral problem in a small-er tank (30 gallons or less) than in a' larger aquarium.

Ecsenius bandanus
Banda Blenny
Max. Length: 1.6 in. (4 cm).

Ecsenius bicolor (variant)
Bicolor Blenny
Max. Length: 4 in. (10 cm).

Ecsenius dilemma
Philippines Blenny
Max. Length: 2 in. (5 cm).

Ecsenius namiyei
Namiye's Blenny
Max. Length: 4 in. (10 cm).

Ecsenius pictus
Painted Blenny
Max. Length: 2 in. (5 cm).

Ecsenius stigmatura
Tailspot Blenny
Max. Length: 2 in. (5 cm).

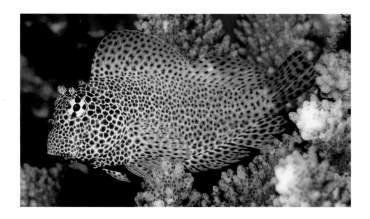

Shortbodied Blenny (*Exallias brevis*): this attractive species presents feeding challenges in captivity and can be destructive to small-polyped stony corals.

Shortbodied Blenny (Genus *Exallias*)

While the Shortbodied or Leopard Blenny (*Exallias brevis*) is a very attractive species, it is also destructive in the reef aquarium. Rather than feeding heavily on algae, this fish feeds on corals. It is thus difficult to feed in captivity and will graze on small-polyped stony corals in the reef aquarium. It is also known to eat some algae, foraminiferans, fish eggs, and sponges. In the wild, it spreads its feeding efforts over a large area, so it rarely kills coral colonies. In the aquarium, there are usually not enough coral colonies to keep the blenny from inflicting serious damage. For these reasons, the Shortbodied Blenny is best left in the wild. I have heard of individuals feeding on frozen, prepared foods, but this seems to be the exception, not the rule. This blenny is very distinct, with a honeycomb pattern on the head, body, and fins. Larger male specimens sport red on the fins and body. It spends its time tucked into crevices or among stony coral branches and is highly territorial, defending its food source from members of its own species.

Yellowtail Fang Blenny (*Meiacanthus atrodorsalis*): despite its intimidating name, this elegant blenny makes a wonderful addition to the reef aquarium.

Lyretailed Fang Blennies (Genus *Meiacanthus*)

These blennies spend most of their time swimming in the water column. They are more brazen because they have venomous fangs, but use them mostly in defense against would-be attackers. They will not nip at corals. Feed them finely chopped seafood, mysid shrimp, vitamin-enriched brine shrimp, and Cyclop-eeze (their mouths are relatively small, so make sure the food offered is small enough). They do best when housed with live rock as they hunt tiny crustaceans on the rock as well as feed on zooplankton produced by rock-dwellers. There are several *Meiacanthus* species that have been raised in captivity. They are demersal spawners that deposit their eggs in a shell or crevice. House only one fang blenny per tank unless you can acquire a pair (males will fight). They rarely bother other fishes, with the possible exception of congeners. They are usually ignored by their tankmates because of their venomous fangs. That said, individuals may be harried by territorial species like dottybacks and damselfishes.

Meiacanthus grammistes
Striped Fang Blenny
Max. Length: 4.3 in. (11 cm).

Meiacanthus mossambicus
Mozambique Fang Blenny
Max. Length: 3.9 in. (10 cm).

Meiacanthus nigrolineatus
Blackline Fang Blenny
Max. Length: 3.7 in. (9.5 cm).

Meiacanthus oualanensis
Canary Fang Blenny
Max. Length: 4.3 in. (11 cm).

Meiacanthus smithi
Smith's Fang Blenny
Max. Length: 3.1 in. (8 cm).

Meiacanthus tongaensis
Tonga Fang Blenny
Max. Length: 3.1 in. (8 cm).

Panamic Fang Blenny (*Ophioblennius steindachneri*): a large, aggressive blenny that is very territorial and must be kept with fishes at least twice its own length.

Biglipped Blennies (Genus *Ophioblennius*)

The members of this genus have a blunt head, cirri over the eyes, on the nape and near the nostrils, and large lips. They have large, nasty fangs far back in the lower jaw that are are used in territorial defense. To feed, they use their expandable jaws to rasp algae and micro-invertebrates off hard substrates. Food-habit studies have shown that they feed almost entirely on algae (including green filamentous algae, blue-green algae [cyanobacteria] and diatoms) and detritus. They get relatively large and are highly territorial, excluding members of their own kind as well as other species that feed on algae or try to enter their preferred hiding places. In the aquarium, they will chase or dash out to nip other fishes that enter their territory. In some cases, they may even kill smaller fishes. Keep this fish with tankmates that are at least twice its length. Even then, the blennies may bite them. Larger individuals are usually more aggressive than smaller specimens. Keep only one per tank, unless you have a larger aquarium and you can find a male-female pair.

Seaweed Blenny (*Parablennius marmoreus*): the ornate head adornment makes this blenny an interesting addition to the smaller reef tank.

Seaweed Blennies (Genus *Parablennius*)

Only one member in this genus regularly makes it into the aquarium trade—the Seaweed Blenny (*Parablennius marmoreus*). This blenny feeds mainly on algae and detritus, although sponges, tunicates, bryozoans, tiny serpent stars, worms, and hydroids have also been taken from their stomachs (these may be ingested incidentally). While it does not usually feed on corals, it may occasionally nip at them. Like most blennies, it needs a good source of plant material if is going to thrive in captivity. A tank with microalgae, as well as supplementary feeding with some algae-impregnated frozen foods, is imperative. Also, like most of the blennies, this species can be rather aggressive toward other herbivores. Only one individual should be kept per small tank, and care should be taken when keeping it with other blennies. If you have a very large tank, aggression problems will be minimal. The Seaweed Blenny attains a maximum length of 4.7 in. (12 cm).

Jeweled Blenny (*Salarias fasciatus*): a commonly employed grazer that leaves telltale "kiss marks" when rasping algae from the inside panes of the aquarium.

Lawnmower Blennies (Genus *Salarias*)

Fishes in this genus are usually not dangerous to corals or clams, but an occasional individual may nip at a stony coral. These blennies will help control filamentous algae, rasping hard substrates with their comblike teeth. They feed on filamentous algae, diatoms, foraminiferans, tiny crustaceans, detritus, and sand. They occasionally consume fish eggs, sponges, and small snails. Their feeding activities often stir up sediment, putting detritus into suspension where it can be removed by mechanical filters. Keep only one *Salarias* species in a smaller tank. In a larger tank, you can house a pair (or possibly more, depending on the aquarium size). While territorial disputes may occur, if there is enough space the combatants can avoid one another. They occasionally attack other fishes. I have had them bite seahorses and try to nip the fins of herbivores. They will consume frozen herbivore foods and may even eat flake food.

Urchin Clingfish (*Diademichthys lineatus*): this unusual clingfish is hardy, though secretive, and one of the most interesting in its genus for the reef aquarium.

Clingfishes (Family Gobiesocidae)

These fishes are usually tadpole-shaped, with a large head, a body that tapers toward the tail, and modified pelvic fins that form a suction disc. The disc allows them to cling to hard bottoms in surgy areas. Several species associate with crinoids or among the spines of sea urchins. Most feed on small benthic invertebrates (including barnacles, limpets, and small crustaceans), although some of the larger species are known to ambush small fishes that swim past (these aggressive species are rare in the aquarium trade). Although few clingfishes are available to aquarists, those that do enter the market are very durable, although often secretive. The most desirable member of the family is the Urchin Clingfish (*Diademichthys lineatus*), which associates with sea urchins or branching small-polyped stony corals. It will not harm corals, but will feed on urchin tube feet, pedicellariae and sphaeridia. Adults have also been observed picking at the mantles of *Tridacna crocea*. Feed it Cyclop-eeze and/or live, gut-packed brine shrimp, two or three times a day.

Green Mandarin Dragonet (*Synchiropus splendidus*) male: a spectacular fish, but one with a specialized diet that makes it a challenge to keep.

Dragonets (Family Callionymidae)

Dragonets are eyecatching beauties that can be ideal for the reef aquarium if you are willing to make the sacrifices necessary to keep them. They will not harm ornamental invertebrates and need to be provided with well-established live substrates to provide the tiny live prey items they require. If you are keeping a sand-dwelling dragonet, make sure you devote some of the aquarium to an open sand bottom. This provides them with a normal foraging ground, as well as substrate in which to bury. These fishes are usually ignored by all but the most aggressive fish tankmates. They may help control brown flatworms that can grow to epidemic proportions in a reef tank (although if you have a tank full of flatworms, you won't be able to eliminate them by adding a single dragonet or even a small group).

Dragonets should not be kept with potent sea anemones, as these predatory invertebrates often eat them. The elephant ear anemone, large crabs, and mantis shrimps are also dragonet predators. Many dragonets species are quite small and thus can be kept in

Moyer's Dragonet (*Synchiropus moyeri*) male: when males display, they erect their oversized dorsal fins. Note the pair of blue ocelli, or eyespots, on this specimen.

smaller tanks. A 10- or 20-gallon tank is suitable for most. A few larger, more active species, like the Finger Dragonet, should be kept in tanks of at least 30 gallons (114 L).

Dragonets have a sharp spine on each "cheek." While these spines may help it avoid becoming the meal of a predatory fish, they also make the fish susceptible to becoming entangled in a fish net. When removing these fishes from an aquarium, it is best to herd them into a plastic specimen container.

Some dragonets have noxious body slime. This may be protective in the aquarium, as they sometimes attract but rarely succumb to common skin parasites. Because these fishes lack scales, the aquarist should not treat them with copper medications or organophosphates (neither of which would be used in the reef aquarium in any case). While keeping a heterosexual pair in the same aquarium is possible, keeping same-sex conspecifics together can be problematic. Most of the dragonets are sexually dimorphic, with males attaining larger sizes than females. The masculine sex typically has a larger first dorsal fin or longer dorsal, anal, and caudal fins than the females. Males can also be more colorful than females.

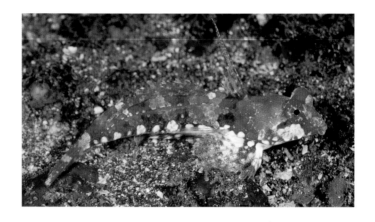

Redblotched Dragonet (*Synchiropus rubrovinctus*) male: many members of the genus live on sand substrate and some bury within it.

As noted above, the biggest dragonet husbandry challenge is feeding. They feed on small invertebrates (e.g., foraminiferans, worms, copepods, amphipods) that live on the seafloor. In the aquarium, they will also eat live and frozen brine shrimp, mysid shrimp, and myriad tiny critters found on healthy live rock or in live sand. It is always best to keep them in an aquarium with live substrates to ensure that they get enough to eat. To maintain a high enough density of dragonet foods, avoid housing them with any other—or many other (depending on the size of your tank)—tank-mates with a similar diet. To boost the production of appropriate foods, replace some substrate on occasion.

You can also "farm" your own dragonet food in a separate aquarium. Some suppliers sell mysid shrimp, amphipods, and other small bottom-associated crustaceans that dragonets love. You can culture these in a smaller tank, then occasionally introduce them to your display aquarium or add a productive refugium to your system where small invertebrates can breed. You can also target-feed your dragonet by using a turkey baster or pipette to introduce food to the area in which the fish hangs out.

Dactylopus dactylopus (Bennett, 1837)
Finger Dragonet

Maximum Length: 7.1 in. (18 cm).
Range: Eastern Indian Ocean and Western Pacific.
Minimum Aquarium Size: 30 gal. (114 L).
Foods & Feeding: Keep in a tank with a bed of well-established live sand, possibly with an attached refugium. It will also eat black worms, live brine shrimp, and mysid shrimp. Target feeding is often needed to ensure it gets enough to eat. Use a turkey baster or pipette to direct food toward the fish. Feed three times per day in a tank without live sand.
Aquarium Suitability/Reef Compatibility:
Aquarium Notes: This larger, active dragonet will need to be kept in a smaller reef aquarium with little live rock or a larger reef with plenty of open sand bottom. When threatened or at night, it will partially bury in the sand. To ensure success with this fish, try to avoid tankmates that will gobble up all the appropriate food before the dragonet gets an opportunity to feed. Keep only one per tank and do not house with other small sand-dwelling dragonets. The high dorsal fin is a likely target of fin-nippers.

Synchiropus ocellatus (Pallas, 1770)
Ocellated Dragonet (Scooter Dragonet)

Maximum Length: 2.4 in. (6 cm).
Range: Eastern Indian Ocean and Western Pacific.
Minimum Aquarium Size: 20 gal. (76 L).
Foods & Feeding: Keep in a tank with a bed of well-established live sand, possibly with an attached refugium. It will also eat black worms, live brine shrimp, and mysid shrimp. Target feeding is often needed to ensure it gets enough to eat. Feed three times per day in a tank without live sand.
Aquarium Suitability/Reef Compatibility:
Aquarium Notes: This interesting little dragonet is usually indifferent toward other fishes, although it may be pestered by more pugnacious fishes. It may quarrel with members of its own kind in a small tank, but if your tank is large enough (has enough surface area) more than one male can be kept, although keeping a male with one or more females is more prudent. All should be introduced simultaneously. Like other members of the family, this species has a hard time competing for food with more vigorous eaters. It is sexually dimorphic, with males getting larger than females and having a larger first dorsal fin.

Synchiropus picturatus (Peters, 1876)
Spotted Mandarin (Psychedelic Mandarin)

Maximum Length: 2.8 in. (7 cm).
Range: Western Pacific.
Minimum Aquarium Size: 75 gal. (285 L) or larger.
Foods & Feeding: Keep in a tank with live rock, possibly with an attached refugium. This species will do better in a tank that contains abundant filamentous algae, which usually harbors rich crustacean fauna. It will also eat black worms, live brine shrimp, and mysid shrimp. Target feeding is often needed to ensure it gets enough to eat. Feed three times per day in a tank without live rock.
Aquarium Suitability/Reef Compatibility:
Aquarium Notes: This distinctive mandarin is a resident of tidal creeks, mangrove swamps, and lagoon patch reefs. Like other dragonets, it usually ignores its tankmates unless they are closely related. Males will fight each other and may attack the Green Mandarin (*Synchiropus splendidus,* page 320). If you want to keep more than one in the same tank, or want to house it with the Green Mandarin, keep only one male and one or more females. Females can also be kept together. It may be picked on by some tankmates, but it exudes a noxious slime that dissuades the attack of many fishes.

Synchiropus splendidus (Herre, 1927)
Green Mandarin (Striped Mandarin)

Maximum Length: 3.1 in. (8 cm).
Range: Western Pacific.
Minimum Aquarium Size: 75 gal. (285 L) or larger.
Foods & Feeding: Keep in a tank with live rock, possibly with an attached refugium. It will do better in a tank that contain lots of filamentous algae, which usually harbors rich crustacean fauna. It will also eat black worms, live brine shrimp, and mysid shrimp. Target feeding is often needed to ensure it gets enough to eat. Feed three times per day in a tank without live rock.
Aquarium Suitability/Reef Compatibility:
Aquarium Notes: This is a great reef aquarium species. It is not a threat to invertebrates and is highly disease-resistant. It has even been known to spawn in reef aquariums. The mandarin will ignore other fish species, but males will attack and bite male conspecifics. (Males are easily recognized by the presence of long dorsal spines.) Choose your fish carefully; bringing a skinny Green Mandarin back to good health is usually an uphill battle. Be sure to note feeding advice on page 316. It always does best in well-established reef tanks without aggressive feeding competition.

Synchiropus stellatus Smith, 1963
Starry Dragonet

Maximum Length: 2.4 in. (6 cm).
Range: Indo-Pacific.
Minimum Aquarium Size: 20 gal. (76 L).
Foods & Feeding: Keep in a tank with live sand, possibly with an attached refugium. It will also eat black worms, live brine shrimp, and mysid shrimp. Target feeding is often needed to ensure it gets enough to eat. Feed three times per day in a tank without live sand.
Aquarium Suitability/Reef Compatibility:
Aquarium Notes: This charming little dragonet is very meticulous when locating and handling its prey. It will typically sit and inspect the food item for a few seconds before ingesting it, allowing more voracious feeders, like dottyback, wrasses, goatfishes, butterflyfishes, and angelfishes, to snatch it right out from under its nose. A male can be housed with one or more females in a larger tank, but males are prone to fighting. It may also be picked on by larger congeners. It has long been known that the best way to keep dragonets healthy is to keep them in a thriving reef tank where they can graze on tiny live prey in the sand and on the live rock.

Rainford's Goby (*Amblygobius rainfordi*): this handsome goby and its congeners will do best if filamentous algae is present in the aquarium.

Hover Gobies (Genus *Amblygobius*)

Hover gobies are wonderful reef aquarium fishes—and accurately named: they spend much of their time hovering in the water column, alert to feeding opportunities and predators. Most are omnivorous, feeding on algae and tiny invertebrates. Some sift sand and debris, filtering out small invertebrates from the sediment. They do much better in captivity when housed in an established tank with some growth of filamentous algae. If the tank does not support an algal crop, they tend to become emaciated. It is possible to get these fishes to accept introduced fare, like vitamin-enriched live and frozen brine shrimp, mysid shrimp, and prepared foods for herbivores. With the exception of closely related species, the *Amblygobius* species are rarely aggressively toward fish tankmates. It is best to keep only one individual of a species per tank, but you may be able to get them to pair up and spawn if your tank is large enough. They do best if housed with peaceful species. They will jump out of open aquariums if they are harassed by aggressive tankmates or if startled when the lights are turned off.

Amblygobius decussatus (Bleeker, 1855)
Crosshatch Goby

Maximum Length: 3.1 in. (8 cm).
Range: Western Pacific.
Minimum Aquarium Size: 10 gal. (38 L).
Foods & Feeding: Feed meaty foods, like vitamin-enriched live and frozen brine shrimp and mysid shrimp, as well as prepared foods for herbivores. It eats large quantities of algae in the wild, and will do better if provided with similar fare in the aquarium. If placed in a tank without algae, live sand, or live rock, feed at least twice a day. If natural foods are present, feed every other day.
Aquarium Suitability/Reef Compatibility:
Aquarium Notes: This attractive goby is ideal for most reef aquariums. Like others in the genus, it may benefit from having access to some filamentous green or red algae. Do not keep it with conspecifics or with similar congeners, although it will typically ignore unrelated gobies and other benthic fishes. It is more likely to be picked on by belligerent tankmates. It is a rather delicate substrate sifter and is thus less likely than its larger relatives to inadvertently bury corals that are located near the bottom of the tank. This species is a capable jumper.

Amblygobius phalaena (Valenciennes, 1837)
Banded Goby

Maximum Length: 5.9 in. (15 cm).
Range: Eastern Indo-Pacific.
Minimum Aquarium Size: 20 gal. (76 L).
Foods & Feeding: Feed meaty foods, like vitamin-enriched live and frozen brine shrimp and mysid shrimp, as well as prepared foods for herbivores. It eats large quantities of algae in the wild, and will do better if provided with similar fare in the aquarium. If placed in a tank without algae, live sand, or live rock, feed at least twice a day. If natural foods are present, feed every other day.
Aquarium Suitability/Reef Compatibility:
Aquarium Notes: This handsome fish will help keep the upper layers of live sand stirred. It spends more time sifting and penetrates deeper into the sand bed than smaller congeners. Although it is usually not a threat to sessile invertebrates, I did have one that pulled zoanthids off a rock. It will also eat noxious flatworms. It tends to be hardier than *A. rainfordi* (page 325). It is rarely quarrelsome with heterospecifics, but will fight with members of its own species. Do not keep it with aggressive species that stay on or near the substrate. If the tank is large enough, it is usually ignored by its tankmates.

Amblygobius rainfordi (Whitley, 1940)
Rainford's Goby (Old Glory, Court Jester Goby)

Maximum Length: 2.6 in. (6.5 cm).
Range: Western and Central Pacific.
Minimum Aquarium Size: 20 gal. (76 L).
Foods & Feeding: Feed small crustaceans, like vitamin-enriched live and frozen brine shrimp and mysid shrimp, as well as prepared foods for herbivores. It will typically do best in a tank with some filamentous algae and live rock. If placed in a tank without algae, feed at least twice a day. If lots of algae is present, feed every other day.
Aquarium Suitability/Reef Compatibility:
Aquarium Notes: A favorite with many reef aquarists, this attractive little fish will not harm sessile invertebrates, and it really thrives if kept in a tank with filamentous algae. If the tank does not support an algal crop, this fish usually becomes emaciated. With the exception of closely related species, it is rarely aggressively toward fish tankmates. Juveniles can be kept together in a medium-sized tank if introduced together, but adults often quarrel. Individuals are often erroneously sold as mated pairs. It is best to keep only one per tank. It should be kept with peaceful species—avoid placing it in a tank with dottybacks, hawkfishes, larger damselfishes, and other bullies.

Amblygobius bynoensis
Freckled Goby
Max. Length: 3.1 in. (8 cm).

Amblygobius esakiae
Snoutspot Goby
Max. Length: 2.6 in. (6.5 cm).

Amblygobius hectori
Yellowstripe Goby, Hector's Goby
Max. Length: 2.2 in. (5.5 cm).

Amblygobius nocturnus
Nocturn Goby
Max. Length: 2.4 in. (6 cm).

Amblygobius semicinctus
Halfbanded Goby
Max. Length: 5.5 in. (14 cm).

Amblygobius sphynx
Sphinx Goby
Max. Length: 7.1 in. (18 cm).

Yellow Clown Goby (*Gobiodon okinawae*): fascinating small fishes that shelter and spawn amongst the protective branches of stony coral colonies.

Clown or Coral Gobies
(Genera *Gobiodon* & *Paragobiodon*)

These beguiling, diminutive fishes usually nestle within branching small-polyped stony corals. They feed on tiny crustaceans, protozoa, coral mucus, and tissue. They may nip at stony corals, but they do not cause irreparable damage, and their movements among the coral branches may help circulate fresh seawater in stagnant portions of the colony. Although rarely aggressive toward unrelated fishes, they may fight with their own kind and congeners. If there is enough habitat, they will disperse or form male-female pairs. If suitable hiding places are available, they are usually ignored by aggressive tankmates. Predatory fishes may feed on them, although they are reported to exude a noxious slime. They are often the first fishes to get ich (*Cryptocaryon*), which shows up as white pimples on the body and fins. Feed them Cyclop-eeze, finely shaved table shrimp, and frozen food for carnivores once a day. These species will spawn in captivity, laying their demersal eggs among coral branches. The eggs are then guarded by the male.

Gobiodon acicularis
Needlespine Coral Goby
Max. Length: 1.5 in. (3.8 cm).

Gobiodon citrinus
Citron Clown Goby
Max. Length: 2.2 in. (5.6 cm).

Gobiodon histrio
Green, Broadbanded Clown Goby
Max. Length: 1.4 in. (3.6 cm).

Gobiodon quinquestrigatus
Fivelined Goby
Max. Length: 1.4 in. (3.6 cm).

Paragobiodon lacunicolus
Blackfin Coral Goby, Panda Coral Goby
Max. Length: 1 in. (2.5 cm).

Paragobiodon xanthosomus
Yellowgreen Coral Goby
Max. Length: 1.6 in. (4.1 cm).

Sharknose Goby (*Gobiosoma evelynae*) cleaning Yellow Goatfish (*Mulloidichthys martinicus*): the tiny goby (arrow) cleans parasites above the client's eye.

Cleaner Gobies (Genus *Gobiosoma*)

This genus contains smaller species perfect for nano-reef systems. Some clean other fishes; others lead secretive lives in sponge lumens. These gobies are not totally dependent on their cleaning behaviors, readily accepting other foods in captivity. They are great for the reef tank, although they may nip at tridacnid clam mantles on rare occasion. They can be housed with larger predators, although if the predators are not fed often enough, they may eat the gobies. Always add them to the tank *before* the predatory species. Although rarely aggressive toward other fishes, cleaner gobies may fight with conspecifics or congeners (especially if space is limited). If a male and female pair up, they often become more aggressive toward conspecifics. It is not uncommon for them to spawn in the aquarium. In most cases, the eggs are laid in a crevice or empty shell, and both parents defend the eggs. Feed them a varied diet that includes Cyclop-eeze, frozen mysid shrimp, finely shaved table shrimp, and frozen food for carnivores. In a reef tank, they can be fed once a day, more often in new or sparsely aquascaped aquariums.

Gobiosoma multifasciatum
Greenbanded Goby
Max. Length: 1.5 in. (3.8 cm).

Gobiosoma evelynae
Sharknose Goby
Max. Length: 1.6 in. (4 cm).

Gobiosoma randalli
Yellownose Goby
Max. Length: 1.5 in. (3.8 cm).

Gobiosoma oceanops
Neon Goby
Max. Length: 2 in. (5 cm).

Gobiosoma punticulatus
Redhead Goby
Max. Length: 1.8 in. (4.6 cm).

Gobiosoma xanthiprora
Yellowprow Goby
Max. Length: 1.6 in. (4 cm).

Archfin Shrimp Goby (*Amblyeleotris arcupinna*): a number of goby species form mutualistic partnerships with snapping shrimps.

The Shrimp Gobies

Shrimp gobies are fascinating to watch in their classic symbiotic relationship with snapping shrimps. The shrimp's burrow provides a sanctuary for the otherwise vulnerable goby, while the goby acts as a "seeing-eye" fish for the relatively poor-sighted shrimp. Because both members benefit, the symbiosis is termed mutualistic. (Some crustacean experts maintain that these shrimps actually see quite well, but their visual acuity is not as good as that of the goby). As the shrimp keeps house or feeds just outside the burrow, the goby stays near the burrow's entrance and stands guard (it also feeds and interacts with conspecifics at this time). The crustacean moves freely in and out of its refuge, but when it leaves the burrow, it keeps in contact with the vigilant goby by placing one of its antennae on the fish. When a predatory fish approaches, the goby rapidly flicks its tail, warning the shrimp of impending danger. If the goby flicks its tail once, the shrimp may not respond, but if the goby executes a series of flicks, the shrimp retreats. If the predator comes within a critical distance, the goby will also dart into its hiding place.

Speckleback Shrimp Goby (*Amblyeleotris japonica*) and Filamented Dartfish (*Ptereleotris hanae*). Dartfishes sometimes join shrimp-goby partners.

Banded Shrimp Gobies (Genus *Amblyeleotris*)

The genus *Amblyeleotris* contains at least 25 species, a number of which show up in aquarium stores labeled as "banded watchman gobies." These gobies are great reef tank residents and easy to keep. Their relatively small sizes and less active lifestyles mean you can keep them in aquariums as small as 10 gallons (38 L). One prerequisite is a cover for the tank, to prevent outbound leaping. They and their shrimp partners do best in a tank with a deep sand substrate. Because these shrimp burrow, be sure to your rockwork rests firmly on the bottom panel of the aquarium with the sand substrate filling in around the rock; if rock is placed on top of the substrate, burrowing shrimp can cause catastrophic collapses of the aquascape. To facilitate burrow construction, mix some pieces of coral rubble, small pieces of live rock, and/or medium-sized shells with the sand. Both the gobies and their shrimp associates will feed on a wide variety of fresh, frozen, and flake foods.

Amblyeleotris fasciata (Polunin & Lubbock, 1977)
Wheeler's Shrimp Goby

Maximum Length: 3.1 in. (7.9 cm).
Range: Indonesia and Philippines.
Minimum Aquarium Size: 10 gal. (38 L).
Foods & Feeding: Meaty foods, including finely shredded frozen seafood, mysid shrimp, frozen preparations, pigment-enriched flake food, and Cyclop-eeze. Feed at least once a day or preferably twice a day.
Aquarium Suitability/Reef Compatibility:
Aquarium Notes: This is one of the more colorful members of the genus and regularly shows up in aquarium stores. It is a hardy aquarium fish, but will sometimes jump out of a tank if disturbed. It is rarely aggressive, and I have even had a male and female pair up in small aquariums. The color of this species varies depending on the color of the substrate where it is found. Those living on lighter sand have bright red bands on the body, while those found on dark sand have burgundy-colored bands. (Taxonomic note: this species was formerly known as *Amblyeleotris wheeleri*. The species formerly known as *A. fasciata* is now referred to as *A. katherine*.)

Amblyeleotris guttata (Fowler, 1938)
Orangespotted Shrimp Goby

Maximum Length: 3.5 in. (8.9 cm).
Range: Western Pacific.
Minimum Aquarium Size: 10 gal. (38 L).
Foods & Feeding: Meaty foods, including finely shredded frozen seafood, mysid shrimp, frozen preparations, pigment-enriched flake food, and Cyclop-eeze. Feed at least once or preferably twice a day.
Aquarium Suitability/Reef Compatibility:
Aquarium Notes: This is one of the most attractive shrimp goby species and is relatively common in the marine fish trade. As with other members of this genus, it is well-suited for aquarium life. It is not aggressive, except possibly toward conspecifics (this applies particularly to males). Keep only one per tank, unless you have a male-female pair or the aquarium is large (100 gallons or more). This species bounces up and down with its fins spread and mouth open wide when displaying. It is usually found on sand or rubble patches of the reef face. If proper hiding places are not available and/or if it is harassed by tankmates, it will jump out of an uncovered tank. When possible, purchase a goby-shrimp duo collected and imported as a symbiotic unit.

Amblyeleotris latifasciata Polunin & Lubbock, 1979
Spottail Shrimp Goby (Metallic Shrimp Goby)

Maximum Length: 6.3 in. (16 cm).
Range: Western Pacific.
Minimum Aquarium Size: 15 gal. (57 L).
Foods & Feeding: Meaty foods, including finely shredded frozen seafood, mysid shrimp, frozen preparations, pigment-enriched flake food, and Cyclop-eeze. Feed at least once a day or preferably twice a day.
Aquarium Suitability/Reef Compatibility:
Aquarium Notes: This is a great reef aquarium fish, beautiful and unusual. It can be aggressive toward related species, especially in a small tank that lacks hiding places. It is also one of the larger members of the genus. A larger nano-reef may suffice, but it will need plenty of open sand/rubble bottom. Individuals that occur on light sand bottoms are pale in color, while those that occur on black sand are dark in color with bright highlights. If possible, purchase the fish with its snapping shrimp partner. This species will pair with the common Tiger Snapping Shrimp (*Alpheus bellulus*).

Amblyeleotris randalli Hoese & Steene, 1978
Randall's Shrimp Goby

Maximum Length: 3.5 in. (8.9 cm).
Range: Western Pacific.
Minimum Aquarium Size: 10 gal. (38 L).
Foods & Feeding: Meaty foods, including finely shredded frozen seafood, mysid shrimp, frozen preparations, pigment-enriched flake food and Cyclop-eeze. Feed at least once a day; twice daily is preferable.
Aquarium Suitability/Reef Compatibility:
Aquarium Notes: This spectacular goby is a great reef tank fish. It can be kept with other shrimp gobies (they may even share a burrow with a heterospecific). They can also be kept with members of their own kind, but individuals will occasionally quarrel. Combative individuals will approach each other with all their fins spread, their mouths open and their gills flared. If aggression escalates, they will bite each other's fins, especially the dorsal. Sometimes this species will not eat for several days after it is introduced to its new home, but it rarely refuses food for long. The large dorsal fin is occasionally a target for species that like to nip fins or remove parasites.

Amblyeleotris diagonalis
Diagonal Shrimp Goby
Max. Length: 3.1 in. (8 cm).

Amblyeleotris periophthalma
Broadbanded Shrimp Goby
Max. Length: 3.1 in. (8 cm).

Amblyeleotris steinitzi
Steinitz' Shrimp Goby
Max. Length: 3.1 in. (8 cm).

Amblyeleotris yanoi
Yano's Shrimp Goby
Max. Length: 5.1 in. (13 cm).

Amblyeleotris sp.
Eyebrow Shrimp Goby
Max. Length: 4.3 in. (11 cm).

Amblyeleotris sp.
Fivebar Shrimp Goby
Max. Length: 2.5 in. (6.4 cm).

Ventralbarred Shrimp Goby (*Cryptocentrus* sp.): more robust than the *Amblyeleotris* species, these gobies pose more of a threat to fancy shrimps.

Stocky Shrimp Gobies (Genus *Cryptocentrus*)

The gobies in this genus are stockier in build and have more capacious mouths than the *Amblyeleotris* species. As a result, larger *Cryptocentrus* species are potentially dangerous to ornamental shrimps. They are reported to inhabit more turbid, silty areas than the *Amblyeleotris* species. The *Cryptocentrus* species also differ in their aquarium behavior. They tend to be more aggressive toward other gobies and smaller bottom-dwelling fishes. If you keep more than one member of this genus in the same aquarium, add them simultaneously or introduce the smaller individual first.

An aquarium with a larger surface area (more usable living space) with lots of hiding places will increase your likelihood of success in keeping these fishes. When initially introduced to the aquarium, it is not unusual for these gobies to hide whenever you enter the room. But they will gradually become accustomed to your presence and allow you to observe them at close range. Because these gobies are typically found in relatively shallow water, they will feel right at home in brightly lit reef aquariums.

Cryptocentrus cinctus (Herre, 1936)
Yellow Shrimp Goby

Maximum Length: 2.8 in. (7.1 cm).
Range: Indo-Pacific.
Minimum Aquarium Size: 10 gal. (38 L).
Foods & Feeding: Meaty foods, including finely shredded frozen seafood, mysid shrimp, frozen preparations, pigment-enriched flake food, and Cyclop-eeze. Feed at least once a day or preferably twice a day.
Aquarium Suitability/Reef Compatibility:
Aquarium Notes: This is one of the most popular members of the shrimp goby group. It comes in several colors, including yellow, light brown, or white overall; all have blue spots on the head, dorsal fin, and flanks (it often has four or five dusky body bars). It readily adapts to aquarium living and has even spawned in reef aquariums. Placing two individuals together in the same tank can be risky unless you can find a male-female pair. This species will attack smaller shrimp gobies, especially in smaller aquariums. If possible, purchase a specimen collected with its symbiotic shrimp partner. It will readily bond with the Tiger Snapping Shrimp (*Alpheus bellulus*).

Cryptocentrus leptocephalus Bleeker, 1876
Pinkspotted Shrimp Goby (Singapore Shrimp Goby)

Maximum Length: 5.9 in. (15 cm).
Range: Eastern Indian Ocean and Western Pacific.
Minimum Aquarium Size: 20 gal. (76 L).
Foods & Feeding: Meaty foods, including finely shredded frozen seafood, mysid shrimp, frozen preparations, pigment-enriched flake food, and Cyclop-eeze. Feed at least once a day or preferably twice a day.
Aquarium Suitability/Reef Compatibility:
Aquarium Notes: This is one of the larger and more aggressive shrimp gobies. Adults will often attack other gobies and even smaller, unrelated fishes like assessors and wrasses. It is more likely to pose a behavioral problem if space is limited and if introduced to the tank first. Aggression usually takes the form of jaw gaping and lateral displays, but can escalate to biting and physical harm to the intruding fish. Conspecifics will usually fight as well if they are not a male-female pair. When housing more than one specimen of undetermined sex, the aquarium should be large (135 gal. [513 L]or more). Adults are a threat to certain ornamental shrimps (even cleaner shrimps [*Lysmata* spp.]).

Cryptocentrus pavoninoides Bleeker, 1849
Blackfinned Shrimp Goby

Maximum Length: 5.1 in. (13 in.).
Range: Western Pacific.
Minimum Aquarium Size: 20 gal. (76 L).
Foods & Feeding: Meaty foods, including finely shredded frozen seafood, mysid shrimp, frozen preparations, pigment-enriched flake food, and Cyclop-eeze. Feed at least once a day or preferably twice a day.
Aquarium Suitability/Reef Compatibility:
Aquarium Notes: This handsome species is a wonderful aquarium fish with two color forms. One is a yellowish orange phase with permanent bars, a few spots on the body, numerous spots on the head, and bold, orange markings on the median fins. The other is a brown to olive-drab color that displays bars when threatened or behaving aggressively, has blue spots on the body and few on the head. Even though it is large, it seems to be a minimal threat to smaller fish tankmates, even other gobies. (It may eat small ornamental shrimps.) I kept an adult individual in a large reef aquarium with other shrimp gobies. They would occasionally display at each other, but that was the extent of their aggression.

Cryptocentrus sp.

Lightbanded Shrimp Goby (Bluespotted Shrimp Goby)

Maximum Length: 3.1 in. (7.9 cm).

Range: Eastern Indian Ocean and Western Pacific.

Minimum Aquarium Size: 10 gal. (38 L).

Foods & Feeding: Meaty foods, including finely shredded frozen seafood, mysid shrimp, frozen preparations, pigment-enriched flake food, and Cyclop-eeze. Feed at least once a day or preferably twice a day.

Aquarium Suitability/Reef Compatibility:

Aquarium Notes: This undescribed goby is usually sold with a large, grayish green snapping shrimp. They make an interesting couple, as the crustacean is usually larger than the goby. Because the shrimp partner is so large, it is capable of doing some major excavating and can cause unstable aquarium rockwork to cave in. The goby itself is a durable little fish. Because it is smaller, it is prone to being picked on by more aggressive members of the clan. Initially, it will be quite shy, hiding when the aquarist approaches until it is fully acclimated.

Cryptocentrus fasciatus
Barred Shrimp Goby
Max. Length: 3.5 in. (9 cm).

Cryptocentrus fasciatus (variant)
Barred Shrimp Goby
Max. Length: 3.5 in. (9 cm).

Cryptocentrus inexplicatus
Inexplicable Shrimp Goby
Max. Length: 3.1 in. (8 cm).

Cryptocentrus leucostictus
Saddled Shrimp Goby
Max. Length: 4.3 in. (11 cm).

Cryptocentrus strigilliceps
Target Shrimp Goby
Max. Length: 2.8 in. (7.1 cm).

Cryptocentrus sp. (variant)
Ventralbarred Shrimp Goby
Max. Length: 4.3 in. (11 cm).

Tangaroa Shrimp Goby (*Ctenogobiops tangaroai*): small but with a prominent dorsal spike, members of this genus make excellent additions to small reef tanks.

Speckled Shrimp Gobies
(Genus *Ctenogobiops*)

Members of the genus *Ctenogobiops* are smaller gobies, many of them very similar in appearance, and all are species that make great additions to the small, passive community tank. These fishes are found in the wild on silty sand, coarse sand, or mixed sand/rubble bottoms on or near coral reefs. The speckled shrimp gobies are not a threat to any invertebrates and will not bother fish tankmates, except for other members in their own genus.

The speckled shrimp gobies can be kept in pairs, although members of the same sex will fight if they are housed in a smaller tank. The tank should be large enough so that pairs, or individuals of the same sex, are able to have at least 16 in. (41 cm) between their burrows.

Magnificent Shrimp Goby (*Flabelligobius* sp.): true to its name, this species hoists a stunning dorsal fin to alarm would-be predators or to attract a mate.

Magnificent Shrimp Gobies
(Genus *Flabelligobius*)

This genus contains one described and possibly one undescribed species. Like other shrimp gobies, any *Flabelligobius* is an amazing addition to the reef aquarium. They are especially well-suited to the nano-reef tank and are harmless to virtually all ornamental invertebrates. When first added to a tank, they will be quite shy. If aggressive fishes are present, you may never see them because they will hide constantly. They are smaller, more docile gobies that are likely to be picked on by *Amblyeleotris* and *Cryptocentrus* species. If you keep them with potential bullies, the tank must be large and the *Flabelligobius* species added first. Their large dorsal fins may be picked at by fin-nippers (damsels, tobies).

Feed magnificent shrimp gobies a varied diet at least twice a day with foods like finely shredded frozen seafood, mysid shrimp, frozen preparations, and Cyclop-eeze (the last is a wonderful choice for these gobies). A productive refugium can provide a much-appreciated constant supply of tiny invertebrate prey items.

Whitecap Shrimp Goby (*Lotilia graciliosa*) is always found in the wild with a large snapping shrimp, *Alpheus rubromaculatus*, but may accept a captive surrogate.

Whitecap Shrimp Goby (Genus *Lotilia*)

The only species in this genus, the Whitecap Shrimp Goby (*Lotilia graciliosa*) is a handsome little fish that is always found with a large snapping shrimp known as *Alpheus rubromaculatus*. The partners usually live in sand patches on coral reefs and are not common anywhere. Because of the shrimp's size, it is likely to do some serious undermining of your tank's reef structure. Be sure your live rock base is on the bottom of the tank before the sand is added. This shrimp will also do a good job of suspending some of the detritus and sediment collecting in the sand bed (this may disturb an aquarist fanatic about a clean tank, but it actually allows the detritus to be filtered out of the tank). This shrimp goby is not likely to do as well in the aquarium without a shrimp. Although *A. rubromaculatus* is preferred, the fish may adopt a smaller shrimp species in captivity. This is one of the more docile shrimp gobies, so do not house it with aggressive tankmates. Offer it foods like finely shredded frozen seafood, mysid shrimp, frozen preparations, and Cyclop-eeze (an excellent choice). A productive refugium will aid in its feeding.

Smiling or Flagfin Shrimp Goby (*Mahidolia mystacina*) an attractive species that varies in color. Inset: color variant.

Smiling Shrimp Goby (Genus *Mahidolia*)

This genus contains one wide-ranging species (it occurs from East Africa to the Society Islands) known as the Smiling or Flagfin Shrimp Goby. Although not common in the aquarium trade, it is a welcome addition to the passive reef community tank that has a substantial portion of the bottom devoted to sand. It is a smaller species, attaining just 3.1 in. (7.8 cm).

Adults are often observed in pairs. When they display at each other, they throw their large first dorsal fin forward and open their capacious mouths extremely wide. Only one should be kept per tank, unless you can acquire a male-female pair. Even then, members of the opposite sex may fight in a tank without enough suitable shelter and/or space. Larger individuals may ingest smaller, more delicate shrimps. A reef tank of 10 gallons (38 L) or more will suffice for a solitary individual. It is yellow, brown, or black overall. Mature males have a dorsal fin that is higher than that of the females.

Yellownose Shrimp Goby (*Stonogobiops xanthorhinica*): species in this genus spend their time hovering above their burrows picking off passing plankters.

Longray Shrimp Gobies (Genus *Stonogobiops*)

The members of the genus *Stonogobiops* are some of the most attractive gobies available to marine aquarists and are a wonderful choice for the reef aquarium, even the nano-reef. Unlike the other shrimp gobies, which spend most of their time resting on the substrate, most of the longray (or highfin) shrimp gobies scull in the water column from 0.4 to 14 in. (1 to 36 cm) above their burrow entrances. Most of them associate with Randall's Snapping Shrimp (*Alpheus randalli*).

These fishes do not require much space (I have kept them in tanks as small as 5 gallons [19 L].) and are easier to observe in a less spacious aquarium. (As with many smaller fishes, they tend to disappear in large reef systems.) This goby is more likely to acclimate if kept without potentially bothersome fish tankmates, although in a tank without dither fish, it may take the *Stonogobiops* a little longer to overcome its initial shyness. Once it does, it will repay the sense of security and lack of competition with more aggressive feeders by staying out in the open where you can watch its behaviors.

Stonogobiops nematodes Hoese & Randall, 1982
Blackray Shrimp Goby (Highfin Shrimp Goby)

Maximum Length: 2 in. (5 cm).
Range: Indonesia and Philippines.
Minimum Aquarium Size: 10 gal. (38 L).
Foods & Feeding: Meaty foods, including finely shredded frozen seafood, mysid shrimp, frozen preparations, pigment-enriched flake food, and Cyclop-eeze. Feed at least once a day or preferably twice a day.
Aquarium Suitability/Reef Compatibility:
Aquarium Notes: This is a popular reef aquarium fish and more durable than its size suggests. At feeding time it will occasionally threaten food competitors by opening its mouth and charging toward them. Although good at aggressive bluffing, these diminutive fishes may not get enough to eat if kept with pugnacious or larger tankmates. They can be kept in pairs, but individuals of the same sex may fight (intrasexual aggression between males is highly likely). Fighting consists of mouth-gaping displays, chasing, and biting. It will sometimes bite an opponent and hold on tenaciously. If startled, it will occasionally bury under fine sand or jump out of an open tank.

Stonogobiops yasha Yoshino & Shimada, 2001
Whiteray Shrimp Goby (Yasha Goby)

Maximum Length: 2 in. (5 cm).
Range: Indo-west-Pacific.
Minimum Aquarium Size: 10 gal. (38 L).
Foods & Feeding: Meaty foods, including finely shredded frozen seafood, mysid shrimp, frozen preparations, pigment-enriched flake food, and Cyclop-eeze. Feed at least once a day or preferably twice a day.
Aquarium Suitability/Reef Compatibility:
Aquarium Notes: This is a wonderful, colorful fish for the reef aquarium, but careful acclimation is critical. It may hide for days or even weeks when first introduced. Do not keep it with aggressive tankmates like pugnacious damsels, dottybacks, larger jawfishes, hawkfishes, pygmy angels, aggressive wrasses, sand perches, and larger, scrappier shrimp gobies (e.g., *Cryptocentrus* spp.). This species may be evicted from its burrow by larger jawfishes, while substrate-disturbing species may collapse its shrimp partner's underground architecture. More than one can be housed in the same tank (75 gal. [285 L] or larger). New individuals are prone to jumping, so it is best if the tank is in an area with minimal human traffic.

Monster Shrimp Goby (*Tomiyamichthys oni*): great specimens for the nano-reef or species tank, these shy fishes provide an up-close view of symbiosis in action.

Tomiyama Gobies (Genus *Tomiyamichthys*)

Although not as stunningly pigmented as other shrimp gobies, these can be fascinating additions to a reef aquarium. There are approximately four species in this genus of shrimp-associated gobies, ranging in size from 2.4 to 3.9 in. (6 to 10 cm). Feed them twice a day with meaty foods, including finely shredded frozen seafood, mysid shrimp, frozen preparations, pigment-enriched flake food, and Cyclop-eeze. They tend not to be overly aggressive and can be shy when first placed in a tank. A single individual can be housed in a tank as small as 5 gallons, while it is prudent to keep more than one (unless a known heterosexual pair) in a tank of 30 gallons or more. They are slender-bodied and are not as likely to do harm to other gobies as some of their larger shrimp goby cousins (e.g., *Cryptocentrus* species). They may be picked on by other benthic fishes, like more aggressive gobies, hawkfishes, damsels, and sand perches. If startled, they will jump out of an open tank. Some sexual dimorphism has been reported—individuals that sport larger first dorsal fins are said to be males.

Orangespeckled Shrimp Goby (*Vanderhorstia* sp.): appealing to the collector of unusual fishes, these gobies need a sandy habitat and peaceful tankmates.

Slender Shrimp Gobies (Genus *Vanderhorstia*)

This is a group for the enthusiast who seeks small, delicate, uncommon fishes. This genus of elongated shrimp gobies contains 11 described species and a number of undescribed forms. While they do not regularly make it into the aquarium trade, they are a welcome addition to a reef tank that duplicates a reef/sand flat interface. They will not harm corals, and the smaller species are not a threat to crustaceans. The larger species, however, may eat delicate shrimps. They vary in size from 2.4 to 4.7 in. (6.1 to 12 cm). Do not house them with aggressive species, especially benthic bullies (e.g., hawkfishes, sand perches). They may be evicted from their burrows by heftier shrimp gobies (like larger *Amblyeleotris* or *Cryptocentrus* species). Keep only one *Vanderhorstia* species per tank, unless the aquarium is large (100 gallons or more). These fishes do not occur in colonies in the wild and usually maintain a greater inter-individual distance than many other shrimp gobies. They are great jumpers that will "go airborne" if frightened. Like other shrimp gobies, they do best in a tank with a deep sand substrate.

Vanderhorstia ambanoro
Ambanoro Shrimp Goby
Max. Length: 4.7 in. (12 cm).

Vanderhorstia flavilineata
Yellowlined Shrimp Goby
Max. Length: 1.6 in. (4.1 cm).

Vanderhorstia lanceolata
Lanceolate Shrimp Goby
Max. Length: 2.4 in. (6.1 cm).

Vanderhorstia sp.
Bluelined Shrimp Goby
Max. Length: 3 in. (7.6 cm).

Vanderhorstia sp.
Spangled Shrimp Goby (female)
Max. Length: 2.8 in. (7.1 cm).

Vanderhorstia sp.
Spangled Shrimp Goby (male)
Max. Length: 2.8 in. (7.1 cm).

Twinspot Goby (*Signigobius biocellatus*): the eyespots on the dorsal fin are thought to mimic a large predator and serve to scare away potential threats.

Twinspot Goby (Genus *Signigobius*)

This unique goby is a heartbreaker—interesting and attractive, but difficult to keep and often starving to death despite the aquarist's best efforts. A sand bed is an imperative if you want to try to succeed, and consider stocking its favorite prey, infaunal animals like worms, copepods, and amphipods. (It doesn't take long for this vigorous substrate sifter to decimate populations of infaunal invertebrates.) This fish will usually eat frozen mysid shrimp and black worms off the sand surface and will need to be fed four or five times a day (more if possible) to increase its chances of survival. If these foods never get to the bottom because of other aggressive feeders in the tank, this goby will starve. An adult Twinspot will disturb the upper 1 in. (2.5 cm) of sand when feeding. When constructing a burrow, it will dig even deeper into the sand bed. It is usually sold in pairs and is thought to do better when such pairs are kept together. It is essential to provide suitable hiding places. Lay a flat rock on the sand surface that this fish can dig under. Deworming may also facilitate its care. If pestered by tankmates, it will not survive.

Bella's Sleeper Goby (*Valenciennea bella*): a less commonly encountered member of an appealing but challenging genus that may suffer from parasites.

Sleeper Gobies (Genus *Valenciennea*)

This genus is comprised of 15 species, many of which get relatively large for a goby. They use their scooplike jaws to take mouthfuls of sediment and sift the debris through their gill-rakers. In doing so, they extract infaunal prey from the substrate, such as tiny crustaceans (usually under 1 mm in length) and occasionally minute snails, larval clams, shelled protozoans, and worms. Although they do not eat corals, they may bury them as they engage in their normal feeding activities. They have a dubious reputation when it comes to their husbandry: many individuals become emaciated and perish. This may result from intestinal worms. To deworm a new sleeper goby, use a commercial preparation or make your own medicated food: add Fenbendazole or Piperazine at a dosage of 250 mg per 100 grams of food and feed it for 7 to 10 days.

Sleeper gobies should be placed in a tank that contains a thick layer of live sand. A good portion of the aquarium bottom should also be free of rockwork. A productive refugium will ensure that sand-dwelling infaunal prey will continue to populate the display

Sixspot Sleeper Goby (*Valenciennea sexguttata*): as with all members of this genus, this is a fish needing frequent feeding and a fully covered aquarium top.

tank substrate. For substrate choices, stay away from dolomite, oyster shell, large grades of crushed coral, or puka shell as these may interfere with normal feeding or even damage the goby.

Your chances of success will increase if you feed these fishes often (at least four times a day) with nutritious foods like mysid shrimp, frozen preparations, and fresh seafood. Sleeper gobies often hide during the acclimation period. Do not disturb the gobies during this critical time. Chunks of rubble will be used by these gobies to help shore up their burrow openings. They also appreciate a flat rock, which they will use for a burrow ceiling.

The biggest cause of sleeper goby mortality is their skill at leaping out of the aquarium. If you do not have a cover, they will definitely jump out, but they can also leap through small holes in the cover. The best way to prevent this disaster is to use fiberglass screen and PVC or eggcrate material to make a full-fitting cover that will allow the necessary gas exchange but keep your fish in the tank.

Valenciennea puellaris (Tomiyama, 1956)
Orangespotted Sleeper Goby (Maiden Goby)

Maximum Length: 5.5 in. (14 cm).
Range: Indo-west-Pacific.
Minimum Aquarium Size: 55 gal. (209 L).
Foods & Feeding: Attempt to feed small crustaceans, like vitamin-enriched live and frozen brine shrimp and mysid shrimp, live black worms, as well as prepared foods for carnivores. Feed four times a day. Also feeds on organisms that occur in live sand.
Aquarium Suitability/Reef Compatibility:
Aquarium Notes: This fish does not eat sessile invertebrates, although it may bury corals that are set near the sand bed. It will eat smaller bristleworms and also desirable infaunal invertebrates. It is very effective at stirring the substrate bed, and its feeding activities take it deeper into the sand than gobies from most other genera. It is often difficult to keep, with many individuals starving to death. This species can be kept in pairs (the natural social unit of adults in the wild) if you can acquire a male and female. Otherwise, they may quarrel with one another and with others in the genus. A mated pair will spawn in burrows they construct. These burrows may topple unstable rockwork.

Valenciennea wardi (Playfair, 1867)
Ward's Sleeper Goby (Tiger Sleeper Goby)

Maximum Length: 5.1 in. (13 cm).
Range: Indo-west-Pacific.
Minimum Aquarium Size: 55 gal. (209 L).
Foods & Feeding: Attempt to feed small crustaceans, such as vitamin-enriched live and frozen brine shrimp and mysid shrimp as well as live black worms and prepared foods for carnivores. Feed several times a day.
Aquarium Suitability/Reef Compatibility:
Aquarium Notes: This attractive goby is often used to stir sand beds, although it is not as effective a sifter as *V. puellaris* (page 357). It tends to be easier to feed than some congeners. To increase your chances of success, keep it in a tank with a live sand bed, which will provide the tiny invertebrates that are its natural prey. It is rarely aggressive toward other bottom-dwelling fishes, with the possible exception of congeners. It can be kept in male-female pairs, but two or more males may quarrel. Juveniles have a spot on the dorsal fin and tail. This may serve to dissuade would-be predators by resembling the "face" of a piscivorous fish. Like all sleeper gobies, it is prone to jumping out of the aquarium.

Valenciennea helsdingeni
Twostripe Sleeper Goby
Max. Length: 6.3 in. (16 cm).

Valenciennea limicola
Muddy Sleeper Goby
Max. Length: 2.8 in. (7.1 cm).

Valenciennea longipinnis
Longfinned Sleeper Goby
Max. Length: 5.9 in. (15 cm).

Valenciennea muralis
Mural Sleeper Goby
Max. Length: 5.5 in. (14 cm).

Valenciennea randalli
Randall's Sleeper Goby
Max. Length: 3.5 in. (9 cm).

Valenciennea strigata
Yellowheaded Sleeper Goby
Max. Length: 7.1 in. (18 cm).

Peppermint Goby (*Coryphopterus lipernes*): one of several smaller members of this genus that lives on hard substrates.

Miscellaneous Sand-dwelling Gobies

A number of gobies are used by aquarists to assist in stirring up the upper layers of an aquarium sand bed. The *Valenciennea* species are sometimes recommended for their sifting habits, but these "super scoopers" are often so aggressive and dig so deep into sand beds that quickly decimate infaunal invertebrates. Because they quickly exhaust their supply of live foods, they tend to be difficult to keep. A number of other sand-sifting gobies are hardier and not as detrimental to the sand bed and its fauna, because they do not dig as deep. Many of these sand-dwelling species graze diatoms and detritus off the sand surface, supplementing their diets with tiny crustaceans and worms. If there is not enough natural fodder available, you will need to feed them at least twice a day. They tend not to be overly aggressive toward heterospecifics, but may quarrel with close relatives or other substrate-bound fishes. These gobies vary in size. When keeping one or more, be sure the aquarium has a secure cover as they have been known to leap from open tanks.

INNERSPOT SAND GOBY (*CORYPHOPTERUS INFRAMACULATUS*)

Coryphopterus spp. (= *Fusigobius* spp.)
Sand Gobies (Fuse Gobies)

Maximum Length: 1.2 to 3.1 in. (3 to 7.8 cm).
Range: Indo-Pacific.
Minimum Aquarium Size: 10 to 30 gal. (38 to 114 L).
Foods & Feeding: Meaty foods, including finely shredded frozen seafood, mysid shrimp, frozen preparations, flake foods and Cyclop-eeze. Feed at least twice a day.
Aquarium Suitability/Reef Compatibility:
Aquarium Notes: These interesting, reef-safe gobies feed off the substrate and will help keep the upper layer of the sand from becoming overgrown or caked. They eat small worms and minute crustaceans, but are less likely to decimate infaunal invertebrates than the more aggressive sand-sifters. These sand-dwelling species are quite aggressive toward conspecifics and congeners—it is best not to house more than one per tank. Provide it with suitable hiding places as it will not do well if pestered by tankmates. Some species (like the Masked Goby [*C. personatus*], page 366, and Peppermint Goby [*C. lipernes*], page 360) live on hard substrate and feed on zooplankton . These latter species can be kept in pairs or small groups.

BEAUTIFUL HIGHFIN GOBY (*EXYRIAS BELLISIMUS*)

Exyrias spp.
Highfin Gobies

Maximum Length: 3.7 to 5.3 in. (9.4 to 14 cm).
Range: Indo-Pacific.
Minimum Aquarium Size: 20 to 30 gal. (76 to 114 L).
Foods & Feeding: Meaty foods, including finely shredded frozen seafood, mysid shrimp, frozen preparations, pigment-enriched flake food, and Cyclop-eeze. Feed at least twice a day in a tank lacking infaunal prey.
Aquarium Suitability/Reef Compatibility:
Aquarium Notes: These larger sand-dwelling gobies are interesting to watch and fairly proficient at keeping the upper layers of a sand bed agitated. Keep just one per tank unless the aquarium is large. Their robust size means that they are likely to bully a wider range of goby tankmates. Still, they are shy gobies and will need good hiding places on the sand bed (like a cave or overhang). Target feeding may be necessary to ensure they get enough to eat. They will quickly decimate worm populations in a shallow sand bed. They are less likely to bury corals than the *Valenciennea* species and are also not as likely to jump out of a tank (although this may happen if they are pestered by more aggressive fishes).

GOLDSPOT GOBY (*GNATHOLEPIS THOMPSONI*)

Gnatholepis spp.
Earbar Gobies

Maximum Length: 1.8 to 3 in. (4.6 to 7.6 cm).
Range: Indo-Pacific and tropical Atlantic.
Minimum Aquarium Size: 10 to 20 gal. (38 to 76 L).
Foods & Feeding: Meaty foods, including finely shredded frozen seafood, mysid shrimp, frozen preparations, pigment-enriched flake food, and Cyclop-eeze. Feed at least twice a day.
Aquarium Suitability/Reef Compatibility:
Aquarium Notes: These small, distinctively marked gobies feed off the surface of the sand substrate—although they will do some surface turning, they are not very proficient at it. Their diet consists mainly of diatoms, detritus, and small crustaceans. The smaller species will do well in the nano-reef aquarium. Keep one per tank unless the aquarium is larger as they will fight if crowded. They are likely to be picked on by larger, more aggressive benthic fishes, including hawkfishes and sand perches. They are also potential prey for the fish-eating Green Brittle Star (*Ophiarachna incrassata*) and carpet anemones. Provide them with a ledge over the sand bottom under which to hide.

ORNATE GOBY (*ISTIGOBIUS ORNATUS*)

Istigobius spp.
Speckled Gobies (Decorated Gobies, Ornate Gobies)

Maximum Length: 3.5 in. (8.9 cm).
Range: Indo-Pacific.
Minimum Aquarium Size: 10 gal. (38 L).
Foods & Feeding: Meaty foods, including finely shredded frozen seafood, mysid shrimp, frozen preparations, pigment-enriched flake food, and Cyclop-eeze. Feed at least twice a day.
Aquarium Suitability/Reef Compatibility:
Aquarium Notes: The members of this genus are often nicely patterned and are proficient at turning the upper half inch of the sand bed. They are less likely to bury corals near the aquarium bottom than the more aggressive sand-sifters. They feed mainly on tiny crustaceans that live on or near the sand surface. In nature, they hide under rocks and rubble or among mangrove roots. They will behave aggressively toward conspecifics and congeners and may even pick on other smaller sand-dwelling gobies. Keep only one per tank unless the aquarium is larger. It may jump out of an open aquarium.

Oplopomus oplopomus (Valenciennes, 1837)
Spinecheek Goby

Maximum Length: 3.1 in. (8 cm).
Range: Indo-Pacific.
Minimum Aquarium Size: 20 gal. (76 L).
Foods & Feeding: Meaty foods, including finely shredded frozen seafood, mysid shrimp, frozen preparations, pigment-enriched flake food, and Cyclop-eeze. Feed at least twice a day.
Aquarium Suitability/Reef Compatibility:
Aquarium Notes: This species is fairly hardy in captivity, readily adapting to aquarium fare, and is proficient at stirring the upper sand surface. It tends not to be aggressive toward heterospecifics, although it is sometimes bullied by more belligerent bottom-dwellers (e.g., hawkfishes and sand perches). While it may hide initially, it will quickly become familiar with its new surroundings and start spending more time in the open (unless bullied). Make sure it gets enough to eat as it usually takes food directly off the substrate. It may jump out of an open aquarium.

Coryphopterus melacron
Blacktip Goby
Max. Length: 1.8 in. (4.5 cm).

Coryphopterus personatus
Masked Goby
Max. Length: 1.2 in. (3 cm).

Exyrias puntang
Puntang Goby
Max. Length: 5.5 in. (14 cm).

Istigobius decoratus
Decorated Goby
Max. Length: 3.5 in. (8.9 cm).

Istigobius ornatus
Ornate Goby
Max. Length: 3.5 in. (8.9 cm).

Yongeichthys nebulosus
Shadow Goby
Max. Length: 6.3 in. (16 cm).

Candycane Dwarf Goby (*Trimma cana*): among the smallest marine fishes, these wee gobies often live commensally with corals are great choices for a nano-reef.

Nano Gobies

Scores of tiny gobies (most under 1 in. [2.5 cm] in total length) are perfect candidates for the small reef aquarium, and many of these Lilliputians of the goby family are both brightly colored and relatively easy to keep. Some are quite secretive, living under ledges, among rubble, or in caves; others sit or hover in the open. Some species live commensally on particular soft or stony corals. They may even benefit the coral in some way, although more research is needed to confirm this. They are microcarnivores, with most preying on tiny planktonic crustaceans. Recently, more of these lovely little gobies have been coming into the aquarium trade. Their small size makes them potential prey for a large number of fish tankmates, including dwarf seabasses, dottybacks, larger cardinalfishes, hawkfishes, and sand perches. If you want to keep one, you will need to be careful when selecting its piscine tankmates. They might also fall prey to crabs, Green Brittle Stars (*Ophiarachna incrassata*), and other piscivorous invertebrates. The pygmy and dwarf gobies will feed on any foods that remain suspended in the water column.

Common Ghost Goby (*Pleurosicya mossambica*): a minuscule male (arrow) guards a clutch of eggs that have been deposited on a tunicate by its mate.

One great food for these gobies, as well as other small zooplankton feeding fishes, is Cyclop-eeze. This nutritious food (high HUFA and protein content) remains in suspension longer, and most fishes love it. Its suspensive property gives smaller zooplanktivores time to pick the food particles out of the water column.

These small gobies may be a problem to house during shipping and before sale in a retail shop. They are so diminutive that if they are placed in a larger holding tank, they are likely to go unnoticed by potential customers. They are also prone to going through the small holes in central system tank dividers and overstand pipes or overflow boxes. One way to keep them safe and separated is to place them in a clear plastic cup with a lid. Holes should be provided to allow gas exchange between the cup and tank water, and the cup should be placed in an area where there is good water circulation. Food will have to be introduced to this temporary holding vessel. Although they may seem a bit expensive for their size, these lovely gobies are worth the extra effort and are ideal fish candidates for the smaller nano-reef.

Nano Gobies

Asterropteryx bipunctatus
Twinspot Filamented Goby
Max. Length: 1.2 in. (3 cm).

Eviota bifasciata
Twostripe Pygmy Goby
Max. Length: 1 in. (2.5 cm).

Priolepis nocturnus
Blackbarred Convict Goby
Max. Length: 1.4 in. (3.6 cm).

Trimma benjamini
Ringeye Dwarf Goby
Max. Length: 1 in. (2.5 cm).

Trimma striata
Stripehead Dwarf Goby
Max. Length: 1.4 in. (3.5 cm).

Trimma tevegae
Bluestriped Dwarf Goby
Max. Length: 1.6 in. (4 cm).

BLUEDOT GOBY OR STARRY GOBY (*ASTERROPTERYX ENSIFERA*)

Asterropteryx spp.
Asterropteryx Gobies

Maximum Length: 1.5 to 2.4 in. (3.8 to 6.1 cm).

Range: Indo-Pacific.

Minimum Aquarium Size: 2 gal. (8 L).

Foods & Feeding: Meaty foods, including finely shredded frozen seafood, mysid shrimp, frozen preparations, pigment-enriched flake food, and Cyclop-eeze. Feed at least twice a day.

Aquarium Suitability/Reef Compatibility:

Aquarium Notes: *Asterropteryx* gobies make wonderful additions to the smaller reef aquarium, where they often hover over the substrate, sometimes in loose groups. They are usually found in the wild close to coral rubble or growths of macroalgae. House them with nonaggressive tankmates. Because of their small size, they are vulnerable to being eaten by larger fish tankmates. They can be kept in groups (especially the Bluedot Goby, *A. ensifera*) in a moderate-sized aquarium. Provide them with a patch of rubble on the sand bottom in which to hide. Some (perhaps all) feed heavily on detritus and diatoms that grow on the sand surface, as well as tiny invertebrates. The most attractive member of the group, *A. bipunctatus* (Twinspot Filamented Goby), has orange spots (page 369).

WHIP CORAL GOBY (*BRYANINOPS YONGEI*)

Bryaninops spp.
Commensal Gobies

Maximum Length: 1 to 2.2 in. (2.5 to 5.6 cm).
Range: Indo-Pacific.
Minimum Aquarium Size: 2 gal. (8 L).
Foods & Feeding: Meaty foods, including finely shredded frozen seafood, mysid shrimp, frozen preparations, pigment-enriched flake food, and Cyclop-eeze (a preferred food). Feed at least twice a day.
Aquarium Suitability/Reef Compatibility:
Aquarium Notes: These gobies, which often escape detection except by sharp-eyed viewers, live on a variety of different invertebrates (such as sponges, whip corals, soft corals, and tunicates). Unless you have multiple potential hosts, keep only one of these fishes per tank. (Usually only one or a heterosexual pair is found on a host in the wild.) They feed on tiny zooplankton. Because of their small size and lack of defenses, they are like candy to many potential fish-eating tankmates. They are also likely to enter overflow boxes or standpipes. If they do not find a suitable host, they are apt to hide incessantly. At least one species (the Redeye Hovering Goby [*Bryaninops natans*]) is found in groups, suspended in the water column above stony corals.

Discordipinna griessingeri Hoese & Fourmanoir, 1978
Spikefin Goby

Maximum Length: 1 in. (2.5 cm).
Range: Indo-Pacific.
Minimum Aquarium Size: 2 gal. (8 L).
Foods & Feeding: Meaty foods, including finely shredded frozen seafood, mysid shrimp, frozen preparations, pigment-enriched flake food, and Cyclop-eeze. Feed at least twice per day. May be difficult to feed.
Aquarium Suitability/Reef Compatibility:
Aquarium Notes: This remarkable little goby is best housed in the nano-reef aquarium where it can be fully appreciated and kept away from would-be predators. It is likely to disappear in a larger reef aquarium, where even modest-sized tankmates would quickly drive it into hiding. It shelters among rubble or under rocks on the sand bottom during the day and is more likely to come out of hiding when it is dark or light levels are subdued. Its small size means a larger number of fish may eat it (including species that are usually not piscivorous). The long dorsal spine is a potential target for nipping tankmates. Keep one per nano-reef aquarium.

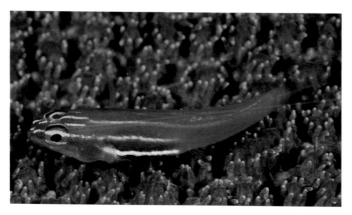

NEON PYGMY GOBY (*EVIOTA PELLUCIDA*)

Eviota spp. Larson, 1976
Pygmy Gobies

Maximum Length: 0.8 to 1.2 in. (2 to 3 cm).

Range: Indo-Pacific.

Minimum Aquarium Size: 2 gal. (8 L).

Foods & Feeding: Meaty foods, including finely shredded frozen seafood, chopped mysid shrimp, frozen preparations, pigment-enriched flake food and Cyclop-eeze (the best food for these fishes). Feed at least once per day.

Aquarium Suitability/Reef Compatibility:

Aquarium Notes: The more than 30 species in this genus of tiny gobies are all ideal additions to the nano-reef. Most spend their time resting on the substrate, while a few hover just over the bottom. Because they are so small, they are potential prey for a wide range of tankmates (like dwarf seabasses, cardinalfishes, hawkfishes, wrasses, and sand perches). They are prone to going into overflow boxes and up siphon tubes. Be aware that some are naturally short-lived—one has a life span of less than 60 days, and about 3 weeks of this time is the larval stage. These gobies will spawn in captivity, with males guarding clutches of benthic eggs.

ORANGE CONVICT GOBY (*PRIOLEPIS* SP.)

Priolepis spp.
Convict Gobies

Maximum Length: 1.4 to 2.8 in. (3.6 to 7.1 cm).

Range: Indo-Pacific and tropical Atlantic.

Minimum Aquarium Size: 2 gal. (8 L).

Foods & Feeding: Meaty foods, including finely shredded frozen seafood, mysid shrimp, frozen preparations, and Cyclop-eeze (a preferred food for these fishes). Feed at least twice a day.

Aquarium Suitability/Reef Compatibility:

Aquarium Notes: These are secretive gobies—sometimes stunningly attractive—that will spend most of their time hiding in reef crevices or under rocks or rubble. Some prefer a cave in which they will perch, upside down, on the ceiling. Because of their cryptic behavior, they are not the best display animals. You may not see them for weeks or even months. Some individuals will pop out of hiding when food is added to the aquarium. Others will wait for the food to make its way into their hiding places before feeding. You are more likely to see them in a nano-reef aquarium with no intimidating tankmates. One species, *Priolepis nocturnus* (page 369), will readily spawn in captivity. Eggs are deposited on the ceiling of a cave or overhang and are guarded by the male.

REDSPOTTED DWARF GOBY (*TRIMMA RUBROMACULATUS*)

Trimma spp. & *Trimmatom* spp.
Dwarf Gobies

Maximum Length: 0.8 to 1.6 in. (2 to 4 cm).

Range: Indo-Pacific.

Minimum Aquarium Size: 2 gal. (8 L).

Foods & Feeding: Meaty foods, including finely shredded frozen seafood, chopped mysid shrimp, frozen preparations, pigment-enriched flake food and Cyclop-eeze (the best food for these fishes). Feed at least once a day.

Aquarium Suitability/Reef Compatibility:

Aquarium Notes: Astonishingly small, the tiny species in these two genera are best suited to the nano-reef. In the average reef aquarium, they are almost sure to be eaten or disappear from sight. They are naturally short-lived and are hermaphrodites: dominant females change to males (which are dominant over females), while males can revert back to females if need be. Their husbandry needs are the same as those of the *Eviota* species (page 373). Keep them singly or in small groups. Some hover in the water column; others prefer to sit in repose on the substrate. Some display a jerky swimming behavior, while others swim in a heads-up fashion. All are potential prey items for a wide array of fish tankmates.

Tryssogobius colini Larson & Hoese, 2001
Dartfish Goby

Maximum Length: 2 in. (5 cm).
Range: Western Pacific.
Minimum Aquarium Size: 5 gal. (19 L).
Foods & Feeding: Meaty foods, including finely shredded frozen seafood, mysid shrimp, frozen preparations, pigment-enriched flake food, and Cyclop-eeze (a preferred food for this fish). Feed at least twice a day.
Aquarium Suitability/Reef Compatibility:
Aquarium Notes: This newly described deep-water goby looks very much like a dartfish with great appeal to many reef aquarists. It is not uncommon, but enters the aquarium trade only on occasion. Like a dartfish, it hovers over the substrate and disappears into a hole when threatened. Keep this species singly, in pairs, or in groups if your tank is of moderate size. Do not house with aggressive fishes or with tankmates that can swallow it whole. If pestered, it will hide and not feed. Firefishes may harass it in smaller tanks. It is ideal for a nano-reef species tank. Although not as likely to jump out of an open tank as a firefish, it is best to keep the tank covered.

Lined Dartfish (*Ptereleotris grammica*): this beautiful deep-water species is less common but more delicate than most in a genus of ideal reef-aquarium species.

Dartfishes (Genus *Ptereleotris*)

Dartfishes are wonderful additions to the reef aquarium as they are no threat to ornamental invertebrates. They are, however, notorious for jumping out of open aquariums, and some sort of top is required. Dartfishes eat most aquarium foods, including finely chopped seafood, frozen preparations, mysid shrimps, Cyclop-eeze, and flake food. They feed on zooplankton in the wild and should be fed twice a day. Because of their very peaceful nature, they can be kept in mixed aggregations and housed with conspecifics. They tend to fare better if you place several individuals in the same tank. The tank should have a sand bed with several flat rocks lying on the surface. Excavate a depression in the sand and place a rock over it or let them dig their own holes. If you place dartfishes in an aquarium with aggressive tankmates, they will often hide and not eat. It is common for them to hide for a week or more during acclimation. They are fairly disease- and parasite-resistant. Be aware that they will swim into the intake tube of canister filters if the protective strainers are left off, and they may also plunge into overflow boxes.

Ptereleotris calliura
Blue Dartfish
Max. Length: 4.9 in. (12.5 cm).

Ptereleotris evides
Scissortail Dartfish, Scissortail Goby
Max. Length: 5.5 in. (14 cm).

Ptereleotris hanae
Filamented Dartfish
Max. Length: 4.7 in. (12 cm).

Ptereleotris heteroptera
Spottail Dartfish, Blue Gudgeon Goby
Max. Length: 4.7 in. (12 cm).

Ptereleotris monoptera
Monofin Dartfish
Max. Length: 4.7 in. (12 cm).

Ptereleotris zebra
Zebra Dartfish
Max. Length: 4.3 in. (11 cm).

Helfrich's Firefish (*Nemateleotris helfrichi*): this deep-water member of the genus, tends to be less aggressive toward conspecfics than other firefish species.

Firefish (*Nemateleotris* spp.)

Firefishes are fault-free reef aquarium residents, as they are colorful, hardy, and "invertebrate-friendly." They are, however, often intolerant of conspecifics or congeners. They are best kept singly or in pairs (if you can acquire a male and female, which can be difficult to ascertain). If you keep more than one, and they do not pair up, the dominant individual will usually harass and injure the subordinate. Fortunately, they are rarely aggressive toward the related *Ptereleotris* species or other fish species. Provide them with plenty of places to hide and feed them a varied diet (they love Cyclop-eeze), at least once a day. An aquarium bottom covered with rubble is an ideal habitat for these fishes. They do best when housed with docile species. Aggressive or larger, active tankmates may cause them to hide and refuse to feed. The most common cause of firefish death is jumping out of uncovered tanks or even through very narrow openings in the aquarium covering. They will also leap into overflow boxes or out of open fish bags as they float on the aquarium surface during acclimation. Be sure all exit paths are blocked.

Nemateleotris decora Randall & Allen, 1973
Purple Firefish (Purple Dartfish, Decorated Dartfish, Flame Firefish)

Maximum Length: 3.5 in. (9 cm).
Range: Indo-Pacific.
Minimum Aquarium Size: 10 gal. (8 L).
Foods & Feeding: Meaty foods, including finely shredded frozen seafood, mysid shrimp, frozen preparations, pigment-enriched flake food and Cyclop-eeze (a preferred food). Feed at least once a day.
Aquarium Suitability/Reef Compatibility: ■ ☀ ☙ ⚘ ✶
Aquarium Notes: This is a great choice for the shallow- or deep-water reef aquarium. It will hover 2 to 4 in. (5 to 10 cm) over the substrate, facing into the current. Provide plenty of hiding places. It is the most aggressive of the firefishes. House it singly or in male-female pairs. (Although sexing is difficult, males are reported to be more robust and slightly longer than the females. Sometimes pair behavior can be seen in a dealer's tanks.) Bullied individuals will hide among tank decor or lie on the bottom against the glass. This species will ignore other fishes, with the possible exception of congeners. The most common cause of death is leaping from uncovered tanks or through holes in the aquarium back strip.

Nemateleotris magnifica Fowler, 1938
Firefish (Fire Dartfish, Magnificent Dartfish)

Maximum Length: 3.1 in. (7.9 cm).
Range: Indo-Pacific.
Minimum Aquarium Size: 10 gal. (38 L).
Foods & Feeding: Meaty foods, including finely shredded frozen seafood, mysid shrimp, frozen preparations, pigment-enriched flake food and Cyclop-eeze (a preferred food). Feed at least once a day.
Aquarium Suitability/Reef Compatibility:
Aquarium Notes: This is a wonderful, justifiably popular reef aquarium fish that does best when housed with other passive species. Select tankmates carefully. Housed with pugnacious or large, hyperactive tankmates, it will hide and not feed. Hawkfishes have been known to chase and nip this fish, while larger wrasses will eat them like candy. Keep one Firefish per aquarium, unless the tank is very large or you are able to acquire a male-female pair. If kept in groups, one individual often nips and chases conspecifics, usually until it succeeds in killing them all. Provide this species with plenty of hiding places. It frequently leaps from uncovered tanks and into overflow boxes.

Orangestripe Wormfish (*Gunnelichthys viridescens*): attractive, unusual, and well-suited to the reef aquarium. Inset: Curious Wormfish (*Gunnelichthys curiosus*).

Wormfishes (Genus *Gunnelichthys*)

These unusual microdesmids are good for the reef aquarium that has a deep sand bed. In the wild, they live in burrows or bury under the sand. The best venue for these fishes is a tank with plenty of open sand bottom. The wormfishes are very passive and will do best with other peaceful species. Dottybacks, hawkfishes, and sand perches will pick on them. You can keep them in pairs or even in small groups. They are prone to being eaten by a number of different predators (like goatfishes, wrasses, and larger gobies); because of their spaghetti-like form, greedy piscivores can literally slurp them up. They should be fed at least once a day and preferably more often. The diet should include finely shredded seafood, mysid shrimp, frozen preparations, and Cyclop-eeze. Although they are not as likely to jump as some of their cousins, they will propel themselves out of a tank if harassed or startled. Most do not exceed 5 in. (13 cm).

Compressed Ribbon Goby (*Oxymetopon compressus*): not an easy fish to keep, but a stunning addition to the home aquarium with exceptional husbandry.

Ribbon Gobies (Genus *Oxymetopon*)

These unusual fishes live on mud or silty sand flats or slopes where groups hover over a home burrow. All three species in this genus attain a maximum length of around 8 in. (20 cm) and are residents of the West Pacific. They are not well-suited to the typical reef tank as they do best in a habitat with plenty of open sand bottom and a deep sand bed. They can be housed in a larger reef tank that has live rock at one end or scattered patch reefs. A flat rock on the sand bottom, with a hollow dug underneath it, makes a great shelter site. They are more likely to adapt in a tank with other passive fishes (wormfishes, gobies, and dartfishes). If kept with aggressive species, they will hide incessantly and starve. Live brine shrimp may be needed to initiate feeding, but switch them to finely shaved seafood, mysid shrimp, and/or Cyclop-eeze once they are acclimated. Feed at least three times a day, and preferably more often. Move toward the tank slowly when these fishes are out in the open. They will spend more time in view in an aquarium that is dimly lit. They are likely to leap out of an open aquarium.

Pinnate Batfish (*Platax pinnatus*): juveniles are thought to mimic noxious flatworms. Undeniably beautiful, they grow into very large, less appealing adults.

Batfishes & Spadefishes (Family Ephippidae)

Although a juvenile batfish can make a spectacular display animal for the larger reef tank, these fishes are not well suited for the invertebrate aquarium—no matter how strong the temptation to bring one home. All members of the family are a potential threat to cnidarians: they are known to eat soft corals, tube anemones, sea anemones, and hydroids. Juveniles are less destructive than adults, but are still not recommended as all ages are prone to skin parasites. The other inherent batfish downside is that they get too large for all but the largest home aquarium. They are deep-bodied and have very large fins (in young fish the fins are proportionally larger). They will need a very deep tank because the fins are easily tattered if the aquarium does not have enough depth and/or unencumbered swimming space. The fins are also a tempting target for any fish tankmates prone to fin-nipping (e.g., some damselfishes, tobies). While some batfishes readily accept aquarium foods, the Pinnate Batfish (*Platax pinnatus*) and Zebra Batfish (*P. batavianus*) can be difficult species to feed.

Chocolate Surgeonfish (*Acanthurus pyroferus*) juv.: a family valued for its algae-grazing habits, but one with some members unsuited to the average reef tank.

Surgeonfishes (Family Acanthuridae)

Surgeonfishes are typically welcome additions to the reef aquarium because of the algae-eating habits of many—but not all—species. The acanthurids are active—some are hyperactive, and many are sizeable fishes that need plenty of swimming room. When keeping larger species, avoid excessive decor to provide more swimming room. It is important to have appropriate hiding places. They do best in "clean," well oxygenated water. Because they eat a lot and produce prodigious amounts of waste, a protein skimmer is recommended.

It is important to provide enough of the right foods to ensure their nutritional needs are met. Algae-eating surgeonfishes require substantial amounts of plant material, including microalgae, macroalgae, broccoli, spinach, *Spirulina* flake food, and dried algae sheets. They tend to do best in tanks with excessive algae growth. Algae-eating species should be fed several times a day. Also add some form of vegetable matter for them to browse on throughout the day. The zooplankton-feeding species should be fed several times a day.

Elongate Surgeonfish (*Acanthurus mata*): this is one of many larger members of the family that will require a huge tank with lots of swimming room.

If the fish has a pinched-in stomach, feed it more. Juveniles have greater metabolic demands than adults. Many surgeonfishes are territorial and will target conspecifics and food competitors. The species vary in their aggressiveness. Many of the less aggressive forms tend to be less colorful, and thus less popular. It is best not to house the more belligerent species with other acanthurids (although it is possible in an extra-large tank). Be aware that these fishes have caudal peduncle spines that can inflict serious lacerations to tankmates or aquarists.

Finally, know that keeping surgeonfishes in a reef tank is not without some drawbacks. They are susceptible to parasitic infections, especially soon after purchase, and an infested fish will have to be removed to administer treatment. Certain surgeonfishes may also develop a taste for large-polyped stony corals. This behavior usually begins when the fish begins feeding on the feces (which include zooxanthellae) that these corals exude from their oral openings. Sometimes the fish will be satisfied with just the fecal material, but in other cases it will begin nipping at the mouth and the polyps. This can irritate the coral and cause it to retract its polyps.

Lined Surgeonfish (*Acanthurus lineatus*): a very active and aggressive member of the genus that will have to be housed in an extra-large reef aquarium.

Acanthurus Surgeonfishes

This is the largest surgeonfish genus and the most popular among marine aquarists. There are three distinct feeding groups: herbivores, which browse on filamentous microalgae or fleshy macroalgae; detritivores, which suck detritus and diatoms off the sand substrate (often ingesting a considerable quantity of substrate in the process) or scrape it off hard surfaces (some specialize in feeding on the feces of carnivorous fishes.); and zooplanktivores, which swim in the water column where they capture minute prey (the group with fewest species). Most need to be housed in a very large aquarium. Many are strongly territorial, driving conspecifics and food competitors from the area they defend. They vary in their tendency to act as bullies in a captive system. The least aggressive include the Atlantic Blue (*Acanthurus coeruleus*), Powder Brown (*A. japonicus*), Brown (*A. nigrofuscus*), and Convict Surgeonfish (*A. triostegus*). The more belligerent include the Achilles (*Acanthurus achilles*), Powder Blue (*A. leucosternon*), Lined (*A. lineatus*), and Sohal Surgeonfish (*A. sohal*).

ADOLESCENT

Acanthurus coeruleus Bloch & Schneider, 1801
Blue Tang (Atlantic Blue Tang)

Maximum Length: 9.1 in. (23 cm).
Range: Atlantic Ocean.
Minimum Aquarium Size: 100 gal. (380 L).
Foods & Feeding: Feed a mixed diet, the bulk of which should consist of vegetable matter. Give it frozen foods that contain the blue-green algae *Spirulina*, slices of zucchini, broccoli, and dried algae flakes or sheets. Vegetable matter should be introduced daily in an aquarium where algae is not present, and frozen foods should also be presented several times a day.
Aquarium Suitability/Reef Compatibility:
Aquarium Notes: The Blue Tang feeds mostly on filamentous algae and is a good choice for controlling undesirable algae. It may eat more desirable macroalgae and occasionally nip the tissue of large-polyped stony corals (especially large-polyped species). Although this species is usually well-behaved in larger aquariums, it can misbehave in smaller tanks. Your safest bet is to keep only one *A. coeruleus* per tank, especially the yellow juveniles which are highly territorial. Small groups of adults can be kept in extra-large aquariums and should be added simutaneously.

Acanthurus leucosternon Bennett, 1832
Powder Blue Surgeonfish

Maximum Length: 9.1 in. (23 cm).
Range: Indian Ocean.
Minimum Aquarium Size: 100 gal. (380 L).
Foods & Feeding: Feed a mixed diet, the bulk of which should consist of vegetable matter. Give it frozen foods that contain the blue-green algae *Spirulina*, slices of zucchini, broccoli, and dried algae flakes or sheets. Vegetable matter should be introduced daily in an aquarium where algae is not present, and frozen foods should also be presented several times a day.
Aquarium Suitability/Reef Compatibility:
Aquarium Notes: While this beautiful acanthurid will feed on filamentous algae, it is also quite aggressive. You will need to pick its tankmates carefully. It is especially prone to attacking other herbivores and fishes with similar body shapes. Do not keep more than one *A. leucosternon* per tank. It is an "ich magnet" and is difficult to treat successfully in a tank with invertebrates. It does best in a spacious aquarium with plenty of unobstructed swimming room. This species is sexually dimorphic, with the males being considerably smaller than the females. When stressed the color fades.

Acanthurus nigricans Linnaeus, 1758
Whitecheek Surgeonfish

Maximum Length: 8.4 in. (21.3 cm).
Range: Pan Pacific.
Minimum Aquarium Size: 100 gal. (380 L).
Foods & Feeding: Feed a mixed diet, the bulk of which should consist of vegetable matter. Give it frozen foods that contain the blue-green algae *Spirulina*, slices of zucchini, broccoli, and dried algae flakes or sheets. Vegetable matter should be introduced daily in an aquarium where algae is not present, and frozen foods should also be presented several times a day.
Aquarium Suitability/Reef Compatibility:
Aquarium Notes: This is an elegant fish that browses fine filamentous microalgae and small fleshy macroalgae off hard substrates. Occasionally it will eat red cyanobacteria. This species is more likely to acclimate than the similar Powder Brown Surgeonfish (*Acanthurus japonicus*). Both are relatively shy when added to the aquarium and will require suitable hiding places. Keep only one of these fish per tank. Although less aggressive than many in the genus, once acclimated some individuals will behave aggressively toward food competitors introduced after them.

LARGE JUVENILE

Acanthurus olivaceous Foster, 1801
Orangeshoulder Surgeonfish (Orangeband Surgeonfish)

Maximum Length: 13.8 in. (35 cm).
Range: Western-Pacific.
Minimum Aquarium Size: 180 gal. (684 L).
Foods & Feeding: Feed a mixed diet, mostly consisting of vegetable matter. Give it frozen foods that contain the blue-green algae *Spirulina* and dried algae flakes or sheets. Vegetable matter should be introduced daily if algae is not present, and frozen foods should be presented several times a day.
Aquarium Suitability/Reef Compatibility:
Aquarium Notes: This species feeds by sucking filamentous algae, diatoms, and detritus off the sand, which helps keep the surface of the sand clean. It rarely grazes algae off hard substrates. It is unlikely to bother corals and usually ignores unrelated fishes. Best housed in an extra-large aquarium with a sand bottom, minimal aquascaping, and plenty of swimming room—perhaps a lagoon-type biotope. It is prudent to house only one per tank, unless you keep an adult and a juvenile specimen in a larger tank together. If keeping with other surgeonfishes you should add it before more belligerent species.

JUVENILE

Acanthurus pyroferus Kittilitz, 1834
Chocolate Surgeonfish (Mimic Surgeonfish)

Maximum Length: 9.8 in. (25 cm).
Range: Indo-Pacific.
Minimum Aquarium Size: 100 gal. (380 L).
Foods & Feeding: Feed a mixed diet, the bulk of which should consist of vegetable matter. Give it frozen foods that contain the blue-green algae *Spirulina*, slices of zucchini, broccoli, and dried algae flakes or sheets. Vegetable matter should be introduced daily in an aquarium where algae is not present, and frozen foods should also be presented several times a day.
Aquarium Suitability/Reef Compatibility:
Aquarium Notes: This durable fish feeds on filamentous algae and diatoms. Its juvenile color (above) mimics either the Lemonpeel Angelfish (*Centropyge loriculus*) or the Half Black Angelfish (*C. vroliki*). As it grows to a size that exceeds that of the angelfish model, it begins to develop its adult coloration, brown with an orange vertical splash behind the gills. It is not one of the more aggressive species, but will defend a preferred hiding place and may pick on a newcomer added to a smaller tank. Keep only one adult per tank. Juveniles of different colors will coexist.

Acanthurus sohal (Forsskål, 1775)
Sohal Surgeonfish

Maximum Length: 15.7 in. (40 cm).
Range: Red Sea and the Arabian Gulf.
Minimum Aquarium Size: 180 gal. (684 L).
Foods & Feeding: Feed a mixed diet, the bulk of which should consist of vegetable matter. Give it frozen foods that contain the blue-green algae *Spirulina*, slices of zucchini, broccoli, and dried algae flakes or sheets. Vegetable matter should be introduced, and frozen foods should also be presented several times a day.
Aquarium Suitability/Reef Compatibility:
Aquarium Notes: This species is one of the true "bad boys" of the acanthurid family. Highly territorial, it will dash from one side of the tank to the other and violently harass other finned tankmates, especially congeners and food competitors. Its caudal spines are very large and are reported to be venomous. It feeds mostly on filamentous algae and fleshy macroalgae, usually off hard, flat substrates. This very active fish needs plenty of swimming room. Adults must be kept in larger aquariums if they are going to be successfully acclimated to captivity. The Lined Surgeonfish (*Acanthurus lineatus*) (page 387) is a very similar fish that is less hardy.

Acanthurus achilles
Achilles' Surgeonfish
Max. Length: 9.4 in. (24 cm).

Acanthurus chirurgus
Doctorfish
Max. Length: 13.5 in. (34.3 cm).

Acanthurus nigrofuscus
Brown Surgeonfish
Max. Length: 8.3 in. (21 cm).

Acanthurus tennentii
Lieutenant Surgeonfish
Max. Length: 12.2 in. (31 cm).

Acanthurus thompsoni
Thompson's Surgeonfish
Max. Length: 10.6 in. (27 cm).

Acanthurus triostegus
Convict Surgeonfish
Max. Length: 10.6 in. (27 cm).

Orangetipped Bristletooth (*Ctenochaetus tomiensis*): most members of this relatively mild-mannered genus have subdued colors and feed heavily on detritus.

Bristletooths (Genus *Ctenochaetus*)

Bristletooth surgeonfishes feed on detritus, bacteria, diatoms, and large amounts of sediment. They have specialized teeth that are elongate and flexible, with spatula-shaped ends that are curved inward. When they feed, they press their jaws against the substrate and then throw the lower jaw upward. This effectively brushes particulate matter off rock, dead coral, and out of turf algae. Most avoid areas with long filamentous algae (if they happen to ingest it they quickly spit it out because it gets stuck in their teeth). Juveniles quickly lose weight if food is in short supply. These fishes rarely bother sessile invertebrates. If these fishes contract a skin parasite, it is difficult to treat them in the reef aquarium. They have poorly developed caudal peduncle spines and tend to be dominated by other, more aggressive surgeonfishes. (These spines can still inflict damage to an aquarist's hand.) They tend to be less aggressive members of the surgeonfish family and are not likely to pick on tank-mates. That said, conspecifics may quarrel, and they may fight with other members in the genus.

Ctenochaetus strigosus (Bennett, 1828)
Goldring Bristletooth (Yelloweye Bristletooth, Kole's Tang)

Maximum Length: 7.1 in. (18 cm).
Range: Hawaiian and Johnston Islands.
Minimum Aquarium Size: 75 gal. (285 L).
Foods & Feeding: Feed a mixed diet, the bulk of which should consist of vegetable matter. Give it frozen foods that contain the blue-green algae *Spirulina*, and dried algae flakes or sheets. Vegetable matter should be introduced daily in an aquarium where algae is not present, and frozen foods should also be presented several times a day.
Aquarium Suitability/Reef Compatibility:
Aquarium Notes: This is a good community fish for the reef aquarium, but one that will do better if a good crop of diatoms happens to be present. Like others in the genus, this fish spends most of its time grazing on hard substrate for detritus and diatoms. This is one of the less aggressive members of the family. Even so, it is best to keep only one per tank. It is also likely to be picked on by more bellicose acanthurids. A number of simliar species once synonymized with *C. strigosus* are now recognized as valid (e.g., *C. truncatus*, page 399).

Bignose Unicornfish (*Naso vlamingi*) juv.: aquarists are most likely to encounter young unicornfishes, such as this, that are destined to grow much larger.

Unicornfishes (Genus *Naso*)

These unusual acanthurids are only suitable for the largest reef tanks. Most get quite large (some sporting a hornlike forehead protuberance) and they are very active, spending most of their time in shoals, high in the water column. They feed on zooplankton and macroalgae. Some species will not thrive unless brown macroalgae is provided. Commercially available dried algae sheets and flakes will suffice for most species. Juveniles and subadults spend their days feeding, so vegetable matter should be introduced daily in an aquarium where microalgae is not present, and frozen foods should also be presented several times a day. Adults feed more on zooplankton and should be fed mysid shrimp, vitamin-enriched brine shrimp, and frozen preparations for herbivores. The caudal peduncle spines of the *Naso* species are stout and fixed in an erect position, making them easily entangled in a fish net. These fishes tend to be rather durable if they are provided with enough swimming space. They are typically not aggressive toward tankmates, except for members of their own species and possibly related forms.

Naso lituratus (Foster & Schneider, 1801)
Orangespine Unicornfish (Naso Tang)

Maximum Length: 18.1 in. (46 cm).
Range: Western Pacific.
Minimum Aquarium Size: 180 gal. (684 L).
Foods & Feeding: Feed a mixed diet, the bulk of which should consist of vegetable matter. Give frozen foods that contain *Spirulina* and some of the dried brown algae available from pet shops or Asian food stores. Spends a major part of the day grazing, so vegetable matter should be introduced daily if macroalgae is not present. Frozen foods should also be presented several times a day.
Aquarium Suitability/Reef Compatibility:
Aquarium Notes: This much-loved fish feeds mostly on brown macroalgae and will usually eliminate these plants from a reef tank. Most individuals will take a variety of foods. A rare individual may nip at large-polyped stony corals and low-growing soft corals. This fish needs plenty of swimming space and suitable hiding places. It is usually not aggressive toward tankmates, except members of its own species and possibly congeners. When stressed or at night, it develops a blotchy color pattern. It may jump out of an open aquarium. *Naso elegans* is the "sister species" from the Indian Ocean.

Bristletooths and Unicornfishes

Ctenochaetus binotatus
Twospot Bristletooth
Max. Length: 7.9 in. (20 cm).

Ctenochaetus hawaiiensis (juv.)
Chevron, Hawaiian Bristletooth
Max. Length: 11 in. (28 cm).

Ctenochaetus truncatus
Squaretail Bristletooth
Max. Length: 7.3 in. (18.5 cm).

Naso brevirostris
Palefin Unicornfish
Max. Length: 23.6 in. (60 cm).

Naso unicornis
Bluespine Unicornfish
Max. Length: 23.6 in. (60 cm).

Naso vlamingii
Bignose, Vlaming's Unicornfish
Max. Length: 10.6 in. (27 cm).

Palette Tang (*Paracanthurus hepatus*): this attractive species depends heavily on zooplankton and will need frequently feeding in the reef tank.

Palette Tang (Genus *Paracanthurus*)

There is a single species in this surgeonfish genus: the electric-blue Palette or Pacific Blue Tang (*Paracanthurus hepatus*). It is shy, especially when first introduced to the aquarium—provide it with branching corals or other suitable shelter. Juveniles can be kept together, but adults will quarrel. It is not overly aggressive toward heterospecifics with the possible exception of close relatives. This fish is very prone to skin parasites, which can be particularly difficult to deal with in a reef aquarium. It is also susceptible to lateral line and fin erosion. Quarantine this fish, and any surgeonfishes, for several weeks before placing it in your display tank. The Palette Tang reaches a length of about 12 inches (30.5 cm) and should be kept in a tank of 100 gallons (380 L) or more. Juveniles often form groups over branching stony corals, in which they shelter. They feed on algae as well as zooplankton. Offer it finely chopped fresh or frozen seafood, mysid shrimp, vitamin-enriched brine shrimp, and frozen preparations for herbivores. Indian Ocean specimens sometimes have a yellow "belly."

Moorish Idol (*Zanclus cornutus*): a fish that is coveted by many aquarists, but one that is difficult to feed in captivity and thus nearly impossible to keep alive.

Moorish Idol (Genus *Zanclus*)

The exquisite Mooish Idol (*Zanclus cornutus*) will either refuse to eat or not take food with gusto in captivity (its diet in the wild consists of coralline algae and sponges). If you do decide to keep one, attempt to feed it a mixed diet that includes finely chopped table shrimp, squid, mysid shrimp, vitamin-enriched live brine shrimp, as well as vegetable matter. Frozen foods that contain the blue-green algae *Spirulina* are a good staple if you can get your Moorish Idol to eat them. Feed several times a day. Individuals that are reluctant to feed may require live rock with rich coralline algae and sponge growth on which to survive until they acclimate to aquarium foods. They do best on their own, often behaving aggressively toward each other. Provide plenty of swimming space as well as some good holes into which they can dive when threatened. The adult gets up to 6.2 inches (16 cm) in length and will need to be kept in a reef tank of at least 100 gallons (380 L) in size. Young *Zanclus cornutus* settle out of the plankton at a large size—up to 3.1 inches (8 cm) in length.

Brown Tang (*Zebrasoma scopas*) juvenile: one of a group of active grazers prized both for their beauty and their ability to help control nuisance algae in the reef.

Tangs (Genus *Zebrasoma*)

These fishes are frequently employed to control algae in the reef tank. They browse on both microalgae and macroalgae. Their long snouts allow them to feed on algae in reef interstices. Although tangs serve a useful function in the reef aquarium, some individuals do occasionally nip at the tissue of hard and soft corals. Large-polyped stony corals are their most frequent targets. They less frequently bother star polyps, gorgonians, zoanthids, and *Tridacna* clams (although they have been known to nip clam mantles). This behavior is more likely in tanks where algae growth is sparse and little food is introduced (i.e., when the tangs are hungry). Adding sheets of dried algae is helpful. Tangs will sometimes consume small fanworms and rasp through the tubes of larger sabellid feather dusters. Unfortunately, they are disease-prone in captivity: they are parasitized by black ich (a turbellarian flatworm), ich, and coral fish disease. They are also notorious for developing lateral line and fin erosion, a malady often blamed on a nutrient deficiency or poor water conditions. Some species in the genus can be quite aggressive.

Zebrasoma desjardinii (Bloch, 1797)
Indian Ocean Sailfin Tang

Maximum Length: 15.7 in. (40 cm).
Range: Indian Ocean.
Minimum Aquarium Size: 135 gal. (513 L).
Foods & Feeding: Feed a mixed diet, the bulk of which should consist of vegetable matter. Give frozen foods that contain the blue-green algae *Spirulina*, slices of zucchini, broccoli, and dried algae. Vegetable matter should be introduced daily in an aquarium where algae is not present, and frozen foods should also be presented once or twice a day.

Aquarium Suitability/Reef Compatibility:
Aquarium Notes: This handsome species is one of the best choices for controlling undesirable algae. An occasional individual will even eat bubble algae (*Valonia*). It will also browse on desirable macroalgae and may occasionally nip (and even eat) the tissue of hard corals (especially large-polyped stony coral species) and low-growing soft corals. It is the least aggressive member of the *Zebrasoma* genus, although it may behave aggressively toward members of its own kind (or, on rare occasions, docile fish added after it). The related Sailfin Tang (*Z. veliferum*) is similar in behavior and husbandry.

Zebrasoma flavescens (Bennett, 1828)
Yellow Tang

Maximum Length: 7.9 in. (20 cm).

Range: Central Pacific.

Minimum Aquarium Size: 75 gal. (285 L).

Foods & Feeding: Feed a mixed diet, the bulk of which should consist of vegetable matter. Give frozen foods that contain the blue-green algae *Spirulina*, slices of zucchini, broccoli, and dried algae. Vegetable matter should be introduced daily in an aquarium where algae is not present, and frozen foods should also be presented once or twice a day.

Aquarium Suitability/Reef Compatibility:

Aquarium Notes: A mainstay in the aquarium trade, this striking fish is a great choice for controlling undesirable algae. Less belligerent than some surgeonfishes, it is still one of the more aggressive in its genus and can be a bully once established. To keep more than one the in same tank, all must be introduced simultaneously. In the aquarium it will often maintain territories from which it excludes conspecifics and similar fishes. It may occasionally nip the tissue of large-polyped stony corals and low-growing soft corals. Its beautiful color will fade if given an inadequate diet.

Zebrasoma rostratum (Günther, 1875)
Black Tang (Longnose Black Tang)

Maximum Length: 8.3 in. (21 cm).
Range: Eastern Central Pacific.
Minimum Aquarium Size: 100 gal. (380 L).
Foods & Feeding: Feed a mixed diet, the bulk of which should consist of vegetable matter. Give frozen foods that contain the blue-green algae *Spirulina*, slices of zucchini, broccoli, and dried algae. Vegetable matter should be introduced daily in an aquarium where algae is not present, and frozen foods should also be presented once or twice a day.
Aquarium Suitability/Reef Compatibility:
Aquarium Notes: This unusual tang has been showing up in aquarium stores with more regularity, with most individuals being collected around Christmas Island in the Central Pacific. This is a good reef aquarium fish and is one of the least aggressive members of its genus. It is likely to be picked on by more belligerent members of the genus and family. As for others in the family, be sure you provide plenty of swimming room. It will eat some filamentous and macroalgae. Adults develop a greenish silver patch along the back. The body and snout also become more elongate as the fish grows.

Zebrasoma xanthurum (Blyth, 1852)
Purple Tang (Yellowtail Tang)

Maximum Length: 9.8 in. (25 cm).
Range: Red Sea.
Minimum Aquarium Size: 100 gal. (380 L).
Foods & Feeding: Feed a mixed diet, the bulk of which should consist of vegetable matter. Give frozen foods that contain the blue-green algae *Spirulina*, slices of zucchini, broccoli, and dried algae. Vegetable matter should be introduced daily in an aquarium where algae is not present, and frozen foods should also be presented once or twice a day.
Aquarium Suitability/Reef Compatibility:
Aquarium Notes: This is another great species, almost luminous in color when well fed, and great for helping to control filamentous algae. It feeds on blue-green algae, red filamentous algae, brown macroalgae, as well as green macro and filamentous algae. *Z. xanthurum* has been known to pick at both large-polyped stony corals and low-growing soft corals. This is an aggressive tang: it will attack others members of its genus and may pick on newly introduced fishes. Only one should be housed per tank. It is best not to keep it with other surgeonfishes, unless you have an extra-large tank.

Indonesian Coral Rabbitfish (*Siganus tetrazonus*): a less common member of a group of active grazers well-suited to large and moderately sized reef aquariums.

Rabbitfishes (Family Siganidae)

Rabbitfishes are some of the best herbivores for helping to control algae growth in the reef aquarium. This includes macroalgae as well as some of the pestilent filamentous forms. A few species will even eat *Valonia* (bubble algae). Some species will eat sessile invertebrates, like sponges and colonial tunicates, but most will not bother either soft or stony corals. That said, individuals have been known to feed on the zooxanthellae expelled by large-polyped stony corals. This can lead to an occasional individual developing the bad habit of picking at large polyps. If you have corals in your tank that are beginning to close up or behave as if irritated, be sure to spend some time closely watching your fish population. If a rabbitfish begins nipping at the corals, you will probably have to remove it. Sometimes feeding more often can discourage these fishes from picking at your sessile invertebrates, but this can also reduce a rabbitfish's desire to consume the pestilent algae in the tank.

As far as other invertebrates are concerned, I have had rabbitfishes chew through the sedimentary tubes of feather duster worms,

Pacific Coral Rabbitfish (*Siganus studeri*): although largely harmless with most invertebrates, some individuals may develop problematic feeding habits.

nip at the feeding tentacles of Christmas tree worms, and on rare occassions nip clam mantles or eat mushroom anemones.

The rabbitfishes are a good selection for the large reef aquarium. They are active fishes that normally cover a lot of territory in their daily pursuits, so swimming room is key. Be aware that rabbitfish species vary in size (some get too large for the home aquarium). When it comes to food, rabbitfishes are usually not finicky. Of course, it is important to include plenty of plant material in their diets. This would include sheets of dried algae, frozen spinach leaves that have been thawed, broccoli, and flake and frozen foods that contain *Spirulina*. They will also eat algae growing on the aquarium glass or decor, or introduced macroalgae, such as *Caulerpa*. Some of the rabbitfishes will eat the fecal matter produced by their piscine tankmates. Feed them often (at least several times a day) to keep up with their fast metabolism.

Some rabbitfishes engage in rapid color change. If a rabbitfish changes colors, lies in a torpor on the substrate, or dashes about or hides incessantly, there is a problem (e.g., poor water quality, low oxygen levels, or bullying by a tankmate). In many cases, these fish-

Goldspotted Rabbitfish (*Siganus guttatus*): although they form large schools in the wild, rabbitfishes may attack congeners in captive confines.

es will adopt the "stressed" coloration when first introduced to their new home and may retain this pattern until they begin to feel more at ease. Fortunately for aquarists, rabbitfishes tend to be very disease-resistant.

The rabbitfishes will take longer to acclimate if they are kept in a high-traffic area. They are not as pugnacious as their surgeonfish cousins, but in some cases they will exhibit intra- and interspecific aggression. This is especially true if the rabbitfish is placed in a tank and allowed to settle in before a conspecific or congener is introduced. Members of the subgenus *Lo* tend to be more aggressive. One way to successfully keep conspecific rabbitfish in the same tank is to obtain a heterosexual pair. This is difficult because the only sexual dimorphism known in siganids is that females tend to mature at a larger size than males. In most cases, obtaining a pair is a matter of luck, not skill.

Siganus doliatus Cuvier, 1830
Pencilstreaked Rabbitfish

Maximum Length: 9.4 in. (24 cm).
Range: Western Pacific.
Minimum Aquarium Size: 10 gal. (380 L).
Foods & Feeding: Consumes a varied diet, mostly vegetable matter. Feed dried and frozen herbivore foods. Supplement with pieces of zucchini, broccoli, leaf lettuce, and sushi nori (dried seaweed). Feed two to three times a day.
Aquarium Suitability/Reef Compatibility:
Aquarium Notes: This hardy, handsomely adorned rabbitfish will do best if kept in a tank with plenty of swimming room and with nonaggressive to moderately aggressive tankmates. It may pick at the fecal material produced by large-polyped stony corals, which could lead to picking at the polyp itself. Heavy feeding will help discourage this behavior. They also will eat macroalgae and are usually effective at helping to control *Caulerpa*. Keep only one or a pair per tank. This is a pair-bonding species, with pair members joining up when they are about 3 in. [7.6 cm] in length. Adult pair members may behave aggressively toward related species. They tend to ignore most fish tankmates.

Siganus (Lo) vulpinus (Schlegel & Müller,1845)
Foxface Rabbitfish

Maximum Length: 9.4 in. (24 cm).
Range: Western Pacific.
Minimum Aquarium Size: 100 gal. (380 L).
Foods & Feeding: Consumes a varied diet, mostly vegetable matter. Feed dried and frozen herbivore foods. Supplement with pieces of zucchini, broccoli, leaf lettuce, and dried algae sheets. Feed two to three times per day.
Aquarium Suitability/Reef Compatibility:
Aquarium Notes: This is a justifiably popular and durable aquarium fish that can even be used to break in a new aquarium. Provide it with plenty of swimming space. Although this fish is usually not a threat to sessile invertebrates, I have had it chew through the tubes of feather dusters as it grazed on the algae growing on the sedimentary tube. There are also reports of individuals eating mushroom anemones. This more aggressive rabbitfish will often quarrel with other siganids and food competitors. Juveniles, usually put up with conspecifics, but adults will fight unless they are of the opposite sex and form a pair. This fish develops a blotchy coloration when sleeping or stressed.

Siganus corallinus
Coral Rabbitfish
Max. Length: 11 in. (28 cm).
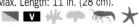

Siganus (Lo) magnifica
Magnificent Rabbitfish
Max. Length: 9.1 in. (23 cm).
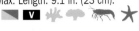

Siganus puellus
Masked Rabbitfish
Max. Length: 15 in. (38 cm).
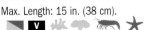

Siganus stellatus
Honeycomb Rabbitfish
Max. Length: 15.7 in. (40 cm).
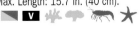

Siganus (Lo) unimaculatus
Onespot Foxface Rabbitfish
Max. Length: 7.9 in. (20 cm).
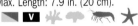

Siganus (Lo) uspi
Bicolored Rabbitfish
Max. Length: 9.4 in. (24 cm).

Banded Sole (*Soleichthys heterorhinos*): flatfishes can be interesting additions to reef aquascapes featuring a generous expanse of open sand substrate.

Flatfishes (Families Bothidae, Pleuronectidae & Soleidae)

The flounders and soles mostly exhibit muted colors to help them blend in with the seafloor, although a few sport bold patterns or bright colors that catch the eye of a reef aquarists. They spend most of their time lying on or under soft substrates. While not a threat to sessile invertebrates, most will eat motile crustaceans and infaunal worms. They need to be housed in a tank with a fine sand bed in which to bury (the bed depth is dependent on the flatfish species). Much of the sand bed should be obstruction-free so that they can freely move about and dig. Avoid keeping stinging corals and sea anemones near the aquarium bottom as the flatfishes are likely to run into or land on them, resulting in severe stings to the fish and subsequent death. Live food may be needed initially to get a flatfish to eat. For larger individuals, gut-packed ghost shrimp should be provided once per day, while smaller soles or flounders will eat live brine shrimp. If kept with voracious competitors, the flatfish may have difficulty getting enough to eat.

413

Bluechin Triggerfish (*Xanthichthys auromarginatus*) male: some zooplankton-feeding triggerfish species can be kept in a reef tank.

Triggerfishes (Family Balistidae)

The vast majority of triggerfishes are not suitable for the reef aquarium. Most are polyphagous, feeding on a wide array of invertebrates, including prized species that we nurture in our reef tanks. A small group of triggerfishes, however, are exceptions to this rule. These reef-tank-suitable species feed mainly on zooplankton and typically ignore invertebrates if they are fed frequently enough by the aquarist. One important caveat: they are likely to "stray" and start eating your desirable invertebrates if they are underfed. Adequate feeding is also very important because they are prone to weight loss if not fed several times a day.

The good triggerfishes for the reef tank are also less likely to rearrange the aquarium decor. This potentially destructive trigger-fish behavior can lead to corals toppling over or falling on each other, causing mechanical damage and subsequent death. Some triggerfish species may leap from an open aquarium or spit water on electrical outlets. This includes members of the genus *Xanthichtys.*

414

Melichthys niger (Bloch, 1786)
Black Triggerfish (Black Durgon)

Maximum Length: 19.7 in. (50 cm).
Range: Indo-Pacific.
Minimum Aquarium Size: 240 gal. (912 L).
Foods & Feeding: Mixed diet of meaty foods, including chopped seafood, mysid shrimp, frozen preparations, and flake foods. Feed at least three times a day.
Aquarium Suitability/Reef Compatibility:
Aquarium Notes: This species is found in tropical waters around the world and is usually seen in aggregations, swimming high above the reef, often with schooling zooplankton feeders. It is also found associating with large floating rafts of *Sargassum*, a species of brown algae. Because it feeds mainly on floating plant material and zooplankton, it is a possible candidate for the reef aquarium. However, in nature, and in captivity, it will occasionally nibble on sessile invertebrates. It may also harass ornamental shrimps that are introduced after it has become adjusted to its captive home.

Melichthys vidua (Solander, 1844)
Pinktail Triggerfish

Maximum Length: 13.8 in.(35 cm).
Range: Indo-Pacific.
Minimum Aquarium Size: 100 gal. (380 L).
Foods & Feeding: Mixed diet of meaty foods, including chopped seafood, mysid shrimp, frozen preparations, and flake foods. Feed at least three times a day.
Aquarium Suitability/Reef Compatibility:

Aquarium Notes: This attractive triggerfish is a potential candidate for the reef aquarium. It is a mild-mannered fish that is even more sociable toward other fishes than most triggers (including the Niger Triggerfish, facing page). It can be kept with peaceful fishes of equal size or larger, or with more aggressive fishes that are slightly smaller. It can be retiring when initially introduced to an aquarium, but will become quite tame in time. Unlike others in the reef-suitable triggerfish category, this species feeds on larger, motile invertebrates (including crustaceans and octopuses) and small fishes. It will sometimes ignore cleaner shrimps introduced before it.

JUVENILE

Odonus niger (Rüppell, 1837)
Niger Triggerfish (Redtooth Triggerfish)

Maximum Length: 19.7 in. (50 cm)—this includes the long fin filaments present in large adults.
Range: Indo-Pacific.
Minimum Aquarium Size: 100 gal. (380 L).
Foods & Feeding: Mixed diet of meaty foods, including chopped seafood, mysid shrimp, frozen preparations, and flake foods. Feed at least three times a day.
Aquarium Suitability/Reef Compatibility: ▪ 🌿 🐢 🦐 ⭐
Aquarium Notes: This triggerfish is primarily a zooplankton feeder and it can be successfully housed in reef aquariums. That said, some have been known to feed on encrusting sponges. I have also seen the rare individual nip at snails and ornamental crustaceans. They are unlikely to harm corals. If you want to attempt to keep a shrimp with this triggerfish, add the crustacean before you add the triggerfish. Provide enough food to keep them from developing problematic feeding habits.

SARGASSUM TRIGGERFISH (*XANTHICHTHYS RINGENS*)

Xanthichthys spp.
Xanthichthys Triggerfishes

Maximum Length: 8.7 to 13.8 in. (22 to 35 cm).
Range: Indo-Pacific.
Minimum Aquarium Size: 75 to 135 gal. (285 to 513 L).
Foods & Feeding: Mixed diet of meaty foods, including chopped seafood, mysid shrimp, frozen preparations, and flake foods. Feed at least three times a day.
Aquarium Suitability/Reef Compatibility:
Aquarium Notes: These are easily the best triggerfishes for the reef aquarium. On rare occasions, these species may nip at sessile invertebrates or attack delicate crustaceans, like anemone shrimp (*Periclimenes* species), but most individuals will behave themselves when it comes to corals. They are rarely aggressive toward their tankmates, unless the latter are much smaller and/or introduced to the aquarium after them. Larger individuals have been known to prey on small fishes. In larger tanks, they tend to ignore smaller fishes. If your tank is large enough (100 gal. [380 L] or more), you can even keep them in male-female pairs (most members of the genus exhibit color differences between the sexes).

Orangespotted Filefish (*Oxymonacanthus longirostris*): a beauty, but almost impossible to keep without its natural diet of live stony coral polyps

Filefishes (Family Monacanthidae)

The diet of the filefishes vary somewhat, but most feed on a variety of algae and sessile invertebrates. In a number of species, soft and/or stony coral polyps are an important part of the diet. The Orangespotted Filefish (*Oxymonacanthus longirostris*) is a smaller species that eats small-polyped stony coral polyps. Some reef keepers have successfully housed this species in a tank with numerous small-polyped stony coral colonies. If there are enough corals to feed on, and only one or a pair of these fish are kept, they may not damage any one colony enough to cause its demise. That said, *O. longirostris* is best avoided by most aquarists. (One in hundreds may accept substitute foods, but most specimens waste away and die.) Most other filefishes are easier to keep, but potentially too destructive to be housed in the reef aquarium. Filefishes will fight if crowded in a small to medium-sized tank, but heterosexual pairs can be housed together in a larger tank. Feed them a varied diet and provide food two or three times a day. They will eat filamentous algae, macroalgae, and some species will also feed on coralline algae.

Spotted Boxfish (*Ostracion meleagris*) male: although undeniably appealing, this fish and its relatives present a risky proposition to most reefkeepers.

Boxfishes (Family Ostraciidae)

These fishes feed mainly on sessile invertebrates such as tunicates and sponges. However, some have also been reported to ingest polychaete worms, algae, small bivalves, and gastropods. Although most do not typically eat corals in the wild, they may nip at them in aquarium confines. They are more likely to ignore larger soft corals, like *Cladiella, Sinularia,* and *Sarcophyton*, but may pick at low-growing soft corals (e.g., *Anthelia, Xenia*) and large-polyped stony corals (e.g., Open Brain and Elegance Corals). They have also been reported to nip at fanworms, tridacnid clam mantles, and echinoderm tube feet. Boxfishes have chemical defenses (ostracitoxin) that they exude when threatened or greatly stressed. I have never had a boxfish cause a reef tank to be wiped out, but the toxin is known to kill some invertebrates and will wipe out a fish community. They are rarely aggressive toward unrelated species so they can be kept with species of similar dispositions. If you want to house more than one boxfish in the same tank, choose a male and a female.

Lactoria cornuta
Longhorn Cowfish
Max. Length: 18.1 in. (46 cm).

Lactoria fornasini
Thornback Cowfish
Max. Length: 5.9 in. (15 cm).

Ostracion cubicus (juv.)
Yellow Boxfish
Max. Length: 17.7 in. (45 cm).

Ostracion meleagris (female)
Blue Boxfish, Spotted Boxfish
Max. Length: 6.3 in. (16 cm).

Ostracion solorensis (female)
Striped Boxfish
Max. Length: 4.3 in. (11 cm).

Ostracion whitleyi (male)
Whitley's Boxfish
Max. Length: 6.1 in. (15.5 cm).

Blackspotted or Dogface Puffer (*Arothron nigropunctatus*): as lovable as they seem, puffers are among the most highly destructive fishes for a reef system.

Pufferfishes (Family Tetraodontidae)

This family contains some of the most invertebrate unfriendly fishes, as many neophyte aquarists have learned. Members of the genus *Arothron* feed on a host of different invertebrates, including stony corals. The larger species will munch on small-polyped stony coral colonies as if they were hard candy. They will also eat sponges, tubeworms, snails, bivalves (including tridacnid clams), sea urchins, serpent stars, and sea stars. Many species also eat coralline algae. Their catholic diets and fused teeth make them risky reef tank inhabitants. They get their name from their ability to inflate the abdomen by filling the stomach with water or air. They also assimilate a highly toxic substance (tetraodotoxin) in their skin and organs. While this rarely impacts the fish they live with in captivity, it is possible that the toxin may be released in the water if a puffer corpse is left to decompose in the aquarium. Dental care is also required for some *Arothron* species. Their teeth can grow long and impede feeding , but can be ground down using a dremel tool and/or wire cutter (the fish must be anesthetized first).

Solander's Toby (*Canthigaster solandri*): this smaller puffer has been kept in the reef tank, but it is a risk to stony corals and some motile invertebrates.

Members of the genus *Canthigaster* (a.k.a. the tobies) have been kept in larger reef aquariums, but their natural diet does include small-polyped stony coral polyps (e.g., several species feed heavily on the tips of *Acropora* coral branches). They feed on a variety of other invertebrates as well, although their smaller size means they are a less of a threat than the *Arothron* species. I have seen these fishes bite off the tips of serpent star arms, the skin knobs of sea stars, and the spines of sea urchins. They eat a variety of algae, including coralline species. All that said, they have been kept in some reef aquariums without causing much harm to their cnidarian tankmates. Feed them two or three times a day to help curb their interest in corals. Vary their diet and include plant material in the form of frozen preparations for herbivores and freeze-dried algae sheets. Some species are notorious fin-nippers. This can be a chronic problem if a toby is kept with a fish that has long, flowing fins (e.g., comets, batfishes, and bannerfishes). They rarely behave aggressively toward other fish species, with the possible exception of congeners. Overgrown teeth can occur in tobies, but this problem is not as common as in the *Arothron* species.

Canthigaster coronata
Crowned Toby
Max. Length: 5.3 in. (13.5 cm).

Canthigaster epilampra
Lantern Toby
Max. Length: 4.7 in. (12 cm).

Canthigaster janthinoptera
Honeycomb Toby
Max. Length: 3.3 in. (8.5 cm).

Canthigaster papua
Papuan Toby
Max. Length: 4.3 in. (11 cm).

Canthigaster solandri
Spotted Sharpnose Toby
Max. Length: 3.5 in. (9 cm).

Canthigaster valentini
Saddled Toby
Max. Length: 3.9 in. (10 cm).

Spiny Puffer (*Diodon holocanthus*): this species, as well as others in the family, can be housed with some stony and soft corals.

Porcupinefishes & Burrfishes (Family Diodontidae)

Unlike the pufferfishes, porcupinefishes and burrfishes will often ignore stony corals and soft corals in a reef aquarium. But reef-keepers should not relax. The members of this family have spines on their body and fused teeth. These stout, beaklike teeth are used to crush sea urchins, sea stars, hermit crabs, crabs, and snails. They have also been known to dine on low-growing soft corals. Porcupinefishes and burrfishes hunt primarily at night, resting in reef crevices or among benthic debris during the day. In the aquarium, however, they can be trained to take food during the day. These personable fishes make entertaining pets, learning to "beg" food from their keeper and readily acclimating to the rigors of captive life. They are well known for their ability to inflate their bellies with water or air. In some cases, they will nip the fins of their tankmates. They are prone to getting ich and may suffer from serious cases of intestinal worms. The former requires that the fish be removed to a hospital tank, and the latter will call for treatment with medicated, antiparasitic foods.

AGGRESSIVE SPECIES: species prone to belligerent behavior toward members of other species, even those that are unrelated. This would include members of the dottyback, hawkfish, pygmy angelfish, damselfish, surgeonfish, and triggerfish groups. *Note*: a species may be more aggressive in certain social/aquarium contexts than in others.

BENTHIC: living on or near the seafloor (the benthos) or substrate.

CONFAMILIAL: a member of the same family.

CONGENER: a member of the same genus.

CONSEXUAL: a member of the same sex.

CONSPECIFIC: a member of the same species.

CYCLOP-EEZE®: a nutritious, protein-rich frozen food comprised of a marine crustacean in the genus *Cyclops*.

DEWORMER: a medication used to eradicate internal, worm parasites. The most common varieties used are Praziquantel, Piperazine, and Fenbendazole. Foods are laced with these medications and fed to aquarium fishes.

DETRITUS: decomposing organic material, including animal remains, plant remains, waste products, and the bacteria and other microorganisms associated with them.

DIANDRIC HERMAPHRODITE: a rare form of protogynous hermaphrodite in which there are two types of males—initial-phase males (which resemble juveniles and females) and terminal-phase males.

DITHER FISH: an active, bold fish that will swim in the water column and cause more timid species to become bolder.

FEEDING STICK: a piece of rigid tubing or bamboo used to skewer and present food to a captive fish.

GUT-PACKING: providing live prey items (e.g., ghost shrimp, mollies) with a nutritious food one or two hours before feeding them to captive fishes.

HETEROSPECIFIC: a member of a different species.

HUFA: highly unsaturated fatty acids (e.g., omega-3s) which are essential to maintain good fish health. Marine fish flesh is a good source of HUFAs.

INITIAL PHASE: phase exhibited by diandric hermaphrodites that consists of juveniles, females, and individuals that start life as males.

LARGE-POLYPED STONY CORALS (LPS CORALS): a common classification of corals that includes members of the genera *Cynarina, Catalaphyllia, Euphyllia, Favites, Goniopora, Plerogyra, Scolymia,* and *Trachyphyllia.*

MOTILE: free-living, mobile.

NANO-REEF: a reef aquarium smaller than 20 gallons.

PASSIVE SPECIES: species that do not typically behave aggressively toward unrelated species and may not bother congeners (e.g., certain gobies and dartfishes). *Note*: species may not exhibit aggression in certain social/aquarium contexts but may bully other fishes in other venues.

PREDATORY REEF AQUARIUM: a reef tank containing fish-eating larger species such as lizardfishes, frogfishes, toadfishes, lionfishes, scorpionfishes, or groupers.

PROTOGYNOUS HERMAPHRODITE: a species that changes its sex from female to male.

PROTANDRIC HERMAPHRODITE: a species that changes its sex from male to female.

SCHOOL: a group of fishes, usually of equal size, that move and act as a single unit and are equal in social status.

SHOAL: a group of fishes in which social attraction occurs but individuals are not equal in social status; movements are not as coordinated as in a school.

SMALL-POLYPED STONY CORALS (SPS CORALS): a common classification of corals that includes members of the genera *Acropora, Pocillopora, Porites, Seriatopora,* and *Stylophora.*

SPECIES/SPECIMEN REEF: a reef aquarium, often a smaller system, that contains only one species and often a single individual of that species.

TERMINAL PHASE: a phase exhibited by diandric hermaphrodites that consists of males that result from sex change (a.k.a. "supermales").

TUBE FEET: the locomotory or feeding appendages of echinoderms, and the excretory end of their water vascular system; often tipped with an adhesive pad; may extend long distances, up to 3 feet (1 m), from the base.

TUNIC: the covering of a tunicate or sea squirt (Class Ascidiacea; Phylum Urochordata); composed of cellulose and some other materials.

VERRUCAE: bumps or tubercles found on the columns of sea anemones; these are adhesive and help stabilize the animal in sediments.

ZOOID: an "individual" of a colonial animal, such as a compound ascidiacean, bryozoan, siphonophore, or soft coral.

ZOOPLANKTON: small animals found living in the water column.

ZOOXANTHELLAE: symbiotic unicellular dinoflagellate algae, in the genus *Symbiodinium,* that live in the tissues of many tropical animals, such as corals, sea anemones, soft corals, tridacnid clams, some sponges, and some foraminiferans.

PHOTOGRAPHY CREDITS

All photographs by Scott W. Michael, except as follows:

Roger Steene: 31, 35(TL), 46(TR), 60, 61(TL, TR), 73(CR, BL), 74(CL), 75, 79(BR), 88, 93, 107(BR), 117(TL, BL), 133(TR, CL, BR, BL), 140(INSET), 150(CR), 166(CL, CR, BL), 178(CR), 180(TL, TR), 183, 190, 192(CL, CR), 196, 197, 200, 201, 213, 214, 215(TL), 216(TR), 219(CL), 220, 221, 228, 246(TL), 258(TR), 263, 270(BL, BR), 283(BL), 286, 287(TL, TR), 291, 297(BL), 307, 310, 315, 319, 326(CL), 328(TR), 330(BL), 333, 337(TL, CL), 340, 341, 343(CR), 347(INSET), 353(TR, BL), 355, 359(CR, BL), 361, 369(TR, CL), 370, 378(CR), 379, 390, 393, 395, 399(CR), 400, 406, 407, 408, 412(BL), 413, 417, 418

Takamasa Tonozuka: 62, 117(CL, CR), 128(TR), 136, 138(CL, BL), 166(TR), 192(BR), 198, 321, 326(TR, CR), 337(CR), 343(CL), 344, 345, 346, 352, 353(CL, BR), 359(TR), 366(BR), 376, 409, Back cover(T)

Janine Cairns-Michael: 18, 24, 29(BL), 43, 45, 46(TL), 48(CL, BL), 49, 51(CL, TR), 52, 54, 119, 155, 260, 290, 324, 371

Rudy Kuiter: 84(BR), 106(TR, CR), 133(TL), 216(CL), 217(TR, BR), 234, 270(TL), 271(TR, BR)

Fred Bavendam: 8, 46(CL, BL), 178(TL), 180(BR)

Toshio Tsubota: 35(BL), 64, 72(CL), 349, 382

Paul Humann: 117(BR), 297(CL), 330(TL, CL)

Aaron Norman: 147, 156, 168(CR)

John P. Hoover: 150(CL), 251(inset), 396, 398

Larry Jackson: 84(BL), 144, 184(TL)

Fenton Walsh: 106(BL), 278, 397

Foster Bam: 61(CR), 128(BL)

Neville Coleman: 180(CR)

Keisuke Imai: 377

Yasuaki Miyamoto: 215(BR)

Robert F. Myers: 128(BR)

Yasuhiro Morita Ogasawara: 157

Hisayuki Onuma: 28

Kiyoshi Yanagiba: 65

SPECIES INDEX

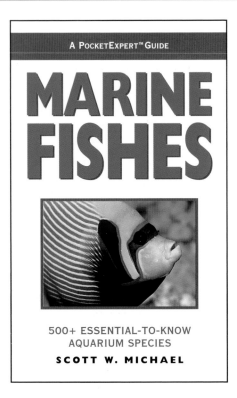

For the perfect companion volume to POCKETEXPERT™ REEF AQUARIUM FISHES, look for POCKETEXPERT™ MARINE FISHES, also by Scott W. Michael. Together they make an indispensable reference for the marine aquarist. Ask for this title at your local fish store or from your favorite bookseller.

Scott W. Michael is an internationally recognized writer, underwater photographer, and marine biology researcher specializing in reef fishes. He is a regular contributor to *Aquarium Fish Magazine* and is the author of the *PocketExpertGuide to Marine Fishes* (Microcosm/TFH), the *Reef Fishes Series* (Microcosm/TFH), *Reef Sharks & Rays of the World* (Sea Challengers), and *Aquarium Sharks & Rays* (Microcosm/TFH).

Having studied biology at the University of Nebraska, he has been involved in research projects on sharks, rays, frogfishes, and the behavior of reef fishes. He has also served as scientific consultant for National Geographic Explorer and the Discovery Channel. His work has led him from Cocos Island in the Eastern Pacific to various points in the Indo-Pacific as well as the Red Sea, the Gulf of Mexico, and many Caribbean reefs.

A marine aquarist since boyhood, he has kept tropical fishes for more than 30 years, with many years of involvement in the aquarium world, including a period of retail store ownership. He is a partner in an extensive educational website on the coral reef environment, **www.coralrealm.com.**

Scott lives with his wife, underwater photographer Janine Cairns-Michael, and their Golden Retriever, Ruby, in Lincoln, Nebraska.

KEY TO SYMBOLS

Aquarium Suitability

These species are almost impossible to keep and should be left on the reef.

Most individuals of these species do not acclimate to the home aquarium, often refusing to feed and wasting away in captivity.

These species are moderately hardy, with many individuals acclimating to the home aquarium <u>if special care is provided</u>.

These species are generally durable and hardy, with most individuals acclimating to the home aquarium.

These species are very hardy with almost all individuals readily acclimating to aquarium confines.

V Venomous: These species have spines or barbs that bear toxins with varying degrees of toxicity. The effects range from mild stings to severe pain and even death. They should be handled with caution and not displayed in systems within reach of children or uninformed viewers.

Reef Compatibility

Safe with stony corals.

Occasional threat to some stony corals.

Threat to stony corals.

Safe with soft corals.

Occasional threat to some soft corals.

Threat to soft corals.

Safe with ornamental crustaceans.

Occasional threat to some ornamental crustaceans.

Threat to ornamental crustaceans.

Safe with other invertebrates.

Occasional threat to some other invertebrates.

Threat to other invertebrates.